The Short Oxford History o.

Italy in the Central Middle Ages

The Short Oxford History of Italy

General Editor: John A. Davis

The Short Oxford History of Italy

General Editor: John A. Davis

Italy in the Central Middle Ages

1000–1300

Edited by David Abulafia

OXFORD
UNIVERSITY PRESS

OXFORD
UNIVERSITY PRESS

Great Clarendon Street, Oxford ox2 6dp

Oxford University Press is a department of the University of Oxford.
It furthers the University's objective of excellence in research, scholarship,
and education by publishing worldwide in

Oxford New York

Auckland Bangkok Buenos Aires Cape Town Chennai
Dar es Salaam Delhi Hong Kong Istanbul Karachi Kolkata
Kuala Lumpur Madrid Melbourne Mexico City Mumbai Nairobi
São Paulo Shanghai Taipei Tokyo Toronto

Oxford is a registered trade mark of Oxford University Press
in the UK and in certain other countries

Published in the United States
by Oxford University Press Inc., New York

British Library Cataloguing in Publication Data

Data available

Library of Congress Cataloging in Publication Data

Data available

ISBN 0–19–924704–8 (pbk)
ISBN 0–19–924703–X (hbk)

10 9 8 7 6 5 4 3 2 1

Typeset in Minion
by RefineCatch Limited, Bungay, Suffolk
Printed in Great Britain by
Biddles Ltd, King's Lynn, Norfolk

General Editor's Preface

Over the last three decades historians have begun to interpret Europe's past in new ways. In part this reflects changes within Europe itself, the declining importance of the individual European states in an increasingly global world, the moves towards closer political and economic integration amongst the European states, and Europe's rapidly changing relations with the non-European world. It also reflects broader intellectual changes rooted in the experience of the twentieth century that have brought new fields of historical inquiry into prominence and have radically changed the ways in which historians approach the past.

The new *Short Oxford History of Europe* series, of which this *Short Oxford History of Italy* is part, offers an important and timely opportunity to explore how the histories of the contemporary European national communities are being rewritten. Covering a chronological span from late antiquity to the present, the *Short Oxford History of Italy* is organized in seven volumes, to which over seventy specialists in different fields and periods of Italian history have contributed. Each volume provides clear and concise accounts of how each period of Italy's history is currently being redefined, and their collective purpose is to show how an older perspective that reduced Italy's past to the quest of a nation for statehood and independence has now been displaced by different and new perspectives.

The fact that Italy's history has long been dominated by the modern nation-state and its origins simply reflects one particular variant on a pattern evident throughout Europe. When from the eighteenth century onwards Italian writers turned to the past to retrace the origins of their nation and its quest for independent nationhood, they were doing the same as their counterparts elsewhere in Europe. But their search for the nation imposed a periodization on Italy's past that has survived to the present, even if the original intent has been lost or redefined. Focusing their attention on those periods—the Middle Ages, the Renaissance, the *Risorgimento*—that seemed to anticipate the modern, they carefully averted their gaze from those that did not, the Dark Ages, and the centuries of foreign occupation and conquest after the sack of Rome in 1527.

Paradoxically, this search for unity segmented Italy's past both chronologically and geographically, since those regions (notably the South) deemed to have contributed less to the quest for nationhood were also ignored. It also accentuated the discontinuities of Italian history caused by foreign conquest and invasion, so that Italy's successive rebirths—the Renaissance and the *Risorgimento*—came to symbolize all that was distinctive and exceptional in Italian history. Fascism then carried the cycle of triumph and disaster forward into the twentieth century, thereby adding, to the conviction that Italy's history was exceptional, the belief that it was in some essential sense also deeply flawed. Post-war historians redrew Italy's past in bleaker terms, but used the same retrospective logic as before to link Fascism to failings deeply rooted in Italy's recent and more distant past.

Seen from the end of the twentieth century this heavily retrospective reasoning appears anachronistic and inadequate. But although these older perspectives continue to find an afterlife in countless textbooks, they have been displaced by a more contemporary awareness that in both the present and the past the different European national communities have no single history, but instead many different histories.

The volumes in the *Short Oxford History of Italy* will show how Italy's history too is being rethought in these terms. Its new histories are being constructed around the political, cultural, religious, and economic institutions from which Italy's history has drawn continuities that have outlasted changing fortunes of foreign conquest and invasion. In each period their focus is the peoples and societies that have inhabited the Italian peninsula, on the ways in which political organization, economic activity, social identities, and organization were shaped in the contexts and meanings of their own age.

These perspectives make possible a more comparative history, one that shows more clearly how Italy's history has been distinctive without being exceptional. They also enable us to write a history of Italians that is fuller and more continuous, recovering the previously 'forgotten' centuries and geographical regions while revising our understanding of those that are more familiar. In each period Italy's many different histories can also be positioned more closely in the constantly changing European and Mediterranean worlds of which Italians have always been part.

John A. Davis

Acknowledgements

I owe a particular debt to the General Editor and to other volume editors in this series. In Summer 2003, when Rome was baking in 95° of heat, John Davis and his family were excellent hosts on the Gianicolo, and John Marino also offered very valuable advice; it was also a pleasure to compare notes with John Najemy a month earlier, in the slightly cooler setting of a conference at the University of Warwick. At Oxford University Press, Andrew MacLennan introduced me to the practicalities of editing this book with his customary enthusiasm and professionalism, and Matthew Cotton has eagerly seen it through to publication. I owe no less a debt to all the contributors. In November 2000, Hiroshi Takayama made it possible for me to discuss this project with him in Tokyo, Kyoto, and on Kyushu island. Alberto Varvaro has been a welcome face in Cambridge for several years.

The reading lists are the work of the chapter authors or of myself as volume editor, or a combination of the two. In accordance with the general practice of the series, works in English are emphasized when possible.

David Abulafia

Gonville & Caius College, Cambridge

Contents

PART III THE OTHER FACES OF ITALY

List of contributors

DAVID ABULAFIA is professor of Mediterranean history at Cambridge University and a Fellow of Gonville and Caius College. His books have a southern Italian flavour and include *The Two Italies* (1977), *Frederick II* (1988), and *The Western Mediterranean Kingdoms, 1200–1500* (1997), all of which have also appeared in Italian. The President of Italy appointed him Commendatore dell'Ordine della Stella della Solidarietà Italiana in 2003.

BRENDA BOLTON was reader in history at Westfield College, London (later merged with Queen Mary College). Her books on the papacy and the Church in the twelfth and thirteenth centuries include *The Medieval Reformation* (1983), *Innocent III* (1995), and *Adrian IV, the English Pope* (2003).

EDWARD COLEMAN is lecturer in history at University College, Dublin. He has written 'The Italian communes: recent work and current trends', in the *Journal of Medieval History* (1999), and 'Sense of community and civic identity in the Italian communes', in *The Community, the Family and the Saint* (1998).

TREVOR DEAN is professor of history at the University of Surrey, Roehampton. His interests include crime in Italy and the history of Este Ferrara; his works include *Land and Power in Late Medieval Ferrara* (1988), *Clean Hands and Rough Justice* (1998, with David Chambers), *The Towns of Italy in the Later Middle Ages* (2000).

STEVEN EPSTEIN is Ahmanson-Murphy distinguished professor of medieval history at the University of Kansas, having previously been professor of history at the University of Colorado. His books make extensive use of Genoese material and include *Wills and Wealth in Medieval Genoa* (1984), *Genoa and the Genoese* (1996), and *Speaking of Slavery* (2001).

DUANE OSHEIM is professor of history at the University of Virginia, with a special interest in the rural society of medieval Tuscany; his books include *An Italian Lordship* (1977) and *An Italian Monastery and its Social World* (1990).

PATRICIA SKINNER is senior lecturer in history at the University of Southampton; her interests include the social history of southern Italy and women's history, and she is the author of *Family Power in Southern Italy* (1995), *Health and Medicine in Early Medieval Southern Italy* (1997), and *Women in Medieval Italian Society* (2001).

HIROSHI TAKAYAMA is professor of European history at the University of Tokyo, and is the author of many books in Japanese on medieval history, mainly concerned with the kingdom of Sicily; his *Administration of the Norman Kingdom of Sicily* (1993) has appeared in English.

MARCO TANGHERONI is professor of history at the Istituto di Medievistica dell'Università degli Studi di Pisa, and among his books on Sardinian history are *Aspetti del commercio dei cereali nei paesi della Corona d'Aragona* (1981) and *La città dell'argento* (1985), while among his works on medieval maritime trade there is *Commercio e navigazione nel medioevo* (1996).

ALBERTO VARVARO is professor of linguistics at the Università degli Studi Federico II, Naples; he has written *Lingua e storia in Sicilia* (1981), *Letterature romanze del medioevo* (1985), and numerous other works linking history and linguistics.

Introduction: The many Italies of the Middle Ages

David Abulafia

I

Writing the early history of a politically fragmented and economically diverse territory which has only been unified in recent times is a difficult task; both medieval Italy and medieval Germany, tied together by their links to the Holy Roman Empire, have posed similar problems in this respect. The difficulties are magnified in the Italian case because of the existence in the south of political structures quite different from those in the north, and because of the ethnic and religious diversity of the south by comparison with the north. And this perhaps explains why most attempts to write a history of Italy in the central Middle Ages have in fact emerged as something slightly different: as studies of power relationships in the towns and great feudal states of the north, in the case of Giovanni Tabacco;[1] as a study of the evolution of the city-state in the case of J. K. Hyde.[2] Hyde's rather Whiggish tendency to see the evolution of north Italian urban society as a path leading to the creation of republics controlled by their citizens forms part of a wider tendency to see the city-states of

[1] G. Tabacco, *The Struggle for Power in Medieval Italy: Structures of Political Rule*, trans. Rosalind Brown Jensen (Cambridge, 1989).
[2] J. K. Hyde, *Society and Politics in Medieval Italy: The Evolution of the Civil Life, 1000–1350* (London, 1973).

medieval Italy as inherently praiseworthy. On the other hand, his interest in the underlying political principles that may have motivated early communal politicians has influenced the outlook of historians of political ideas, notably Quentin Skinner.[3] However, no one can fault Daniel Waley for entitling his widely disseminated account of the high Middle Ages in northern Italy *The Italian City-Republics,* since he does much to explain the distinctive forms of government that emerged in the cities of Lombardy, Tuscany, and adjacent regions.[4] Waley's admirably cool-headed ability to steer a steady course between the rocky shores of Guelf and Ghibelline territory gives his work a non-partisan flavour that even contemporary historians have not found it easy to avoid.[5]

Of course, the result of attention to city republics in the north is that very little attention is generally paid to the south in surveys of medieval Italy; and this book seeks to redress the balance by looking at north and south side by side, and, when appropriate, together. Still, there are exceptions that prove the rule about neglect of southern history in accounts of northern Italy. Even though its main emphasis is naturally elsewhere, Philip Jones's magnificent and monumental *The Italian City-State* looks closely at the economic relationship between north and south and poses the question why urban liberty did not develop in the same way in the Sicilian kingdoms as it did in northern and central Italy (even within the papal domains, which had certain structural similarities with, and close ties to, the south Italian kingdom).[6] Brian Pullan's *History of Early Renaissance Italy* makes a strong case for taking account of the political machinations of the south Italian rulers when trying to make sense of the convoluted politics of northern Italy in the thirteenth and fourteenth centuries.[7] Among older works one could single out Evelyn Jamison's account of medieval Italy in a survey of Italian history published by the Clarendon Press in 1919; given her strong interest in Norman Sicily, this learned

---

[3] Q. R. D. Skinner, *The Foundations of Modern Political Thought*, i. *The Renaissance* (Cambridge, 1978).

[4] D. P. Waley, *The Italian City-Republics* (three editions: London, 1969, 1978, 1988).

[5] To indulge in self-criticism, it now looks to me as if there are anti-Guelf swipes and pro-Ghibelline sentiments in my own *Frederick II* (London, 1988).

[6] P. J. Jones, *The Italian City-State* (Oxford, 1997).

[7] B. Pullan, *A History of Early Renaissance Italy from the Mid-Thirteenth to the Mid-Fifteenth Century* (London, 1973).

Oxford historian gave significant attention to the politics of the south, though her principal message was that 'both in religion and in secular relations, the passion for equality and liberty conditioned Italian developments', and that social duty exercised a powerful claim in religion as in politics, a view of Italian society which still assumes that it was in the north that the basis for modern ideals of liberty was laid as far back as the twelfth century.[8]

The sense that social duty mattered profoundly was expressed in a very different way in Jacques Heers's challenging studies of late medieval Italy. In one work he examined family clans, mainly using Genoese examples, though ranging beyond Italy itself, to argue that the 'horizontal' bonds between kinship groups were more important to the political life of medieval Europe than the 'vertical' structures of class beloved of old-fashioned Marxist historiography.[9] His books were conceived as an unapologetic attack on Marxist tendencies within western, and particularly French, historiography, and Heers took pride in his own right-wing political position. Still, writing about medieval Italy should not be simply an opportunity to trumpet modern political positions, and the question remains whether, prior to Heers, historians had tended to play down the importance of the family clan and kinship allegiances in city politics. Contemporary Marxist historians such as Chris Wickham and Larry Epstein have used Marxist theory as an explanatory tool and have understood class conflict as a broad historical framework, while being prepared to accommodate a variety of interpretations that would not have suited the dogmatists of the past.[10] Among those dogmatists it is impossible to ignore Gaetano Salvemini, whose attempt to analyse the political conflicts of late thirteenth-century Florence in terms of class was rightly derided by the Russian émigré Nicola Ottokar, not that Ottokar lacked a political agenda of his own.[11] Apart from anything

[8] E. M. Jamison, C. M. Ady, and others, *Italy, Mediaeval and Modern* (Oxford, 1919), especially pp. 117–18.

[9] J. Heers, *Family Clans in the Middle Ages* (Amsterdam, 1979); *Parties and Political Life in the Medieval West* (Amsterdam, 1977).

[10] C. J. Wickham, *Land and Power: Studies in Italian and European social history 400–1200* (London and Rome, 1994); S. R. Epstein, *Freedom and Growth: The Rise of States and Markets in Europe, 1300–1750* (London, 2000). Stephan R. ('Larry') Epstein should not be confused with Steven A. Epstein, who writes in this volume.

[11] G. Salvemini, *Magnati e popolani in Firenze dal 1280 al 1295* (2nd edn., Milan, 1974); N. Ottokar, *Il comune di Firenze alla fine del dugento* (2nd edn., Turin, 1962).

else, the Salvemini–Ottokar debate had the depressing effect of making the historiography of medieval Italy revolve once again around Florence, which was actually late to develop economically and politically by contrast with Pisa, Lucca, or even Siena.

The chapter in this book on the communes, by Edward Coleman, rightly insists on the need to assess the city communes in their own terms, and not according to modern values. Yet there exists a powerful historiographical tradition that lays emphasis on republican institutions and ideals and looks less intently at the development in government which, as Trevor Dean shows in this volume, came to characterize the Italian cities by about 1300: the domination over city affairs of a *signore*, a term often mistranslated 'tyrant' or 'despot', who might or might not occupy an actual office of state, who might or might not preserve the existing communal institutions intact, and whose declared purpose was to put to an end the deep internal rivalries between Guelfs, Ghibellines, and other factions which had riven so many communes apart during the thirteenth century. Of course, *signori* might themselves have strong loyalties to pope, emperor, or king of Naples, and the early examples of *signori* from north-eastern Italy show how the Este and the da Romanos were able to lever themselves into positions of great regional power as a result of backing either the papacy or Emperor Frederick II. Still, the historiography has tended to turn its back on the *signori*, which is strange when it is considered that one of the founding fathers of Italian history, Jacob Burckhardt, laid great emphasis on their role as patrons of culture from the thirteenth century onwards, and John Addington Symonds was also adamant that the very individualism of the despots was of fundamental importance in moulding Renaissance values.[12]

Instead, the historiography of medieval Italy has fallen victim to the idealization of Florence and Venice: the former is seen as the great centre of the arts and of industry, admittedly much disturbed by faction fighting; and the latter is seen as an aristocratic republic that proved the success of Aristotelian formulae in government, balancing monarchy (in the form of the Doge), aristocracy (in the Senate), and a small measure of democracy (in the popular assembly, powerless

[12] J. Burckhardt, *The Civilization of the Renaissance in Italy*, trans. S. G. C. Middlemore (London, 1950), and other, generally less well-illustrated, editions; J. A. Symonds, *A Short History of the Renaissance in Italy* (London, 1893).

though it was). This idealization can be linked to the work of historians writing in the nineteenth century, notably Sismondi, who began his history of the Italian republics in 1804, when the shadow of Napoleon Bonaparte stretched across much of Europe; here we can identify a very different outlook from that of Burckhardt and Symonds, for Sismondi related the artistic and literary genius of medieval Italy to liberty, exemplified in the political freedom of Florence above all. If anything, despotism sowed the seeds of decline, whether in Sforza Milan or indeed the supposedly republican Florence of the Medici, for Sismondi had no illusions about the real nature of the power of Lorenzo il Magnifico.[13]

One of the fundamental problems of the more recent historiography of medieval Italy has been a failure to escape from these nineteenth-century debates. The idea that the city republics deserve a certain priority because they stand for values that modern democrats can share is often not far from the surface. Thus even so impartial a judge as Daniel Waley uses the term 'enlightened' in describing the participation of citizens in the government of the Italian communes, while also recognizing the great diversity among cities and the lack of progeny left by the city republics: by the mid-fourteenth century Florence, Venice, and Genoa, admittedly three of the most important cities in Italy, were virtually the only city republics still untamed by *signori*, and Genoa was torn apart by factionalism and (like Florence) not averse to appointing a *signore* when times were hard. Some cities, such as Lucca, gained and lost republican governments. However, it is no disrespect to the republic of San Marino to suggest that the unique survival of this *Comune del Popolo* offers little proof that, after about 1350, republican systems of government were highly valued by those able to exercise political power in Italy.

II

Interpreting medieval Italy as a whole is not simply a question of placing north and south side by side and contrasting the two. The

---

[13] J. C. L. de Sismondi, *A History of the Italian Republics, Being a View of the Origin, Progress and Fall of Italian Freedom*, ed. W. K. Ferguson (New York, 1966); a longer version is that of W. Boulting (London, 1906).

links between north and south, in politics, economy, even demography, were very intense, and in that sense it is still possible (though with care) to use the term 'Italy' (or 'the two Italies') to describe the area stretching from the Alps to the toe of Calabria, as well as the two largest Mediterranean islands, Sicily and Sardinia, the latter of which was drawn in the period of this book into the web of Genoese and Pisan trade and power politics. Marco Tangheroni explains the interaction between Sardinia and the rest of Italy in the last chapter of this book, which not merely brings to light often ignored aspects of medieval Italian history but illuminates, as does his chapter on the commercial revolution, the special role of Genoa and Pisa in the evolution of medieval Italy. No doubt claims can also be made for including Corsica (though it was less often the focus of Pisan–Genoese rivalry, being poorer in resources) and some of the towns along the coasts of Istria and Dalmatia, towns that developed close trade links with Italy and were inhabited in part by speakers of Italian dialects; Malta was a dependency of the Sicilian kingdom, though with a distinctive culture, but it certainly deserves a mention at the appropriate points. However, a different decision has been made here: this book is concerned with the territory we would now regard as Italy, specifically in order to show the great ethnic, religious, linguistic, political, and economic diversity of the peninsula and islands.

Having already become associated with the idea of 'two Italies', north and south, coexisting in the twelfth century, I may be accused of gilding the lily by arguing that these are only two of a great many more.[14] It is not just that the relationship between the supplier of raw materials and foodstuffs (represented in the ties linking Sicily or Sardinia to Genoa) is replicated a hundred times in the relationship between the agricultural regions within northern Italy and the urban centres of demand (as in the case of the Sienese Maremma), or on a smaller scale still in that between the countryside or *contado* and the controlling town. The *contado*–city relationship was by no means a closed one; one of the distinctive features of the Italian town was the existence of lively trading networks that facilitated exchange, so that town and country were able to concentrate on specialities—in the

---

[14] G. Fortunato (1848–1932) used the term 'two Italies' to describe the contrast in his own lifetime: G. Fortunato, *Le due Italie*, ed. M. Rossi-Doria (Lecce, 1994); and for its use in a medieval setting see D. Abulafia, *The Two Italies: Economic Relations between the Norman Kingdom of Sicily and the Northern Communes* (Cambridge, 1977).

cities, these might be different types of cloth, made of cotton, linen, wool, and eventually silk, fibres that themselves might have to be imported from as near as the Apennines or as far as Egypt and Byzantium. Some cities, too, were important sources of metal goods, as was Milan with its easy access to Alpine sources of metal, or Pisa with its control over Elba, rich in iron. Meanwhile, the countryside was also a place of specialization, since even the famed hard wheat of Sicily and Sardinia was difficult to reproduce in the soils of Tuscany and Lombardy, and there was considerable diversity in the food crops that grew in central and northern Italy, as can be seen in the long catalogue of agricultural produce offered in the manual of agronomy of Pietro de' Crescentiis, writing at the start of the fourteenth century. Indeed, the growth in urban population created ever increasing strains as local supplies ran out, especially in times when the harvests were poor. Another important source for the agrarian history of northern Italy at the end of this period is Domenico Lenzi's chronicle of the grain market of Orsanmichele in Florence in the 1320s and 1330s. Here Lenzi portrays clearly the massive difficulty faced by the public authorities in feeding a city whose population had become bloated by the rapid expansion of the textile industry.[15] Imports from overseas came from ever further afield, at least to the maritime cities and to Florence, as Marco Tangheroni shows in this volume. The Crimea was identified as a particularly important source of grain for Genoa and other port cities as early as the late thirteenth century; even the hefty cost of transporting Black Sea grain to Italy did not make the grain unaffordable, since food prices in the big cities had already risen to a level where the importers could make substantial profits. Yet the roots of this trade in primary foodstuffs can certainly be traced back to the twelfth century, and a particularly important moment was the treaty between the Genoa and the Norman kings of Sicily of 1156, which permitted the Genoese large-scale exportation of both wheat and cotton. Even if the relationship between Genoa and Sicily had many ups and downs, the presence of the merchants of one or another of the maritime republics in the markets of Sicily helped to redirect its trade gradually away from the Islamic world (and North Africa in particular) towards northern Italy, at a time when it

[15] See the edition of Domenico Lenzi's work by G. Pinto, *Il Libro del Biadaiolo: carestie e annona a Firenze dalla metà del '200 al 1348* (Florence, 1978).

was also becoming more involved in the politics of Italy as a whole, and when it was undergoing a slow but thorough transformation from a mixed Arabic and Greek society into a Latin one. These themes are taken further in the chapters by Hiroshi Takayama and myself in this volume, while Patricia Skinner's innovative study of material life brings together north and south and enables one to see how the movement of commodities affected daily existence. The interaction between the agrarian economy and civic Italy is also a theme of the chapter on rural Italy by Duane Osheim.

III

Any study of rural Italy displays to view the Church as a landholder. The role of the Church in economic life, politics, attitudes to the family and to wealth, and cultural developments is a constant theme of this book, though, as will be seen, in the deep south we can observe greater religious variety. Certainly, the period covered by this book was one when the Church in Italy was undergoing major transformations, of European and Mediterranean significance. This, after all, was the age of the crusades, and Italians participated vigorously in the naval wars that brought the ports of the Holy Land under Christian control from 1100 onwards; they also participated in the crusading armies, whether they were Normans from the south of Italy or Alpine lords such as Boniface of Montferrat, a key participant in the Fourth Crusade, which conquered Constantinople in 1204. The Genoese saw their role in the First Crusade not simply as an opportunity to acquire trading stations and to bring home booty; the booty itself was God's reward for their prowess in fighting for him, and the green glass *sacro catino* that is still displayed in Genoa cathedral was believed to be the dish used at the Last Supper; it was taken from a mosque in Caesarea and became one of several candidates for the dubious title of the Holy Grail. Thus the First Crusade in particular tapped the religious enthusiasm of the inhabitants of the peninsula.

The upsurge in religious feeling was closely linked to changes that were taking place within the organization of the Church in Italy. The Papal Reform Movement was itself profoundly rooted in wider

European Reformist movements, notably the monastic reforms initiated at Cluny in the late tenth and eleventh centuries. The increasing expectation that priests would meet higher standards of conduct, sending away their wives or concubines and no longer acquiring office through purchase or bribes, had significant political implications, as Edward Coleman shows in his discussion in this volume of the power of the bishops in the north Italian cities. High ecclesiastical office tended less often to remain in the hands of the local elites; either side of 1100, this stimulated those elites to exercise power directly through the commune rather than by way of the bishop's court. However, the effects of the Reform Movement were also felt lower down the political scale, notably among the Patarines of Milan in the eleventh century; there we observe populist preachers, encouraged by Pope Gregory VII, challenging the authority of the Ambrosian Church of Milan, which had its own rituals and a tradition of clerical marriage.[16] Rome sought to suppress variant liturgies; liturgy, indeed, proved to be an effective way to spread papal influence throughout Europe. Yet the Patarine movement also reveals an increasing degree of popular enthusiasm for religion; untamed, this could easily develop into unorthodox beliefs, as happened both in France and Italy in the twelfth century. By stimulating religious life, the Reform Movement also stimulated what would come to be seen as heresy. The term 'Patarine' came to be applied to heretics in the twelfth century, and not just to a populist reforming movement that still stood within the Church. It should also be stressed that anticlericalism, which was expressed, for instance, by the Roman revolutionary leader Arnold of Brescia in his denunciations of papal political power, did not necessarily signify cynicism about the Church and its teachings: rather the opposite, a sense that the leaders of the Church were failing to provide the spiritual support many craved. A conspicuously wealthy Church, rich in lands and drawing on massive revenues from clerical tithes and other taxes, even, by 1300, closely linked to the great banks of Florence, became the target of those who asserted the need to return to the principle of pristine poverty. Such criticism might be contained within the Church, as in the case of

---

[16] H. E. J. Cowdrey, 'The Papacy, the Patarines and the Church of Milan', *Transactions of the Royal Historical Society*, ser. 5, 18 (1968); C. Violante, *La società milanese nell'età precomunale* (Rome and Bari, 1974).

Francis of Assisi; or it might turn against the entire Church, as in the case of the Cathar and Waldensian heretics.

The difficulty in defining heresy was that the position of the Church on several important dogmatic issues still needed to be set out clearly. It is significant that the decisions of the Fourth Lateran Council of 1215 begin with a profession of faith. In part this was aimed at the Greek Church, nominally under papal control since the Fourth Crusade of 1204. However, this profession of faith was also a direct riposte to the alternative theologies of contemporary heretics, of whom the most outrageous (from a Catholic perspective) were the Cathars.[17] In the twelfth and early thirteenth centuries Catharism was the largest heretical movement in Italy. However, whereas in southern France the Cathars were the victims of a brutal crusade that began in 1209, in Italy concerted military action against Catharism did not occur, and such action as was taken generally fell into the hands of a papal inquisition which sought to root out heresy on the ground by investigation, arrest, and interrogation. Progress against heresy was slow, however. In part this was the result of the conflict between Frederick II and the papacy. Frederick was second to none in his dislike for heretics — 'heretics tear the seamless robe of God', his law-book of 1231 proclaimed. However, the emperor was not prepared to let papal inquisitors exercise authority in the areas of northern Italy under his control. He was not the first ruler to see the Inquisition as a means by which the papacy might undermine the authority of secular rulers. Thus the conflict between Frederick (d. 1250), and then his son Manfred (d. 1266), and the papacy provided little real opportunity for the suppression of heresy. The conquest of southern Italy by Charles of Anjou, and the success of the pro-papal Guelf party in northern and central Italy, enabled the inquisitors to extend their work in some areas. Clearly it would be a gross simplification to suggest that Guelfs, as 'the party of the Church', were all orthodox Catholics, while Ghibellines, as 'the party of Empire', showed sympathy to heresy. On the other hand, a few allies of Frederick II in the north, notably Ezzelino da Romano, appear to have enjoyed cocking a snook at the Church by entertaining heretics, and a crusade was launched against Ezzelino in 1254.

[17] C. Lansing, *Power and Purity: Cathar Heresy in Medieval Italy* (New York, 1998) is in fact mainly concerned with Orvieto; see also M. Lambert, *The Cathars* (Oxford, 1998), though M. Barber, *The Cathars* (London and Harlow, 2000) concentrates on Languedoc only.

The basis of Cathar beliefs was a rejection of the material world as inherently evil and as the domain either of the devil or of an Evil Principle who is matched by the Good Principle, God, who controls the world of the spirit; the latter must ultimately prevail. This was not a particularly original answer to the problem of why evil exists in the world. There has been intense argument about the origins of the dualism of the Cathars; the most ambitious, and least rigorous, interpretations seek the origins of Cathar beliefs in the Manichaeans and even the Zoroastrians of the East. Links between the Cathars and the dualist Bogomils of the Balkans are not in doubt, and contact was easily maintained across the Adriatic. The Cathar heresy in Italy seems at first to have preached a moderate or 'mitigated' form of Cathar beliefs, as opposed to the extreme dualism of the French Cathars; this mitigated dualism was closer to the beliefs of the Bogomils in Bosnia and Bulgaria, and spoke of the power of the devil over the material world (the extreme dualists matched the Good and Evil Principles more evenly as, to all intents, a good God and an evil one). But the intense persecution of heretics in southern France during the Albigensian Crusade, from 1209 onwards, led to the flight of extreme Cathars into Italy, changing the configuration of Italian Catharism. Another difference between Italian and southern French Catharism was that Italian Catharism appears to have secured bigger bases in the cities than it did in southern France. Florence in the early thirteenth century was a major centre of heresy. Orvieto, in the Papal State, was another city in which heretics gained great influence, as Brenda Bolton explains in her chapter on papal Italy in this book. There were also rural centres (the moderate Cathar Church of Concorezzo, in the area of Milan, for example); and the activities of the inquisitors and of hostile town governments or other lords led to a flight of Cathars in the years around 1270, to Sirmione on Lake Garda, near an existing centre at Desenzano, the base of a bishop of the extreme sect. However, their concentration in one place exposed them to attack by the Scaliger lords of Verona, who burned 174 Cathars from Sirmione in the great arena of Verona in 1274.[18] This was the last great act of suppression, and Catharism thereafter lingered only in remote areas of Italy. Numerically, it may never have

[18] B. Hamilton, 'The Albigensian Crusade and heresy', in D. Abulafia (ed.), *New Cambridge Medieval History*, v. c.1198–c.1300 (Cambridge, 1999), p. 177.

been very strong; its existence depended on the efforts of a select group of the 'Perfect' (*perfecti*), and there were many laymen who seemed able to keep a foot in both the Catholic and the Cathar camp, admiring the devotion of the Cathars without committing themselves to Catharism, at least until they were on their deathbed. Among women, however, the appeal of this and other heresies was greater, largely because they accorded much higher status to women than the Catholic Church.

The second heresy that was often named in conjunction with Catharism by heresy-hunters was that of the Waldensians, whose origins can be traced back to Valdes of Lyons around 1174; by 1200 they had established bases on the Italian side of the Alps. Their views changed over time, but at this period they appear to have emphasized poverty, preaching, and prayer, and to have had radical views about who (including women) could perform the sacraments and about the right of the laity to preach. Valdes had been made to sign a profession of faith in 1179 which was in fact quite orthodox, and the original source of disagreement between him and the archbishop of Lyons was the right of Valdes and his followers to preach without licence.[19] Valdes, a rich merchant, had renounced his wealth, and a central tenet was the emphasis on the virtue of poverty. Later, Waldensianism spread as far south as the kingdom of Naples, and became a matter of some concern to the Angevin rulers of southern Italy in the early fourteenth century. However, the preference of the Waldensians for remote mountain valleys preserved them from continuous persecution, and the movement remains in existence. Other Waldensians became reconciled to the Church as 'Poor Catholics' and 'Poor Lombards' early in the thirteenth century, when Pope Innocent III realized that the gap between their beliefs and orthodoxy was much narrower than that between Catharism and Catholicism.

Several of the themes which have arisen in discussing heresy also had a major impact on the Catholic Church: the big issue of poverty; the connected desire to reject worldly materialism. One typically Italian expression of this materialism was held to be the concupiscence of the merchant in search of profit; worse still, there was the problem of the usurer, who sought to make his money grow in

---

[19] G. Audisio, *The Waldenisan Dissent: Persecution and Survival, c.1170–c.1570* (Cambridge, 1999).

contravention of biblical commandments (it should be stressed that usury in Italy was not at this period linked to Jews). Valdes had rejected worldly wealth, but had given his name to a proto-protestant movement, whether or not he sought to found one. Francis of Assisi also renounced wordly wealth, around 1208, and chose a life of evangelical poverty, preaching in Umbria, gathering a small group of like-minded apostles, and even inspiring a group of women, led by Clare of Assisi, to establish a group of 'poor recluses', who, as women, were obliged to live as a community rather than going out into the world. The most important development, however, was the approval of Francis's aims by Pope Innocent III, who realized that Francis's initiative, though in many ways similar to that of Valdes, could and should be contained within the Church.[20] More problematic was the reluctance of Francis to address the consequences of the growth of his small brotherhood into what became, by 1223, a religious order with a rule sanctioned by the pope, and with material assets, even if they were technically the property of the Church and not of the Franciscan Order of Friars Minor. This also marked the beginning of a long history of disputes between those dedicated to the simple life of imitation of Christ and those who saw the future in a more rigid organization under papal surveillance. By the middle of the thirteenth century, a further question arose concerning the role of scholarship within the order. Then, at the end of the thirteenth century a powerfully apocalyptic 'spiritual' wing of the Franciscans gained much favour at several royal courts, notably that of Naples, and was highly critical of the wealth of the Church, although the papacy condemned the Spirituals for their belief in the absolute poverty of Christ. These controversies did not, however, prevent vigorous expansion in the Italian towns, where Franciscan houses were established with the aim of reaching a rapidly growing population, often inhabiting suburbs with little or no pastoral care on offer. On the other hand, there was an increasing tendency after 1250 to build rather splendid convents within the city walls, and this was encouraged by the fascination of the city elites with the friars. Handsome donations to the Franciscans served to expiate the sins of those still wedded to wealth and glory. The sight of magnificent convents with frescoed walls then, in turn,

[20] A. Vauchez, 'The Religious Orders', in D. Abulafia (ed.), *New Cambridge Medieval History*, v. *c.1198–c.1300* (Cambridge, 1999), pp. 232–55.

excited the rejectionist wings of the movement, with their emphasis on genuine poverty.

The other major mendicant order, the Dominicans or Friars Preacher, had come into existence in southern France, targeting Cathar heretics; in Italy, as elsewhere, they remained a more intellectual order (the order, after all, of Thomas Aquinas), and they remained more heavily involved in the battle against heresy, functioning in the Italian cities as papal inquisitors, a role which some Franciscans also later acquired. Alongside these two mendicant orders, any large Italian city also provided space for many other religious groups: members of the military orders of the Hospital and the Temple; friars of the Sack, Carmelites, Augustinians, and others who aimed to live in the community, not to mention the enclosed convents of Poor Clares and of monks whose own convent was within or close to a big city. And in the countryside, ascetic figures such as Joachim of Fiore at the end of the twelfth century and Pietro Morrone (the only pope to resign his office) at the end of the thirteenth century acted as focal points for new movements, founding new houses and setting an example by their life or writings.

These are only the better known themes in the religious life of Italy during the period of this book. What needs to be stressed is that intense religious activity also gripped many laymen and laywomen. In the localities, confraternities among the laity became widespread, and sometimes became a headache for local bishops, who wished to exercise some control over their conduct: the fear of heresy remained alive throughout the thirteenth century. In 1260 a movement promoting public penance emerged in Perugia; penances were characterized by mutual flagellation, and the penitents processed from town to town.[21] Such movements made it plain that the institutional Church was not capable of controlling how the inhabitants of medieval Italy expressed their religious devotion. The major challenge was, rather, to ensure that religious enthusiasm was channelled into types of observance that could be accommodated within the Catholic Church, and that confraternities and other groups did not become breeding-grounds for heresy.

[21] A. Vauchez, 'The Church and the laity', in D. Abulafia (ed.), *New Cambridge Medieval History*, v. *c.1198–c.1300* (Cambridge, 1999), pp. 202–3; G. Dickson, 'The flagellants and the crusades', *Journal of Medieval History*, 15 (1989), pp. 227–67.

IV

The tendency to describe medieval Italy in Tuscan, and more particularly Florentine, terms is nowhere so marked as in the case of letters and the arts. In a book which lacks illustrations it would not make sense to offer a detailed account of the fine arts in medieval Italy, and no chapter has been included on that theme. Still, there is a strong sense here as elsewhere in the history of medieval Italy of diversity. External influences betray the commercial and political links between Italy and lands to the east: Byzantine mosaics were commissioned by one Norman king of Sicily after another, and were put to excellent use in the glorification of what, from a Byzantine perspective, was a pirate kingdom whose rulers had no true title to govern. Therefore it is hardly surprising that images of the king himself, dressed in robes strongly reminiscent of Byzantine imperial costume, appear in the mosaics of Palermo and Monreale. Mosaicists working for the papacy on the great basilicas in Rome might also be seen as agents for the papal view that the vicar of Christ resided in the Old Rome and not in the New Rome of Constantinople; this was also perhaps subtly suggested by the use of porphyry marble, the purple stone reserved for past Byzantine emperors, for the sarcophagi of several twelfth-century popes and, in imitation either of the popes or of Constantinople, by the Norman and Hohenstaufen kings of Sicily for their own tombs (which now survive in the cathedrals of Palermo and Monreale).[22] Byzantine influence was also paramount in the decoration of the Church of St Mark in Venice, a Doge's chapel that had grown out of all proportion, just as Venice itself had broken loose of Byzantine tutelage (never very strong) to become mistress of 'a quarter and half a quarter of the Byzantine Empire' after 1204. Echoes of Byzantium might appear elsewhere too, when links to Constantinople were being invoked, as in the cathedral of Ancona, which had intimate ties to Byzantium in the late twelfth century.

On the other hand, the presence of Islamic influences in the art and architecture of medieval Italy does not convey a particularly clear

---

[22] J. Deér, *The Dynastic Porphyry Tombs of the Norman Period in Sicily* (Cambridge, Mass., 1959).

political message. The use of exotic motifs in the decoration of Italian churches took a particularly lively form in Pisa, Rome, and some other cities, where the practice developed in the eleventh century of inserting pieces of highly glazed Islamic ceramics in the façade or bell-tower of churches, creating a jewel-like effect. Some of these *bacini*, or 'basins', were almost certainly booty (for example from the Pisan raid on Mahdia in Tunisia in 1087), but the *bacini* also fascinated contemporary Italians because the technology to create high glazed ceramics did not really develop in central and northern Italy until after 1200.[23] Islamic motifs could also be used to boast of wide trading connections, as one can see in the late medieval palaces of Venice or in the palaces built by the merchant elite of Amalfi and Ravello (the palace of the Rufolo family in Ravello still preserves these echoes of the Orient).[24] But it is also important to be wary of assumptions that 'orientalizing' features were an attempt to adopt wider features of the art and culture of the East. In their relationship with the Levant and the Greek world, the Tuscans of the twelfth and thirteenth centuries AD were unlike the Etruscans of the seventh and sixth centuries BC. The medieval Tuscans strongly asserted western artistic styles as well as imitating those of their wealthy neighbours in the Orient.

Characteristic of the Tuscan and Ligurian architecture of the twelfth century, and found further afield in Ferrara, many a Lombard town, and elsewhere, was the practice of building churches and other monumental structures in bands of white and dark marble (the dark colour could be a deep black, or as light as the green used by the builders of the cathedral in Ferrara). This style, most magnificently developed in the great complex of buildings around Pisa cathedral, also spread to the Pisan and Genoese settlements in Sardinia and Corsica, as can be seen at the convent of Santa Trinità di Saccargia in northern Sardinia, for example. It can almost be seen as the trademark of north Italian Romanesque architecture. The presence of

---

[23] D. Abulafia, 'The Pisan bacini and the medieval Mediterranean economy: a historian's viewpoint', *Papers in Italian Archaeology, IV: the Cambridge Conference*, pt. iv, *Classical and Medieval Archaeology*, ed. C. Malone and S. Stoddart (British Archaeological Reports, International Series, vol. 246, Oxford, 1985), pp. 287–302, repr. in D. Abulafia, *Italy, Sicily and the Mediterranean, 1100–1400* (London, 1987).

[24] D. Howard, *Venice and the East: The Impact of the Islamic World on Venetian Architecture, 1100–1500* (New Haven, 2000); R. E. Mack, *Bazaar to Piazza: Islamic Trade and Italian Art, 1300–1600* (Berkeley, 2002).

marble quarries to the north of Pisa, around Massa and Carrara, made the right stone readily available. The Pisan ascendancy in Sardinia was further celebrated in the massive Romanesque pulpit sent from Pisa to Cagliari cathedral. Further south, the banded marble featured less prominently, but dazzling white Romanesque churches in Bari (the shrine of St Nicholas above all) and in Trani bear eloquent witness to the presence of a Latin Church, building in Latin styles, on the lands conquered from the Byzantine emperors by the Norman invaders. Even so there are plenty of exotic features: elephants on the outside of St Nicholas in Bari, for example, while the tomb of Bohemond of Antioch in Canosa di Puglia is built in a flagrant imitation of Islamic styles, to commemorate the crusading conquests of this Norman hero.

More problematic is the development of sculpture in medieval Italy. Classical models were consistently important, and fragments of ancient sculpture were freely incorporated in monumental buildings, as can be seen at Tuscania in northern Lazio, where an ancient Etruscan sculpture was levered into the façade of the church of San Pietro; and Etruscan and Roman sculptures apparently served as models for the monumental fountain of Perugia, begun in 1277. The sculptors who worked for Frederick II in southern Italy cultivated a self-consciously classical, imperial style, represented on the surviving sculptures from the early thirteenth-century gateway at Capua and at the hunting lodge Frederick II commissioned at Castel del Monte in Apulia. The same classicism can be detected on Frederick's innovative golden coinage issued for the kingdom of Sicily in 1231, the *augustales* which carry an image of the emperor wearing a Roman-style wreath. Yet some scholars have seen in this 'classicism' an attention to form which was in many respects the first move towards the development of Gothic styles of art in Italy; and certainly under Charles I of Anjou an out-and-out Gothicism prevailed, heavily influenced by the court styles of St Louis, king of France and brother to Charles of Anjou. On the architectural side, this can still be detected in such great Neapolitan monuments as the Church of Santa Chiara, while among sculptures of the period nothing compares with the life-size portrayal of King Charles attributed to Arnolfo di Cambio and presented to the citizens of Rome. Here we can see the transition from the somewhat flat classicism of the sculpture of Frederick's age to the richer and warmer Gothic styles that were coming to dominate western

European art at this period. The presence of powerful patrons from the south of Italy serves as a reminder that artistic changes were by no means confined to the north and centre, a point to which it will be necessary to return. Indeed, the great sculptors Niccolò Pisano and his son Giovanni, celebrated for their work in Pisa, Siena, and elsewhere, may well have been of southern origin; they paid close attention to classical models, which were ready to hand in Pisa. Giovanni, for his part, seems to have become aware of French Gothic models as well. This confirms the sense that the coming of 'Gothic' to Italy was the result of a fusion between continental European styles and the rich native artistic traditions of the Italian regions.

The paintings on panel and on vellum of this period also betray Byzantine and continental European influences which converged on the peninsula in the twelfth and thirteenth centuries. Byzantine portrayals of Christ, the Madonna, and the major scenes in the New Testament narrative served as models for artists working in Tuscany, and illustrate the strong commercial as well as cultural bonds between Tuscany and the Greek world at this period, although a vibrant local tradition of religious art also persisted in areas such as Lombardy, in the frescoed churches of Bardolino on Lake Garda, for example. Since the sixteenth century, when Vasari wrote his lives of the great artists, the development of a more intense, kinetic relationship between the figures portrayed and a more powerful sense of drama in religious art has been attributed to Cimabue, though the Tuscan tradition, further enhanced by the genius of Giotto, was paralleled by developments at Rome, where Cavallini acquired great fame; both he and Giotto were invited south to work for the kings of Naples, so it is clear that the transformations in the fine arts were appreciated and paid for by patrons in north and south. There were indeed Florentine connections: Arnolfo di Cambio worked on the Badía outside Florence, and he and Giotto worked on the cathedral of Florence, which was around 1300 a great boom town. Giotto was influenced by classical styles, and Florence was the location of superb late Romanesque churches such as San Miniato al Monte, with its profound debt to classical architectural models and proportions. But these artists served several masters (the Pisanos worked for Ghibellines). The innovative art works of late thirteenth- and early fourteenth-century Italy are situated in Rome, Pisa, Siena, and Perugia, and there was much more in Naples than now survives; we can talk of a 'central Italian tradition' and not, or not yet, of the cultural flowering of Florence. Indeed, cities competed in grandeur, with Siena in particular becoming carried away by the idea of building the biggest and most beautiful cathedral in Italy when the city was well past its peak as an economic and political power. In addition, Tuscan art had an impact further afield, as is clear from the styles of manuscript painting in the thirteenth-century kingdom of Jerusalem.

Literary developments followed patterns that were not dissimilar. The Roman past was inescapable: it was there for all to see. Boncompagno da Signa opened his account of the German attempt to capture Ancona in 1173 with an elegiac description of the monuments of ancient Rome, setting off nicely the barbarians from the north against the true Romanism of the inhabitants of the peninsula.[25] Sensitivity to classical remains did not have to await Petrarch and Boccaccio in the mid-fourteenth century; indeed, the Florentines were apparently convinced that their Baptistery was in reality a converted Roman temple; nor were such converted buildings unknown in Italy. This sense of continuity from the Roman past has been masked by the insistence of Petrarch and hordes of his successors that the Middle Ages marked a break with the Roman past. And yet, as Alberto Varvaro shows in Chapter 9, the evolution of the vernacular is not the history of the emergence of a national language; the many Italies of the Middle Ages were many linguistic Italies as well.

V

It is a minor irony that, in order to study aspects of the Roman past, Italians of the late twelfth century onwards created a new institution without close classical parallels: this was the university, beginning with the law schools of Bologna, whose teachers have traditionally been assumed to have helped formulate Frederick Barbarossa's legal claim to authority in northern Italy. Particularly important was the impact of Gratian's *Decretum*, written in the 1130s and 1140s; this work provided a structure for the study of canon law and showed

---

[25] Boncompagno da Signa, *The History of the Siege of Ancona*, ed. and trans. A. F. Stone (Archivio del Litorale Adriatico, vol. vi, Venice, 2002).

mastery of the Roman law codes at the same time.[26] Strictly speaking, the university in Bologna consisted of several separate schools of study, and it would be more accurate to write of 'the universities' of Bologna, or better still, the *studia*. At the start of the thirteenth century the university in Bologna began to acquire imitators, and universities emerged in Padua (1222), Naples (1224), Siena (1246), Rome (1240s), Perugia (1308), with a new wave to follow from the middle of the fourteenth century.[27] Among these, Padua was particularly successful. The university has to be understood as a product of communal Italy, in several ways. In the first place, its function was to train young men in the arts so that they could participate in the increasingly literate society of the mercantile cities. At the highest reaches of the universities, the doctors of civil law, experts in the codes of ancient Rome, could aspire to appointment as the *podestà* of a commune, taking charge of its government for about a year and acting as impartial arbiters of its affairs; or the doctors in canon law could hope for speedy preferment in the Church; the papacy took a growing interest in the universities, for example by conferring the right on a university to confer the *ius ubique docendi*, the 'right to teach everywhere', and the title of *studium generale*, indicating the institutions that gave degrees with the right to teach everywhere.

The second way that the university was a product of communal Italy was the way it was organized. It was a civil association like a commune, in which the students performed the role of citizens, taking charge of the government of the university and paying the professors as employees (employees subject to harsh terms, such as the ban on leaving for rival universities, notionally on pain of death). This was a different model for university organization from that which developed in Paris, Oxford, and Cambridge, where the doctors and masters exercised authority subject to a Chancellor, and where the teaching of theology rather than law was dominant. Although the university was a product of communal Italy, Frederick II saw great value in the rigorous training of administrators that a university could provide, and set up his own university in Naples in 1224, the first university that was a royal foundation; although it had as many

---

[26] A. S. Abulafia, 'Frameworked individuality: intellectual and cultural creativity, c.1000–c1300', in D. Power (ed.), *Europe in the Central Middle Ages* (Short Oxford History of Europe, Oxford, 2004).

[27] P. F. Grendler, *The Universities of the Italian Renaissance* (Baltimore, 2002).

quiet as active periods, the university of Naples (still in existence and now known as the 'Frederick II University') played an important role in maintaining interest in Roman law under the Angevin rulers of southern Italy, following its revival under Charles I, Charles II, and Robert of Anjou. Not surprisingly Frederick was unsympathetic to the Bologna model of 'student power'; he also attempted to forbid his south Italian subjects from attending Bologna University, compelling them to study in Naples instead; and technically it was the king of Naples who conferred doctorates. Less successful were the fortunes of the separate medical school at Salerno, which withered away under Frederick and the Angevins; but Salerno's loss was Padua's and Bologna's gain, and the study of medicine began to flourish in northern Italy in the thirteenth century. Here was a subject that once again well suited a city-based civilization: there was plenty of employment for physicians and surgeons in the mercantile cities of northern and central Italy—demand for their services and money to pay for them, as well as easy availability of the raw materials for their pharmacopeia of drugs, from concoctions of syrup to ground-up Egyptian mummy, brought along the sea routes from the Levant, Spain, and elsewhere by the Italian merchants who had been pioneers in the opening of trading stations around the Mediterranean.

VI

The university was a community, not so much an organization. Community is the key to understanding the civilization of northern and central Italy in the central Middle Ages, and the significance of the theme should not be underestimated in the south, either, even if the cities of Sicily and southern Italy never achieved the exceptional autonomy of several northern cities (and in Sardinia, as the case of Sassari shows, communal ideas were far from absent). Community does not, then, signify city government alone; the concept is also essential to any understanding of many aspects of Italian life in this period. The fact that the first commune in Genoa was known as the 'company' (*compania*) serves as a reminder that there were common features tying together the business associations of merchants trading across the seas or mountains and the much larger 'company' that pooled the resources of nobles and merchants to build a fleet for the First Crusade and to govern the city of Genoa in that fleet's long absence. But 'companies' or 'societies'—the same word, *societas*, was used for the Lombard League of cities as for the short-term association of two merchants trading from Genoa to Sardinia, Sicily, or beyond—permeated Italian society. The greatest trading companies, the banks and trading enterprises of Florence soon after 1300 such as the Bardi, Peruzzi, and Acciaiuoli, were renewable, largely family based, but also politically powerful, able to mediate between the city of Florence and the kings of Naples, France, and England. The public and private fronts of the family are well illustrated in Steven Epstein's chapter on the family in this book.

Company, companionship, bonds of kinship, neighbourhood, and friendship, all were in no way unique to Italy; but what was perhaps unusual was the lack of interference by remote and sometimes rapacious royal governments in the forms of civil association that developed in northern and central Italy in both town and country (for one must not forget the rural as well as the city commune). As Brenda Bolton shows, even in the Papal State communes functioned with little serious interference from the papal *curia*. The attempt by Frederick Barbarossa in the twelfth century to impose his will on the Lombard cities was nothing less than a wasteful failure. His grandson Frederick II actually attempted nothing similar in the early thirteenth century. In reality, the battle between Barbarossa and the Lombards was not just a political conflict over taxes and service; it was also a conflict between mental worlds, since (as Barbarossa's uncle Otto of Freising made clear in his chronicle) the German court had little understanding of the principles that bound the commune together, even though Germany too possessed areas crowded with prosperous towns, and even though the devolution of political power to princes and cities was a dominant feature of German political life. Nor did Sicily appear much more familiar to northern observers, with its autocratic traditions of monarchy borrowed from ancient Rome, Byzantium, and Islam, its centralized bureaucracy, and its exotic mix of religions and cultures.

The image of Italy presented in this introduction is still closer than perhaps it should be to the idea that there existed an underlying homogeneity in the greater part of the peninsula, if not the islands. In fact, the message of this book is that it would be wrong to underestimate the heterogeneity of Italy. By including a chapter entitled 'The Italian other' the volume may appear to have tied itself to fashionable views of 'alterity' or Otherness and thus, in a certain sense, to have established a homogeneous norm, presumably Roman Catholic and Romance speaking, possibly also male, against which to measure, as outsiders, the Greeks, Muslims, and Jews of the peninsula and islands, not to mention heretical groups such as the Cathars. These waters have been muddied further by the cult status that Edward Said's verbose and irrelevant book *Orientalism* has acquired even among some medieval historians.[28] But the term used here is 'Italian Other', underlining the fact that the different religious and ethnic groups were also part of the fabric of Italian society in the Middle Ages; not for nothing do the Jews of Rome still cite the tradition that they have been in the city since ancient Roman times, making them more 'Italian', in some respects, than the many Italians of Lombard, Catalan, or Balkan descent. This means that the history of relations between groups should be written not simply as a history of confrontation, of the tense moments that punctuated what were often long periods of peaceful coexistence.

And yet Italy was the historic seat of empire and the residence, until the end of the period addressed in this book, of the pope. Its Roman heritage, expressed in both the secular and the religious history of Italy, was simply overpowering in many areas. Setting aside the reality of urban decline, invasion, depopulation, the creation of new political structures in the early Middle Ages, what is clear by about 1200 is that the politically active inhabitants of large areas of Italy wished to imitate their Roman predecessors, forming communes consisting of citizens on the model of the Roman Republic, in the case of the city republics, or expounding an imperial ideology with Roman overtones, in the case of the Hohenstaufen emperors and the Roman civil lawyers. The tension between these two versions of Romanness dominates the history of Italy in the period of this book.

[28] E. W. Said, *Orientalism: Western Concepts of the Orient* (London, 1978), which has nothing to say to historians of the Middle Ages, and arguably nothing to say to historians of any period.

PART I

RULERS AND SUBJECTS

Cities and communes

Edward Coleman

Introduction

'Communal Italy' is historians' shorthand for the highly urbanized areas of Lombardy and Tuscany between the twelfth and the early fourteenth centuries. It was here, in cities located in the plains of the rivers Po and Arno, and in the foothills of the Alps and the Appennines, that self-governing communes first emerged around 1080–1120; most of them followed a similar path to institutional maturity over the course of the next century. In the 1200s, however, the communes struggled to accommodate the aspirations of groups hitherto excluded from civic politics that coalesced in opposition to the established regime under the much heralded banner of the *Popolo*. These pressures, combined with an inability to find a *modus vivendi* with the Church, and an incurable predilection for factionalism and feud amongst the urban nobility, led to a crisis in many cities by 1300. In the following decades, against a backdrop of worsening economic conditions, communes were widely replaced by the rule of a single powerful family of *signori*, a term often mistranslated as 'despots' or 'tyrants'.

The spatial and temporal limits of this chapter are therefore relatively easy to define. Yet 'city' and 'commune', for all that they are habitually associated in historical parlance, are not entirely interchangeable terms. Communes were also created on the basis of demographic units other than cities, such as small towns and villages, parishes and castles. And within cities communal or quasi-communal organizations sprang up as a consequence of association through social class, domicile, profession, or local religious affiliation (*consorteria, vicinanza, compagna, confraternità*). All of these bodies shared certain characteristics, such as collective decision-making, pooled finances, elected office-holders, and written statutes. Even city communes themselves were not entirely 'stand-alone' bodies, but were part of wider networks which also display communal features—city leagues.

The north Italian propensity to use the commune as a solution to a variety of problems has been widely noted: according to one historian, communes exhibited 'amoeba-like' tendencies.[1] Yet even though communes appeared in various guises, the specific marriage of city and commune, and the increasing identification of the two as one, remains a (perhaps the) crucial development in northern Italy in this period. It begins with the directive public role communes exercised inside cities from the early twelfth century onwards. There has been much debate amongst historians about the 'public' nature of the early city commune. An earlier school of thought denied this even existed, and posited instead a 'private commune' composed of a nexus of prominent urban families pursuing vested interests, oblivious, ignorant, or unheeding of the traditions of civic office and notions of *respublica* stretching back to Late Antiquity. However, few now would disagree with the conclusions of Giovanni Tabacco and his followers that the founders of the first communes did indeed draw on these notions and traditions, and that they did so not least because of the legitimacy it lent to their own position.[2] Cities, then, provided the context in which the commune found its classic and most elaborate form and for this, if for no other reason, the city commune is fundamental to our understanding of what made north Italian society distinctive and dynamic in so many spheres during this period.

[1] J. K. Hyde, *Society and Politics in Medieval Italy: The Evolution of the Civil Life, 1000–1350* (London, 1973), p. 54.
[2] G. Tabacco, *The Struggle for Power in Medieval Italy: Structures of Political Rule*, trans. R. Brown Jensen (Cambridge, 1989), pp. 321–44.

Origins of the communes

It is generally supposed that the rise of city communes was predicated on decentralization, localism, and an absence (or collapse) of the 'state'. In broad terms this is correct, though it had not always been so. The north of Italy had in fact formed the core of the tenth-century Italian kingdom (*regnum italicum*), itself a successor to, and roughly coterminous with, the earlier Lombard (568–774) and Carolingian (774–875) kingdoms. But in spite of the legitimization of a continuous history stretching back to the sixth century, the *regnum italicum* showed clear signs of failing soon after the first millennium. Its rulers from 1024, the German Salian emperors, were not present often enough to impose their authority, and the period between the 1020s and 1040s was marked by a series of city revolts, including those in the capital Pavia (1024), Cremona (1030–1), Parma (1037), and (repeatedly) Milan (1036–7, 1040, 1042–3); hard on the heels of these disturbances came further troubles associated with the Patarine movement (1056–75) and the increasing embroilment of the German king Henry IV (1056–1106) with the papacy over ecclesiastical investitures and other matters. Henry's successors, his son Henry V (1105–25), Lothar II (1125–37), and Conrad III (1138–52) came ever more rarely to Italy.

When present in Italy, the emperors were crowned in Monza, held court in Pavia, and from time to time summoned general assemblies of the kingdom at Roncaglia, near Piacenza. But the day-to-day running of the Italian kingdom was in the hands of local representatives, the majority of whom in the eleventh century were bishops. Bishops had gradually taken on this overtly political role in the course of the previous 200 years, consolidating their position at moments when central monarchy was weak, absentee, or too preoccupied with other concerns to devote time and energy to local issues. Bishops operated simultaneously as imperial functionaries and community leaders: linkmen, one might say, between crown and subjects. They were ideally suited to this task for a number of reasons. The urban nature of northern Italy meant that it was most conveniently administered from cities, and bishops held a central position in city life on account of the prestige associated with episcopal office, their extensive landed wealth, and their network of social connections. They were also generally well educated, good administrators, and theoretically celibate, which in turn meant that they were theoretically unlikely to promote narrow family interests, even if in reality the relationship between the bishop and the vassals of his *curia* bordered on familial. Numerous imperial diplomas issued in favour of bishops as representatives of their cities are testimony to a time-honoured and proven system. But in the eleventh century the system was coming under severe strain. The end result was a weakened monarchy and a definitive devolution of control to the localities, in part through formal grant, in part through informal usurpation, though often retrospectively cloaked as confirmation of ancient 'customs' (*consuetudines*).

The decline of the Italian kingdom, and the atrophy of its military, judicial, and fiscal institutions in the course of the eleventh century, produced what has been called 'a pullulation of little powers';[3] in other words a realignment of authority along far more localized lines. Historical factors dictated that cities were bound to become important in this mix. The Po and Arno valleys were heavily urbanized by the standards of the time. Lombard and Tuscan cities were, with very few exceptions, Roman foundations. Consequently, they were deeply rooted in the landscape, and had been continuously occupied over many centuries; they contained large concentrations of population relative to the surrounding countryside, and were nodal points of trade and communications. They possessed significant infrastructural assets: fortified walls and gates, warehouses and workshops, secular and religious public buildings, a large private housing stock and water supplies. Naturally, the maintenance and extension of this infrastructure required capital investment. Although kings and emperors had concerned themselves with the upkeep of palaces, city defences, and public highways, their approach to these projects had always been more geared towards the extraction of revenue rather than the input of resources. As the crown's role in these affairs declined, that of the city population, or specifically its leading citizens (*cives*), expanded commensurately. When, by c.1100, the kingdom had ceased to function in any meaningful sense, the cities found themselves independent but wholly dependent on their own initiatives.

[3] C. Wickham, *Early Medieval Italy: Central Power and Local Society* (London, 1981), p. 168.

This was certainly one of the general reasons underlying the emergence of communes.

Cities had also seen steady growth in their populations in the eleventh century, fuelled by immigration from the countryside, and this meant that the urban social mix inevitably became more complex. The language used in imperial diplomas to describe citizen bodies is usually generic (*populus*) but occasionally there are hints of socio-economic differences within the city in phrases such as *cives maiores et minores* (greater and lesser citizens) or *cives divites et pauperes* (rich and poor citizens). There is enough evidence to lead historians to think that alongside the landed nobles and cathedral clergy, who were the traditional associates and supporters of the bishop, other groups with fewer ties, or no ties, with the bishop were also becoming socially prominent. These new groups too were composed of landowners, but in this case with more diversified interests and backgrounds, for example in commerce and trade, or professional expertise in law and notarial practice. The bishop thus increasingly appears not so much as a representative of all *cives* but as head of a tight and privileged elite, a self-serving clique. In itself the rise of new mercantile and professional families in the city might have had little impact in political terms, as the bishop and his supporters were firmly entrenched in their positions of command and control, and viewed these practically as a hereditary right, a way of life. Yet the entire edifice of what we might reasonably call episcopal lordship in cities crumbled rapidly from *c.*1050 onwards as a consequence of two extraneous but inter-related political changes of wide import which, combined with the altered demographics just mentioned, created the conditions for an irresistible shift towards a more pluralistic civil regime.

The first of these changes—the decline and eventual disappearance of centralized monarchy in northern Italy—we have already discussed. As imperial power became increasingly remote and irrelevant the bishop's position was obviously undermined. But it was the movement for ecclesiastical reform which, in addition to plunging the empire into crisis, administered the *coup de grace* to episcopal lordship in the cities. Not only did reformers such as Peter Damian, Anselm of Lucca, and Bonizo of Sutri condemn simoniac and nicholaistic bishops and oppose imperial investitures—the emblematic flashpoint being the disputed election of the archbishop of Milan in 1075—but they also called into question the whole range of secular powers hitherto wielded by bishops; involvement in judicial and military matters was seen as particularly inappropriate. Pressure was thus brought to bear on bishops to renounce their leading civic position and, as the Reform party was clearly in the ascendancy by the end of the eleventh century, most did so. Those who did not, such as Arnulf of Cremona (1078), Benzo of Alba (1090), and Arnulf of Bergamo (1098), were removed. Naturally this withdrawal of bishops, voluntarily or enforced, from a sphere in which they had been dominant for so long created a vacuum, and this vacuum was filled by the first communes.

This process is notoriously difficult to trace, however, as it has left few explicit clues in the sources. Our main records here are the series of imperial diplomas issued in Italy by the German emperors. Their purpose from the imperial point of view was to secure local support against the papacy and the main papal supporter in northern Italy, the countess Matilda of Canossa (d. 1115). Until around the third quarter of the eleventh century such diplomas were issued in favour of bishops, as representatives of cities, as was mentioned. Thereafter when grants of property or rights in or near a city were conceded the documents were often addressed not to the bishop but directly to the citizens (*cives*). It would seem from this semantic shift that the bishop was no longer considered as the legitimate representative of the city, no doubt for the reasons already outlined. But it is less clear who had taken over the bishop's role. If what we would call a commune was already in existence by this stage it is never called this in the diplomas which refer to the city (*civitas*), but not to the commune. Occasionally, though by no means always, individuals described as 'worthy men' (*boni homines*) are also mentioned, as in a diploma issued to the citizens of Pisa by the German king Henry IV in 1081.[4] We may assume that these men are in some sense representatives of the citizens and that they had petitioned for these grants from the emperor, but they are not named, and their relationship with the preceding episcopal regime, if any, is not explained. Many diplomas make no mention of *boni homines* at all, but are simply addressed generically to all the citizens of the city (e.g. *cives pisani, cives mediolanenses, cives veroneses, cives cremonenses*). They are emphatically

---

[4] D. Gladiss and A. Gawlik (eds.), *Henrici IV Diplomata*, MGH Dip. Reg. et imp. Germ, 3 vols. (Weimar and Hanover, 1953–78), vol. ii, pp. 442–3, n. 336.

not charters of communal foundation, however, convenient though it would be for historians if they were. We might sense that the commune is there in many places by c.1100, but the sources will often not offer definitive confirmation until decades later.

This vagueness and ambiguity in the documentation is naturally frustrating for historians seeking to identify a clear-cut 'beginning' to such an important development as the emergence of the city communes.[5] But it may in itself be significant. It strongly suggests that there was no communal 'big bang', but that on the contrary communes emerged gradually, almost imperceptibly over a period of decades, perhaps even longer. There is certainly evidence to show that cities had been acting collectively for a very long time, whether in association with their bishops or indeed in opposition to bishops, before the chronological 'window' (c.1080–1120) in which it is usually assumed communes appeared. At the other end of the chronological scale it might be noted that the typical political institutions of the commune are not widely recorded before the third decade of the twelfth century, whilst we have to wait until as late as the 1150s to witness the first moves towards the general regularization of communal constitutional arrangements in written law, and only then because Emperor Frederick I threatened to revoke all the concessions made by his predecessors. It may therefore be misplaced to seek to tie down communal origins too closely in time. We should perhaps be thinking in terms of a long transition between pre-communal and communal worlds, of interface rather than interruption. It may be more pertinent and interesting to ask for how long, and in what ways, the old coexisted with the new, rather than when and how the old was displaced by the new.

Curiously enough, the most famous description of the early commune comes not from an Italian source but from the pen of a German cleric, Bishop Otto of Freising (c.1112–58). Otto, who was the maternal uncle of the emperor Frederick I, was a highly educated and intelligent observer. He visited Italy twice and makes reference to events in the peninsula in his *Deeds of Frederick Barbarossa* (1149). The importance of Otto is that he grasped, in a way that no contemporary Italian writer seems to have done, that momentous change was taking place

---

[5] 'No comparable movement in Western history is so imperfectly recorded': Philip Jones, *The Italian City-State* (Oxford, 1997), p. 141.

in the northern half of Italy. Briefly and succinctly, he lays out the salient points:

The entire land is divided amongst the cities; each of them requires its bishop to live in the cities, and scarcely any noble or great man can be found in all the surrounding territory who does not acknowledge the authority of a city. And from this power to force all lands together they are wont to call the several lands of each their *contado* [*comitatus*]. Also that they may not lack the means of subduing their neighbours, they do not disdain to give the girdle of knighthood or the grades of distinction to young men of inferior status and even to some workers of the vile mechanical arts whom other people bar like the plague from the more respected and honourable pursuits. From this it has resulted that they far surpass all other states of the world in riches and power.[6]

Otto thus defines the city commune in terms of urbano-centric political geography encompassing the Church and aristocracy, highly fluid and flexible social structures, and the arrogance of newly acquired wealth. As it is from a non-Italian, who by reason of his birth, upbringing, and experience would be likely to be hostile to the communes, this definition has to be treated with due caution. But it remains highly interesting and evocative.

The sketchy and ambiguous documentary and narrative evidence can be supplemented with evidence from other types of sources, which provide occasional hints at the changes that were taking place. One such example is a sculptural relief on the tympanum of the church of St Zeno in the city of Verona. This shows two heavily armed groups, one on horseback, and the other on foot holding a banner, on either side of a bishop who raises his hand in blessing. An inscription below reads: 'the bishop gives the people an ensign to be prized, Zeno bestows the standard with a happy heart'.[7] Bishop Zeno (d. 372) was credited with bringing Christianity to Verona, and from the eighth century his relics were kept in this church. It has been suggested that the relief is an allegory on the foundation of the commune at Verona, with Zeno personifying the city, the horsemen representing its nobility (*milites*), and the group on foot the non-nobility

---

[6] Otto of Freising, *The Deeds of Frederick Barbarossa*, ed. and trans. C. C. Mierow (New York, 1953), section II, p. 13.

[7] 'Dat presul signum populo munime dignum | Vexillum Zeno largitur corde sereno' (English trans. in D. Webb, *Patrons and Defenders: The Saints in the Italian City States* (London, 1996), p. 62.

(*pedites*). It has been dated to about 1135–8, which is remarkably consistent with the earliest documentary evidence for the Veronese commune (1136). However, if it is some kind of memorial to the founding of the commune, it is unique and shows a precocious awareness of the importance of a change, which was profoundly to affect not only Verona but cities right across northern Italy.

Civic institutions, office-holding, and law

By *c.*1150 communes had been established in all the major towns and cities in Lombardy and Tuscany. Despite differing local circumstances and variations in terminology, most communes are remarkably similar in the phasing of their institutional development and the character of their political structures. All set up regular assemblies of citizens to discuss matters of common concern; all elected officials, commonly called consuls, who took responsibility for internal law and order, and 'external affairs'; all embarked on a policy of bringing the territory around the city, the *contado*, under their authority; all began to collect and keep a diverse body of legal material which ultimately formed the basis of the first city statutes. In this sense it is legitimate to speak of a 'communal movement' in north and central Italy. It does not necessarily follow, however, that the communes always formed a unified front or shared a common ideology. In many respects nothing could be further from the truth, even if on exceptional occasions they did unite in leagues against the German Empire. Even so, the similarities between communes are undeniable and cannot be coincidental. Most probably they result from the fact that faced with common problems cities found common solutions. Their physical proximity to one another, and the ease of communication between them, are likely also to have been factors in the spread of parallel ideas.

The practice of convening a citizens' assembly was not an invention of the communes; city-dwelling Italians had been habitually meeting together for many centuries, primarily to elect their bishop. As far back as 643 an Edict of the Lombard king Rothari refers to an urban 'assembly before the church' (*conventus ad ecclesiam*), and the chroniclers Arnulf and Landulf Senior mention assemblies held in pre-communal Milan in the eleventh century.[8] The emergence of the communes raised the profile of what must have been in many places an already venerable civic institution. The communal assembly (variously called *colloquium, concio, arenga, parlamentum*) was summoned by bells (*ad sonum campane convocatum*) to meetings in the city's central square, more often than not in front of the cathedral, an appropriate meeting place as the cathedral was considered to be the symbolic heart of the city. Meetings appear to have been *ad hoc* rather than regular at first, though it could simply be that only the records of important meetings survive whilst those from more routine occasions have been lost. Business seems to have included declarations of war, ratification of truces and alliances, the election of consuls, the passing of judicial sentences, and the approval of statutes. As regards procedures, it is likely that there were speeches but little in the way of debate. As the numbers attending would quite probably have been in the hundreds, and perhaps thousands in the largest cities, decision-making would have been fairly crude and appears to have been achieved by use of the *Fiat*, or collective cry of assent. So the Genoese annalist Caffaro writes of an assembly held in his city in 1162: 'all those in the assembly cried immediately and with one voice *Fiat! Fiat!*'[9] A major drawback about the assembly was its unwieldiness, and this can only have been compounded as the city population continued to grow. It is for this reason that we see public business also being transacted in smaller councils (*consilia*) from an early stage in most communes. Such councils filled an ancillary or facilitating role alongside the assembly and consuls at first, but gradually acquired more power. Ultimately consuls had to seek their approval rather than that of the assembly on all-important matters. As much of the work of councils was legal, lawyers and jurists (*iudices, causidici*) came to exercise a significant influence in this arena.

The most characteristic office of the early commune was the consul; indeed the period until the late twelfth century is often referred to as the consular phase of communal history. In the past historians often dated the foundation of the commune in a given city

---

[8] Arnulf, *Liber gestorum recentium*, ed. C. Zey, MGH, Script. rer. ger. in usum schol. separatim editi, lxvi (Hanover, 1994), II, 13–20; Landulf, *Historia mediolanensis*, ed. A. Cutolo, RISS², iv/2 (Bologna, 1940), III, 9.

[9] *Annali Genovesi di Caffaro e de'suoi continuatori*, ed. L. T. Belgrano, Fonti per la storia d'Italia, XI/1 (Genoa, 1890), p. 71.

to the first recorded appearance of consuls but, as was said earlier, the imposition of a rigid chronological scheme on a process of gradual and subtle change is artificial. Despite the Roman echoes of the title, the office of consul appears to be new in the twelfth century, though the *boni homines* who acted as representatives of some cities in the eleventh century may have been in certain respects their forerunners. Consuls should not be thought of as rulers of the commune; rather they seem to have been elected representatives of the various social groups that made it up. The number of members of the college of consuls varied considerably from city to city, and even within cities the numbers could increase or decrease over time (never less than two, but sometimes over twenty). It has been plausibly proposed that the number and distribution of consular offices may be related to the balance of political power within a city, with various groups struggling for representation appropriate to their influence. A Milanese document of 1130, for example, records twenty-three consuls, ten of whom are described as being from the upper nobility (*capitanei*), seven from the lower nobility (*valvassores*), and six from the *cives*.[10] It may even be that in some cities—Milan again has been suggested as a possible example—the commune itself arose as a form of settlement (*pax et concordia*) between warring parties. The tripartite social division of *capitanei, valvassores,* and *cives* may be typical particularly of Milan and western Lombardy; it is certainly more frequently documented there than elsewhere. Interestingly, though, Otto of Freising specifically links it to the choice of consuls, and in the same passage also sheds light on the reasons for another feature of consular office, namely its short tenure. He writes:

They are so desirous of liberty that they are governed by the will of consuls rather than rulers. There are known to be three orders amongst them: *capitanei, valvassores* and *cives*. And in order to suppress arrogance the aforesaid consuls are chosen not from one but from each of the three aforesaid classes. And lest they should exceed bounds through lust for power they are changed almost every year.[11]

The terms and conditions of consular office appear in a number of surviving texts of oaths that consuls swore on taking up office

[10] C. Manaresi (ed.), *Gli atti del comune di Milano fino all'anno MCCXVI* (Milan, 1919), p. 7 n. 3.

[11] Otto of Freising, *Deeds of Frederick Barbarossa*, section II, p. 13.

(*brevia*). The oath sworn by the consuls of Pisa in 1162 gives a sense of what was involved:

In the name of the Father, Son and Holy Spirit and in invocation of the Mother of God, always Virgin Mary, the year of the Incarnation of Our Lord Jesus Christ, 1162. From January 1st next for an entire year I will dedicate myself to the prosperity of the city of Pisa in word and deed, on land, on the sea, in all places, in peace and in war, to the honour of the cathedral church of Pisa, dedicated to the Blessed Virgin, to the archbishopric and to the college of canons, to the maintenance of the cathedral, other churches, hospices, bridges, to the clergy, to the city of Pisa on both sides of the river, as enclosed in the new walls, to the prosperity of the Pisan people and those who live from Cintoria to Pontedera, on both sides of the river as far as the sea, from Ripafratta to Filetto on both sides of the river as far as the sea, and as far as the castle of Capoalbo.[12]

The text goes on to discuss how the consul will organize the election from amongst the citizens of councillors, legal officers, treasurers, moneyers, financial regulators, night watchmen, supervisors of buildings, roads, and waterways. He will raise a force of 300 knights and maintain them in readiness, and similarly twenty galleys. There are some peculiarly Pisan aspects to these provisions, notably the concern with the sea and a fleet. But much else is characteristic of the preoccupations of many communes: justice, defence, public finance, urban infrastructure, the Church, and the *contado*. All of these fell under the consuls' remit. The burgeoning bureaucracy of the communes is also here clearly revealed. Although precise population statistics for twelfth-century Pisa are lacking, it seems reasonable to believe that a significant number of the city's adult males were already finding employment of one sort or other in what we might term the 'public sector', even if for many it would have been part-time work;[13] moreover, all the offices mentioned were salaried posts, which also made it imperative that the commune raise revenue by whatever means were open to it.

Consuls had a wide and diverse range of responsibilities, and given that the consular college commonly numbered a dozen or more

---

[12] F. Bonaini (ed.) *Statuti inediti della città di Pisa dal XII al XIV secolo*, i (Florence, 1854), pp. 3–15.

[13] Jones, *Italian City-State*, pp. 409–10, gives a figure of 81 officials (minimum), excluding the 300 knights and those involved in building and crewing the galleys, on the basis of the information contained in this document.

persons it seems probable that some division of labour took place. This can be seen to be formaled with the appointment in some cities of consuls with specific legal or commercial briefs—'consuls of the pleas' or 'consuls of justice' (*consules de placitis, consules causarum, consule iustitiae*) and 'consuls of markets' or 'consuls of the merchants' (*consules mercatorum, consules negotiatorum*). Another major administrative area, public finance and taxation, also developed as a separate office under a treasurer (*camerarius*); the records of this office in Siena, where it was known as the *Biccherna*, have been exhaustively studied. Similarly, a chancery or writing office and archive was created to produce and manage the growing volume of public records. Henceforward, these major 'departments' of communal administration further subdivided themselves, resulting in an impressive, if labyrinthine, array of governmental bodies in the major cities of the late thirteenth and fourteenth centuries.

Oath-taking was not restricted to communal office-holders. Citizens also took oaths, which set out their duties and responsibilities to the commune. In an oath sworn in 1157 the citizens of Genoa pledged to abide by decisions of the consuls, attend the assembly, do military service, and not to help non-Genoese merchants.[14] From uncertain beginnings citizenship developed as a highly complex form of legal status, made more interesting on account of the fact that it was effectively classless, insomuch as it cut across the boundary of noble and non-noble. In many respects it became a class of itself. The communes, like modern states, always knew whom they wished to become citizens and whom they did not and were selective in their approach to conferring citizenship. Yet for all the accretions and variations that it accrued in the medieval centuries it remained essentially a trade-off involving obligations and money in return for privilege and protection.

One further significant constitutional innovation brought in by most communes towards the end of the twelfth century remains to be considered in this section—the office of *podestà* (*potestas, rector, gubernator*). The *podestà* was a single supreme official who took over responsibilities for justice, finance, and defence. Just as in the first quarter of the twelfth century the consulate spread quickly from city

---

[14] *Il Codice Diplomatico della Repubblica di Genova*, ed. C. Imperiale di Sant'Angelo, FSI 77 (Rome, 1936), vol. i, pp. 350–9.

to city, so in the last quarter city after city appointed *podestà*. It could be argued that the recourse to *podestà* actually represents an inversion of the consular commune, in that the college of consuls was intended to be a safeguard against rule by one individual and 'lust for power', as Otto of Freising put it. Moreover, *podestà* were first introduced to Italian cities by the emperor Frederick I during his wars with the communes (1160–76): not a happy beginning. On the other hand, *podestà*, like consuls before them, were not really rulers of cities so much as appointed officers who remained in place for a short period of time, six months or a year, and were answerable to their employers. Even so, their emergence does indicate that the consular system had conspicuously failed to deliver in one important area: the maintenance of law and order within the city. The spread of noble *consorterie* and fortified towers, and the frequent outbreaks of civil strife on the streets were testimony to the struggles for power and influence amongst the ruling elites. The new approach was to try to defuse this situation by investing authority in the hands of a figure who would be neutral and *super partes*.

To preserve this neutrality it became common practice for *podestà* to be drawn from cities other than those in which they served. They had to bring with them their own retinue (*familia*) of judges, notaries, and, of course, troops. They were assigned special quarters in the city (*palazzo del podestà*) and their contact with the population was strictly controlled. At the end of their term of office they had to undergo an audit of their accounts (*sindicatus*), which could result in the withholding of salary if any irregularities were discovered. *Podestà* were usually noblemen for the simple reason that only noblemen would be able to sustain the requisite household and retinue. They were, that is to say, similar in social background to the consular families and would have shared their outlook and assumptions, factors that may have eased their task. In particular, they were likely to be well versed in the art of war, and this was becoming an increasingly sought-after skill in the hostile environment of the late twelfth and early thirteenth centuries. Acting as a *podestà* became a tradition in some families, the role being taken up by more than one family member or in successive generations; some individuals made a career out of being *podestà*, moving from city to city. Movement was not entirely free, however. The patterns of alliances between cities, rather than individual choice, dictated who went where; allied cities tended to exchange *podestà* as a mark of respect and co-operation. Overall the use of *podestà* was an experiment which enjoyed a degree of success. By the early thirteenth century they had become effectively professional administrators and soldiers, and a fixed and accepted feature of Italian political life, as is evidenced by the standardization of their terms of service and even the production of handbooks of advice for *podestà*, the best known of which is the so-called *Oculus pastoralis* (*c.*1212–20).[15]

The *podestà* are closely associated with another development which signals the 'coming of age' of the communes towards the end of the twelfth century, the codification of the first civic statutes (*statuta*). In Milan in 1216 and in Genoa in 1239, for example, statutes were codified on the direct initiative of the *podestà*. In what was perhaps a semi-conscious preparation for this development a number of communes had for some time been collecting and copying all the imperial diplomas, papal bulls, pacts, treaties, charters, and all manner of other documents relating to their city into great compendia, known as 'books of rights' or 'books of privileges' (*libri iurium, libri privilegiorum*). The idea was clearly to gather together all documentation which had a bearing on the legal status of the commune, its rights and claims, particularly with regard to territory. Interestingly, in the absence of founding charters, of the kind which are familiar to north European historians of towns, some of these *libri iurium*, such as the *Registrum Magnum* of Piacenza, include at the beginning a copy of the famed Peace of Constance (1183), under which Emperor Frederick I effectively granted all communes constitutional autonomy.[16] Insistence on the right to issue statutes (*ius statuendi*) was a confident expression of this newly won legal independence.

Cities took great pride in their statutes (the earliest statutes of Ferrara, of 1173, were inscribed on the walls of the city's cathedral); and in time they came to supersede all other forms of law, a point made forcibly by the rhetorician Boncompagno da Signa (1165/70–?1235):

---

[15] *Oculus pastoralis*, ed. G. Franceschi, Memorie dell'Accademia delle Scienze di Torino (Turin, 1966).

[16] *Il 'Registrum Magnum' del Comune di Piacenza*, ed. E. Falconi and R. Peveri, 4 vols. (Milan, 1984–8).

In this way whatever city in Italy makes its own statutes and constitutions, according to which the *podestà* and consuls conduct public business, and punish transgressors, notwithstanding other laws which may contradict statute, [it is so done] because they have sworn to uphold those statutes and constitutions in their entirety.[17]

With successive additions (*addimenta*) and reissues (*reformationes*) the statutes became voluminous and complicated. True to form, the communes created the post of statute inspector (*statuarius, emendator*) to check their accuracy. The actual drafting of statutes was of course a highly specialized task, which in all important cities was carried out by experts in law (*jurisperiti*), trained in the university of Bologna, who were able to bring to bear knowledge of Roman law, canon law, and the whole complex raft of royal, imperial, papal and princely legislation, case law, and custom. Indeed it is fair to say that, without the twelfth-century florescence of legal studies in Bologna, city statutes would not have been the great achievement that they are. The end products are sophisticated and comprehensive, generally divided into several books relating to different branches of law, amongst which constitutional, criminal, and civil law (*de regimine, de criminalibus, de civilibus*) were held to be the most important.

The foregoing discussion of assemblies, councils, consuls, and lawmaking may give the impression that the communes were orderly and well organized. Up to a point, allowing for medieval conditions, this is true. However, there was a dark side to communal society too, which cast a constant shadow over the progress in the fields of law and government.

Warfare and city leagues

Leaf through any of the city annals compiled in Lombardy and Tuscany in the twelfth and thirteenth centuries and one theme immediately stands out—the frequency of war. Here are a few typical lines from the Annals of Cremona, compiled some time before the 1180s:

---

[17] Boncompagno da Signa, *Cedrus*, in *Briefsteller und Formelbüchern des elften bis vierzehnten Jahrhunderts*, 2 vols. (Munich, 1863), vol. i, pp. 121–2.

1150: When the Milanese and Cremonese met in battle at Castelnuovo, and many men and horses were killed; and the Milanese shamefully abandoned their *carroccio* there on 5 July.

1151: When the Cremonese sold Castelnuovo to the Piacentines, in the month of December.

1152: When Medesano (Parma) was captured on 13 July, and the Cremonese remained there for seven weeks.

[in the next year (1153) the city of Ascalon was captured in the month of August].

1155: When Tortona was captured by the emperor Frederick. And in the same year in November the minting of coin was begun in Cremona. And when he retreated the aforesaid emperor burnt Senigola (Cremona).

1157: When there was the third war with Crema, on 8 May.[18]

The city communes were geared for war, they expended the greater part of their income on war, and their citizens were exhorted to war. Civic literature and civic art glorified war; Simone Martini's fresco of the *condottiere* Guidoriccio di Foligniano against the background of a tented army camp in the *palazzo pubblico* in Siena (1330) is a good example. It is also no accident that one of the most potent civic symbols of all—the *carroccio*—was a war chariot. War was endemic, and in more ways than one communal Italy was at war with itself.

An obvious starting-point in any discussion of war is the territorial rivalry that existed between city communes. All cities were gripped by a desire to control the territory surrounding their walls (*comitatus/contado*). In this they were motivated by purely practical considerations. First and foremost the food supply of cities derived from the *contado*, and it was paramount that this be guaranteed. This led communes to intervene actively in the cultivation, sale, and distribution of basic foodstuffs such as grain. Statutory legislation was routinely introduced to regulate prices and prevent hoarding or profiteering. Some cities went further, limiting or even banning the export of corn to other cities, and dictating which crops could be grown and where. It was vital too that roads be maintained and kept secure for the transport of produce from the *contado* to the city, and also for the free flow of exports out of those cities that produced manufactured goods. Commercial traffic also brought significant fiscal benefits to the cities in the form of road, bridge, gate, and market

[18] *Annales Cremonenses*, ed. O. Holder-Egger, MGH, SS, xxxi (Hanover, 1903), pp. 1–21.

tolls. The interchange between city and *contado* is quintessentially captured in a scene from another fresco in Siena's *palazzo pubblico*, this time by Ambrogio Lorenzetti: the artist depicts a party of urban nobility on their way to hawk and hunt in the countryside passing a *contadino* driving his pigs into market at the city gate.

If the basic economic reliance of the city on the *contado* was fundamental, it was not the only reason why the cities wished to control their rural hinterlands. Human resources were also crucial. The communes exploited the manpower of the *contado* most obviously in the production and supply of food, but it was also put to work on infrastructural projects such as road and canal building and the construction of fortifications and planned settlements (*castelli, borghi nuovi*). The rural population also provided a significant proportion of the rank and file of communal armies, as military service extended from the city to the countryside. And, finally, it was a source of tax revenue, particularly so following the introduction of general taxes known as the *estimo, allibramento*, and *catasto* in the fourteenth century, fiscal initiatives in which Tuscan cities appear to have led the field.

From an early stage, then, the city communes attempted to push their territorial authority to its limits. Precisely what the limits were was an open question, however. Just as the rise of the communes involved a reshaping of the administrative and institutional structures of the old *regnum italicum*, so too it was necessary to redraw the map of political geography. The new map, as Otto of Freising once again noted, was basically one of intersecting city territories, at least on the Po and Arno plains. But it was highly fluid and unstable for most of the twelfth and thirteenth centuries, only becoming more simplified after 1300 with the rise to dominance of a few major cities. The tactics most commonly employed by cities in their struggles for territory were to attempt to make secular communal jurisdiction mirror the ecclesiastical jurisdiction of a city's diocese. This had certain advantages in that it provided well-defined boundaries at which to aim and, as the territorial extent of most dioceses had been more-or-less fixed for centuries, it legitimized the extension of urban authority to the countryside by appeal to historical precedent. The process evolved in two, broadly sequential, phases. First of all, the communes extended their control over their own *contado*. This was achieved largely through negotiation, often involving financial transactions, with the holders of rural lordships and leaders of rural communities, and not generally, as an earlier historiography supposed, by an aggressive 'conquest of the *contado*'. Geographical factors certainly played a part in how easy or difficult it was to control a *contado*: those cities with partly mountainous hinterlands—virtually all the Tuscan cities and the Lombard cities on the fringes of the Alps and Apennines—tended to experience more resistance and require greater commitment of time and resources to achieve their ends.

The second part of the process involved securing the frontiers of the *contado*. This was effected by the foundation of the entirely new settlements mentioned earlier, the *borghi nuovi*, mostly laid out between 1150 and 1250. Population was shifted and concentrated into these fortified *borghi nuovi* which were strategically sited along the borders of city territories, on road and river crossings, or at the heads of valleys. On the western Po plain where the tributaries of the main river, the Ticino, Adda, Oglio, and Mincio, formed natural boundaries between city territories, the *borghi nuovi* of Soncino, founded by Cremona in 1118, and Orzivecchi, founded by Brescia in 1120, stared confrontationally at one another from opposite banks of the river Oglio; a similar situation existed in Veneto where the Paduans constructed Cittadella in 1220 in response to the Trevisan foundation of nearby Castelfranco (1195). These settlements were the strongpoints and often the flashpoints of inter-communal warfare, its border skirmishes. Their inhabitants were as much garrisons as cultivators, as is shown by the charters of privileges granted to them by communes in which the responsibilities of guard duty figure prominently. By investing in these elaborate defensive measures on the periphery of their territories the communes were attempting not only to safeguard their land and supply lines, but to reduce the frequency with which the communal militia (in which the citizens themselves served) took the field. This propensity to pay others to do their fighting was to become ever more marked in the thirteenth-century communes, culminating ultimately in the widespread use of mercenary forces.

Territorial rivalries naturally led city communes to seek friends and allies. Almost as soon as they came into existence in the early twelfth century they began to form defensive alliances, usually with relatively distant neighbours, with the aim of protecting their interests and territory against the ambitions of more immediate neighbours. In time these alliances evolved into wider coalitions or leagues (*societates*). The greatest leagues of all, the first and second Lombard Leagues (1167–83, 1231–50), saw dozens of cities in alliance against the German emperors Frederick I Barbarossa (1152–90) and his grandson Frederick II (1220–50), the first of whom made unsuccessful attempts to impose stronger and more direct imperial rule in Italy. In addition to common political and financial structures, which were in many respects scaled-up versions of those to be found in the cities, the Lombard Leagues also raised a common army, drawn from the citizen militias of their member cities. Thus on the battlefield, as in most other aspects of north Italian society during this period, communalism prevailed.

The long-running quarrel between the empire and the communes had its roots in the period of the Investitures Contest. As was discussed earlier, the struggle between pope and emperor at that time formed an important part of the background to the rise of the communes. By the time of the election of the emperor Frederick I Barbarossa in 1152, city communes had been electing civic leaders and officers, operating their own courts, collecting taxes, defining their territorial boundaries, and generally running their own affairs for half a century. Frederick was determined to change this situation, however, driven perhaps by a nostalgic notion of recreating the glories of Ottonian and even Carolingian rule south of the Alps, and certainly by a desire to recoup what he regarded as revenue lost to the imperial treasury during more recent decades of neglect. He used the occasion of an imperial diet assembled at Roncaglia in 1158 to lay out his two essential demands: first, the restoration of the imperial right of appointment to positions of authority throughout the old *regnum italicum,* and second the payment of *regalia,* that is, monies owed on a range of royal prerogatives, amongst which judicial fines, commercial tolls, and *fodrum* (a kind of poll tax) were particularly lucrative. There was no possibility that the communes would accept these demands; therefore conflict became inevitable. It was to last nearly two decades.

The details of the military campaigns need not concern us long here. Resistance to Frederick was co-ordinated by Milan which soon suffered for putting itself in the vanguard. In 1162 Frederick and his Italian allies (Milan's enemies) besieged, evacuated, and destroyed the Lombard capital. This proved a turning-point, for instead of cowing the rest of the cities into submission, as Frederick no doubt hoped, the action backfired. Groups of cities, first in north-eastern Italy, and soon also in Lombardy, sank their differences and banded together in leagues against the emperor. The foundation of the first Lombard League in 1167 is a watershed not only because the military campaign became unwinnable for Frederick as a result, but also because in forming a league the cities recognized that communalism was in their common interest. Backed by Pope Alexander III (1159–81) they struck back at Frederick, rebuilt Milan, resisted his siege of the newly constructed fortress of Alessandria, and finally defeated him in battle at Legnano in May 1176. The emperor and the communes made peace at Constance in 1183 in a settlement of paramount importance.[19] Although the treaty was couched in the language of a gracious imperial concession, Frederick had in fact been forced into a humiliating climbdown, and had to withdraw the demands he had made at Roncaglia in 1158. The city communes were effectively given carte blanche in the running of their affairs and were even allowed to reform their league if they felt threatened once again: little wonder the text of the Peace of Constance was copied into so many communal statute books.

A smaller Lombard League returned to the fray between 1236 and 1250. By then the emperor was the grandson of Frederick Barbarossa, Frederick II. Suspicions of his intentions towards the cities may have been aroused by his legislation in southern Italy, which was hostile to urban liberties, though it is fair to point out that the Constitutions of Melfi of 1231 had no force north of the frontier of the Sicilian kingdom. Several north Italian towns actively supported Frederick, and both David Abulafia and Daniel Waley have tended to see in this conflict an internal conflict among the Lombards in which opposing sides appealed to the emperor, the pope, Frederick's son Henry, and other forces, rather than a united front of the sort visible in the 1160s. Still, the military campaign also followed a pattern similar to the first Lombard war: initial success by the emperor, Cremona, and the pro-imperial cities (Cortenuova, 1237) was followed by stalemate and then a reversal of fortune (Parma, 1248). The anti-imperial communes were once again led by Milan and backed by successive popes,

---

[19] *Frederici Diplomata*, ed. H. Appelt, MGH Dip. reg et imp. Ger., X, 1–5 (Hanover, 1975–90) part 4, 848.

Gregory IX (1227–41) and Innocent IV (1243–54), though Gregory was brought in gradually, having initially sought to work cautiously with Frederick to pacify the region. After the death of Frederick in 1250 imperial efforts in Lombardy became dissipated, and attention switched to the south where a Guelf (i.e. pro-papal) army, led by Charles of Anjou, pursued and destroyed Frederick's heirs in two battles in 1266 and 1268, and to Tuscany where Siena continued to uphold the Ghibelline (i.e. pro-imperial) cause against its deadly rival Florence. This serves as a powerful reminder that cities did not automatically and instinctively oppose the emperor and his heirs. Those who supported the Hohenstaufen could expect favours in return, and not simply the dismantling of communal institutions.

In all this war, over such a long period, it is surprising at first sight how few battles were fought: a mere handful of major encounters: Legnano (1176), Cortenuova (1237), Benevento (1266), and Tagliacozzo (1268), the showdowns between Florence and Siena at Montaperti (1260) and Campaldino (1289). The third and the fourth of these were fought in southern Italy between claimants to the Sicilian throne, and the communes were not directly involved. On further reflection, however, it is apparent that major field battles in open country were few and far between because most of the fighting took place *within* cities. It took the form of street skirmishes, assassinations, and the demolition of private fortifications. The city itself was the real battlefield in communal Italy.

Urban elites and factionalism

On approaching a Lombard or Tuscan city in the Middle Ages the first thing that would have come into view would have been its towers. Veritable forests of tall towers crowd the skyline of Italian cities in artistic representations and literary descriptions. The most remarkable thing about them is that they were not external defences. They were constructed inside the city, sometimes freestanding, more often attached to fortified residences. Few survive today, but those that do, for example in Bologna, Pavia, and most famously at San Gimignano, are eloquent testimony to the feud and faction-fighting that threatened to tear Italian city communes apart.

The causes of this strife were complex and overlapping: familial, factional, and sectional. Contemporaries liked to explain it away by references to primordial feuds, archetypically the murder of Buondelmonte dei Buondelmonti in Florence in 1216, as described by Dino Compagni (1246/7–1324) and Giovanni Villani (1280–1348). But it was far from being so simple. Certainly anyone who believed in an earlier golden age of honesty, modesty, peace, and love, as Dante seems almost to have done in his more sentimental moments, was subject to delusion. Many communes may well have been born as settlements of conflict amongst urban elites. It remained ever thus. The fundamental flaw of civic oligarchy was that not all of the families could hold all of the offices all of the time. Consequently they plotted, they schemed, they built alliances within the city and outside, and, of course, they fought. The result was constant social tumult.

Two related phenomena epitomize this unrest. The first is the *consorteria*, or noble clan. In its simplest form the *consorteria* was a mutual interest group, bound together by oath in the usual manner, which held common property and provided common defence for its members (*soci*). The nucleus was more often than not a single noble family, or an extended kin, their household, and vassals. Friends, neighbours, business associates, clients, and political allies could also join, so a *consorteria* could end up including a large number of individuals, only some of whom were blood relations. At this level it became a faction or party in city life which chroniclers found it convenient to associate with the name of the predominant family: so we have 'the party of the Guidi' in Florence, 'the party of the della Torre' in Milan, and so on.

The second phenomenon is the proliferation of fortified towers, already mentioned. As early as 1090 a noted judgment by Archbishop Daimbert of Pisa regulating the height to which towers could be built indicates that the threat they posed to public order was already appreciated.[20] (This judgment is also referred to in the Pisan consular oath of 1162, discussed earlier.) The *consorterie* and fortified towers were inextricably associated. The *consorterie* had the funds and the organization to facilitate their construction. One of Milan's leading

[20] G. Rossetti, 'Il lodo del vescovo Daiberto sull'altezza delle torri: prima carta costituzionale della repubblica pisana', in *Pisa e la Toscana Occidentale nel Medioevo*, 2 (1991), pp. 25–41.

noble factions in the second half of the thirteenth century was actually called 'of the tower', as we have seen. Boncompagno da Signa, in his discussion of statutes notes:

In the same way many who build towers make a statute, which is called 'breve' in the vulgar tongue, and in which is contained what must be done for the construction and upkeep of the tower, and what one is bound to swear to the other.[21]

The exact functions of fortified towers—places of refuge or permanent residences, lookout positions or fighting platforms—has been debated, but there can be little doubt, given their imposing size and appearance that they were designed to impress and intimidate. Their height (up to 70 or 80 metres), as with modern skyscrapers, probably had as much to do with reasons of prestige as with any practical considerations.

The defeat of the emperor Frederick Barbarossa by the first Lombard League can be linked to a further flourishing of *consorterie* and towers in the city communes. In the absence of a permanent royal court in Italy the cities had always been the only arena in which noblemen could measure themselves against their peers, compete in patronage and influence, flaunt their birthright, satisfy their honour, arrange marriages, see and be seen. This was important enough before 1183, but even more so afterwards. The autonomy henceforward enjoyed by all cities, and the political clout wielded by a few, substantially enhanced their attractiveness in terms of power and prestige. The expansion of communal authority in the *contado*, and the pacts of *comitatanza* made with rural noblemen, also had the effect of drawing more families into intensive participation in civic politics. With the stakes thus raised the levels of violence and contumacy within the city increased accordingly.

The resort to the use of *podestà* (*c.*1180–1220) seems to have been a genuine, even altruistic, attempt to rein in the power and lawlessness of *consorterie*. It was partly successful: *podestà* did stand up to noble clans in a number of cities, razing their palaces and towers to the ground in punishment for transgressions. In 1190, for example, the *podestà* of Genoa, Manigoldo di Tetocio, in armour and accompanied by his retinue, destroyed the palace of a nobleman implicated in a

---

[21] Boncompagno da Signa, *Cedrus*, vol. i, pp. 121–2.

politically motivated murder (and is depicted doing so in a surviving manuscript of the Genoese annals which record the event). Similar instances occurred in Florence and Bologna; the offending parties were forced into exile. However, nowhere did *podestà* really grasp the nettle and challenge noble privilege head on. Perhaps their social affinity with the communes' elites made them temperamentally reluctant to do so, but it meant that when a confrontation did come it was played out along much more overtly class lines.

From the beginnings of the commune until the thirteenth century cities were dominated by ruling elites whose composition scarcely changed. Despite the increasing in-fighting amongst noble families, the same names appear with regularity in the lists of members of the college of consuls and the other major communal offices, year after year, decade after decade, even generation after generation. However, a variety of forces combined to alter this picture dramatically after 1200. It must be remembered, first of all, that the expansion in urban population in northern Italy, which is first discernible in the eleventh century, had continued apace throughout the twelfth century. The scale of growth is graphically illustrated by the building of new city walls which occurred at least once in all major cities, and twice in many, as the built-up area continued to expand. In the last quarter of the twelfth century in Lombardy, for example, new wall circuits were in course of construction, recently completed, or planned at Bergamo (1190), Bologna (1176–7), Brescia (1174–86), Como (1190s), Cremona (1169–87), Milan (1170s), and Reggio (1199), to name only some of the largest and best-documented projects. In Tuscany, the walls of Pisa, completed in 1162, enclosed 114 hectares, but a new circuit was required by the end of the thirteenth century to enclose a further 70 hectares; the famous Florentine third circle (the first was Roman), completed in the early fourteenth century, enclosed a staggering 630 hectares. It is widely accepted that the population of Florence and of northern Italy's other three 'super-cities' (Milan, Genoa, and Venice) had reached 100,000 by c.1300, whilst a further six north Italian cities (Bologna, Brescia, Cremona, Pisa, Siena, and Verona) had more than 40,000 inhabitants. By medieval standards these were very large urban populations. They must also have been infinitely more socially complex than when the communes were first created in the early twelfth century, particularly so because much of the economic prosperity of the cities stemmed primarily from the growth of their commercial and manufacturing sectors. So in a great city like Milan, by the thirteenth century, as the chronicler Galvano Fiamma (1283–1344) noted, there were to be found many men 'who live by buying and selling, and not by manual labour, such as merchants and men halfway between wealth and poverty'.[22]

The noble-merchant or merchant-noble was a figure that had always existed in Italian cities and was accorded social status and a political role, but the numerous middling merchants, tradesmen, and skilled artisans, of the kind Galvano Fiamma had in mind, not to mention the members of the legal and notarial professions who staffed the intermediate and lower levels of communal bureaucracy, were underrepresented or unrepresented. It was from this kind of moderately well-off, tolerably educated, politically hungry groups— Dante's *gente nuova*[23]—that the pressure for change originated. Yet acting alone would be pointless: only by somehow coming together could they effect it.

The principal cohesive element, which facilitated the transformation of these disaffected but disparate groups into a united political movement, was the guild. In all cities there are increasing references to guilds (*societates artium, società d'arti*) in the course of the twelfth century. They are particularly well documented in Florence, the city par excellence for the study of the growth of guilds. In Florence, as is well known, they were divided into major guilds (*arti maggiori*), numbering four (the cloth merchants, the dealers in silk and other materials, the moneychangers, and the judges and notaries) and the minor guilds (*arti minori*). There was wide variation in the importance of guilds and in the wealth and social standing of guild members, but it is important to stress that they were not anything like unions in the modern sense of the word. Broadly speaking they represented the interests of small employers and the self-employed, and their aims (for example with regard to price regulation and taxation) reflect that fact. The unskilled urban workforce was excluded from guilds, just as it was excluded from all other forms of participation in the public life of the city commune.

---

[22] Galvano Fiamma, *Chronicon Extravagans, Chronicon Maius*, ed. A. Ceruti, *Miscellanea di storia italiana*, vii (Turin, 1869) p. 745.

[23] Dante, *Inferno*, xvi. 73–5; *Purgatorio*, vi. 125–6, 133.

Guilds, like noble *consorterie,* had a military aspect too; they were prepared to fight to defend their interests. But they differed from *consorterie* in that, unlike noblemen, guild members were not trained in combat as a way of life from birth. Consequently, the military wing of the guilds tended to develop as a separate organization, though with strong links to guilds, which is often called *societas armorum* or *società d'armi* in the sources. The forces which made up this militia were raised from particular districts of the city (*viciniae, rioni*), and were naturally non-noble (*pedites*). But it was almost always led by a nobleman, as noble military background was the ideal preparation for such a role. In time, the various *società d'arti* and *società d'armi* began to act in concert in defence of their common interests, and to constitute themselves as an entirely new force in the politics of the city commune—the *societas populi,* or the *Popolo.*

Between 1200 and 1250 the *Popolo* achieved a measure of power in a number of cities. In Cremona in 1210, an agreement was brokered by the bishop whereby the commune's offices and revenues were divided between *nobiles* and *populares*; in Piacenza in 1223 the same two groups chose a mutually acceptable *podestà.* The first *Popolo*-dominated regime in Florence (*Primo Popolo*) was established in 1250. The *Popolo* also prevailed in Piacenza in 1250–2, but here there was extensive fighting, which serves as a reminder that, unlike the transition from episcopal lordship to commune more than a century earlier, the rise of the *Popolo* was resisted. There was conflict, violence, destruction, and exile. Nevertheless, the *Popolo* was in control also in Lucca in 1250, Siena in 1253, Bologna in 1255, and Genoa in 1257.

The *Popolo* sought change on three fronts. First, it aimed to break the stranglehold of old noble families over office-holding in the commune and to introduce its own representatives. This involved abolition of the office of consul and its replacement with that of prior or elder (*priore, anziano*) which existed also in guild administration. In similar fashion, the *podestà* would be replaced by the leader of the guilds' militia, the Captain of the *Popolo* (*Capitano del Popolo*). New palaces were constructed for each. Secondly, the *Popolo* was pledged to introduce more equitable taxation. The exemptions and immunities traditionally enjoyed by the nobility and the Church would be ended, and there would be a shift from indirect taxes on goods to direct, property-based taxation. Thirdly, it tried to re-establish law and order. The disorders perpetrated by noble *consorterie* had never been systematically tackled, as has already been said. The *Popolo* curtailed blood feuds and the carrying of weapons, demanded financial pledges for good behaviour from the nobility, and forbade the wearing of livery or insignia which demonstrated party or family allegiance. Transgressors were dealt with severely through use of exile, imprisonment, and the confiscation and destruction of property.

The programme of the *Popolo* is often described as 'anti-magnate', for which reason some historians have been tempted to see it as class based, and its struggles as an early example of class warfare. Yet this is difficult to reconcile with the leading role taken by noblemen as Captains of the *Popolo* and the political co-habitation of the *Popolo* and parties of Guelf noblemen in several cities. Moreover, anti-magnate policies had the effect of drawing some noble families into the orbit of the *Popolo*, through marriage alliance, for example, in order to escape their effects. As a result class lines became blurred rather than sharpened. The aspirations of the *Popolo* found their most extreme manifestation in Florence between 1293 and 1295, when a regime dominated by the prior Giano della Bella (in fact of noble birth) issued a draconian package of anti-magnate laws, known as the Ordinances of Justice (1293). This extreme piece of legislation, containing an infamous 'black list' of around 150 noble families, provoked a backlash and proved the undoing of Giano della Bella himself. But the power of the old nobility had been seriously damaged. Fourteenth-century Florence was dominated by new elites, drawn from the *arti maggiori* and including, amongst others, the Medici, who were to become the city's rulers in the fifteenth century.

The *Popolo* was perhaps more successful in Florence than in any other city. Elsewhere it had less impact, or became enmeshed in the struggles of the nobility, losing its distinctiveness and becoming just another party. Though some elements of its programme were progressive, especially when compared to the unending feuding of the nobility, in the end it simply contributed to the general anarchy. At this point there were no more oligarchic solutions. Consequently in many cities opportunities arose for powerful individuals, almost always noblemen (*signori*), to seize power and turn it into something more personal and permanent. The first *signori* to gain power in the cities emerged during the wars between the emperor Frederick II, the pope, and the second Lombard League. The two most famous examples—Oberto Pallavicino (d. 1269)—and Ezzelino III da Romano

(d. 1259)—were champions of the Ghibelline party in Lombardy and the Trevisan March, and owed their rise in part to the financial and military support they received from the emperor. However, both continued to flourish independently for some time after Frederick's death in 1250; Ezzelino concentrated his efforts on cities such as Verona, Vicenza, and Padua, whilst Oberto held at various times Cremona, Pavia, and Piacenza. They were precocious, but also atypical as *signori*, in that their interests were widely spread. The long-lasting lordships (*signorie*), which followed, were often built up in a single city.

Though many *signori* ultimately swept to power as a result of *coups d'état*, they had often worked their way up through the system. Usually they had held an office such as *podestà* or Captain of the *Popolo*. However, the previously short and fixed duration of these appointments tended to become extended, until ultimately they became lifelong positions (*perpetuus dominus*). The traditional relationship between consuls and priors on the one hand, and *podestà* or captain on the other, was gradually reversed. Rather than the former appointing the latter, the *signori* came to choose the ruling executive and naturally sought to pack it with their own men. The prudent *signore* often also abolished or suspended civic statutes; Oberto Pallavicino led the way here in Cremona in 1264. Like the *Popolo*, city lordship (*signoria*) became established unevenly in terms of geography and with varying durability. Indeed there is a certain reciprocity between the presence or absence of popular and signorial regimes in cities, in that the *signoria* took hold where there was a strong nobility and was less successful where there was a strong *Popolo* to check its progress. The *signoria* was particularly prevalent in the Trevisan March, Emilia-Romagna, in north-west Lombardy and Piedmont; in Tuscany, on the other hand, it appeared sporadically in some cities, such as Florence, and not at all in others, such as Siena. Most *signori* were noblemen of long lineage whose families had been active in city or regional politics from the beginnings of the commune, or even earlier. However, the fact that some of the most successful—for example, Martino della Torre in Milan, Mastino della Scala in Verona, Alberto Scotti in Piacenza, and Azzo d'Este in Ferrara—had been captains of the *Popolo*, undermines the notion that in some way a 'feudal reaction' to the success of the *Popolo* was taking place. In fact the rise of *signori*, by its very nature individualistic and opportunistic, was much less a product of class conflict than the rise of the *Popolo*.

Yet the change was fundamental. Decision-making was now in the hands of one man: no more consuls, councils, or committees. It amounted to nothing less than a closing of the communal era. Until recently historical opinion tended to be very negative about this, seeing the rise of the *signori* as representing a decline from the greater freedom and plurality of the commune. This was reflected in the language used to describe *signori*—'tyrant', 'despot', 'dictator', rather than the more neutral 'lord', which was the term used by contemporaries. Naturally, individual *signori* attracted criticism in the thirteenth and fourteenth centuries too, none more so than Ezzelino III da Romano, 'a limb of the devil himself', according to Salimbene,[24] and also his great rival Azzo d'Este (d. 1264) whose son, Obizzo, was given, in the bitter comment of Riccobaldo da Ferrara, 'fullest dominion [over Ferrara] . . . so that he may do everything, just or unjust, by the power of his will. The new ruler thus has more power than the Eternal God, who cannot be unjust.'[25]

But one can easily counterpose more favourable comments about *signori*: Bonvesin della Riva, for example, is positively gushing about the benefits of Visconti rule in Milan in the 1280s, as is Galvano Fiamma in the 1330s.[26] Most tellingly of all there are very few voices raised in defence of communalism on principle. Strong men who could deliver strong rule in a crisis, as ever, had their appeal. The weary commune, torn apart by faction, in the end signed its own death warrant.

Conclusion

In the last analysis, a kind of pattern can perhaps be discerned in all of this change between the early twelfth and the late thirteenth centuries. An alternation between oligarchy and autocracy, however nuanced and attenuated, is visible: episcopal lordship replaced by the

[24] *The Chronicle of Salimbene de Adam*, ed. and trans. J. L. Baird (New York, 1986), p. 369.

[25] Ricobaldo da Ferrara, *Chronica parva Ferrarienses*, RIS, VIII (1726), coll. 487–8.

[26] Bonvesin della Riva, *De magnalibus Mediolani/Le Meraviglie di Milano*, ed. M. Corti (Milan, 1974); for a partial English translation see T. Dean, *The Towns of Later Medieval Italy* (Manchester, 2000), pp. 11–16.

consulate, replaced by the *podestà*, replaced by the *Popolo*, replaced by the *signoria*. But whatever model is proposed to try to make sense of the flux of events in northern Italy over two centuries, the leading role of the Lombard/Tuscan city remains constant in spite of internal upheavals, and indeed, in the fourteenth century, economic and biological disaster. The age of the city communes was coming to a close by 1300, but the age of the city-state was just beginning.

Law and monarchy in the south

Hiroshi Takayama

In modern scholarship, medieval southern Italy (understood here to mean Sicily and mainland southern Italy) has been discussed, first and foremost, in relation to the formation of Western Europe. To some scholars, it was a gateway through which western Europe received Byzantine and Islamic cultures. Translations into Latin of a number of important Greek and Arabic texts, ranging from philosophy to natural science, were undertaken here. Knowledge of Byzantine art and architecture was also transmitted to Europe through medieval southern Italy. To other scholars it was the nurturing place of the first modern state in western Europe to have a highly developed royal administration and bureaucracy. On the other hand, southern Italy has been discussed with a negative connotation in the context of the formation of Italy. Regardless of how the Norman and Hohenstaufen kingdom dominated the central part of the Mediterranean and had so much influence over the politics, economy, and cultures of this region, it might be seen as a glorious historical anecdote or even as a serious obstacle to the unification of Italy in the 'history of Italy'.

Southern Italy in the Middle Ages should not be treated just as a frontier of Europe or a part of the Italian entity. Both frameworks, Europe and Italy as fixed geo-political or historical entities, prevent us from understanding the history of southern Italy. We could certainly take different viewpoints or use different frameworks to see its history, but it should not be forgotten that southern Italy itself was not an everlasting geo-political entity either. Many of the phenomena that happened in southern Italy must be considered and understood in a far larger context extending beyond its geographical limits. A large part of its history was not self-contained at all, but a reflection of power relationships in a wider context, even though it sometimes became a powerful engine to effect change further afield. Although obvious, it should also be noted that the history of southern Italy cannot be fully understood without putting it in the context of the history of the Mediterranean. The sea could be a serious obstacle to transportation, and become a natural border. But, at the same time, it could be a busy road along which goods and people went back and forth. In the case of southern Italy, the hinterland of which was extremely mountainous, most of the important cities were located along the coastline, and were connected to each other and with foreign cities by sea. In the Middle Ages, southern Italy was more often a part of the Mediterranean than a part of the European Continent.

Norman unification

From the seventh century, the Mediterranean region consisted of three major cultural zones: Latin-Christian Western Europe, the Greek-Christian Byzantine East, and Arab-Islamic North Africa and Spain. Southern Italy was located on their borders, and as a result had a remarkably complicated history. In the eleventh century when Norman warriors arrived from Normandy in northern France, Calabria and Apulia were under the control of the Byzantine Empire. The three duchies of Naples, Amalfi, and Gaeta were nominally subject to Byzantine authority, and the three Lombard principalities of Salerno, Capua, and Benevento were to all intents independent. Sicily was divided among local Muslim warlords.

The Normans first worked for Lombard rulers and Byzantine governors as mercenaries, but were soon drawn to Aversa and Melfi, which became centres for the Norman warriors. By the middle of the eleventh century, the Normans in southern Italy had already become a strong force affecting international politics, and had grown into perhaps one of the most active political elements in western Europe besides the papacy and the German Empire. In fact, they had a strong bearing on the papacy. They fought with Pope Leo IX and captured him in 1053, while they supported Pope Nicholas II against his rival. They were to play important roles during the Investiture Controversy. Without their military support the popes could not have fought against the German emperors so persistently.

In 1059 Richard, a leader of the Normans at Aversa, and Robert Guiscard, a leader at Melfi, received from Pope Nicholas II the investiture of the principality of Capua, and the duchy of Apulia, Calabria, and Sicily respectively. The duchy of Apulia rapidly developed into a powerful principality under Robert Guiscard. He conquered the Byzantine territory in Apulia and Calabria (Bari fell in 1071), and unified southern Italy. Although he faced serious baronial revolts, Robert Guiscard basically succeeded in keeping his authority over the duchy. He also played an important role in international politics. He fought with Pope Gregory VII at first, but, after making peace with him in 1080, maintained a good relationship thereafter. When the German king Henry IV made an expedition to Italy and besieged Gregory VII in 1082, Robert Guiscard marched on Rome, sacked the city, and rescued Gregory VII. He mounted two large expeditions against the Byzantine Empire. During the first in 1081–2, he took Avlona (modern Vlorë), Corfu, and Durazzo (Durrës, Dyrrachium), which were lost after his return to Italy. In the second expedition in 1084–5, he reconquered Avlona and Corfu and occupied Butrint, but he fell ill and died in Cephalonia in 1085.

After the death of Robert Guiscard, the duchy rapidly lost its integrity. His son Roger Borsa (duke from 1085 to 1111) and his grandson William (duke from 1111 to 1127) failed to maintain his strong authority, and allowed many of the Norman barons within the duchy to become effectively independent; this tension between the aspirations of the barons and that of the rulers is a constant in the history of medieval southern Italy. Count Roger I of Sicily, brother of Robert Guiscard, became the most powerful ruler in southern Italy. Prior to his brother's death, Roger I had patiently been conquering Sicily with a few hundred knights under his command. When he took Noto, the last city retained by the Muslims, in 1091, he had already spent thirty years in this endeavour since the capture of Messina in 1061. Even though technically inferior to the duke of Apulia, he transformed Sicily into a cohesive and wealthy state, and became one of the most influential monarchs in western Europe. An agreement with Pope Urban II endowed him with authority over the Church in Sicily, even though the exact terms of this arrangement gave rise to argument for the next six centuries. Powerful princes in Europe sought to make alliances with him. His daughters were married to King Coloman of Hungary, the count of Toulouse, and Conrad, son of Emperor Henry IV of Germany. Roger I died in 1101, and left two boys, Simon and Roger II. During their minority, their energetic mother Adelasia (Adelaide), from Savona in northern Italy, managed to maintain authority and order in Sicily as regent. In 1112 she left Sicily for Jerusalem to marry King Baldwin (who before long repudiated her, having only sought to benefit from the wealth of Sicily); Count Roger II began independent rule.

The Norman conquest redrew the political map of southern Italy. The old political order in this region, balanced among several states with different cultural traditions, was destroyed, and new political circumstances emerged under the Norman rulers. Some of the old political units were simply destroyed, while others remained with their rulers replaced by Normans. Almost all regions in southern Italy were placed under Norman rulers. Thus, in a political sense, one of the most important strategic points and most important trading centres in the Mediterranean ceased to be the border region of the three cultural zones, and became a part of Latin-Christian Europe.

From a demographic point of view, however, the Normans were a minority in terms of numbers, and most of the inhabitants remained almost the same as before. The majority of Sicilians were Muslims and Greeks. Many of the inhabitants in Calabria and a part of Apulia were Greeks, while the majority in Apulia and Campania were those with Latin-Christian traditions. These people with different cultural backgrounds preserved their own customs and traditions under the new rulers. Despite the change of rulers, some of the old political units survived the 'Norman conquest' as Norman political entities or as regional boundaries within the Norman monarchies. However, the links between Adelaide of Savona and northern Italy helped stimulate large-scale migration by so-called 'Lombards' into Sicily from the end of the twelfth century onwards, leading to the gradual latinization of the island and the spread there of Italian vernacular dialects in place of Arabic and Greek.

The Norman kingdom of Sicily

When his cousin's son Duke William of Apulia died without heirs in 1127, Count Roger II of Sicily quickly took over the duchy of Apulia. Having subdued discontented barons, he succeeded in receiving the investiture of the duchy of Apulia from Pope Honorius II in 1128. In 1130, taking advantage of a papal schism, Roger II obtained from the anti-Pope Anacletus II the crown of the kingdom of Sicily, Calabria, and Apulia, the principality of Capua, the honour of Naples, and the protectorate of the men of Benevento. This was the beginning of the Norman kingdom of Sicily and marked a watershed in Italian as well as Mediterranean history. Italy had been ruled by a series of outsiders after the fall of the Western Roman Empire, and its southern part had been divided into small states with different cultural backgrounds. This fragmented situation in the south came to an end when Roger II unified this region and transformed it into a mighty kingdom. This kingdom was a sound political entity with a stable governing system, far more cohesive than the dominion of Robert Guiscard, which had lacked a stable governing system and was dismembered at his death. Its rulers became powerful and influential players in Mediterranean and European politics.

Thus, the creation of the new kingdom in 1130 symbolizes a great historical change in southern Italy and the Mediterranean. But the actual condition of the kingdom should not be misunderstood. Roger II's authority was not yet recognized in a vast area of the peninsula, which was still under the control of independent warlords and cities. At this moment the political extent of the kingdom was far smaller than its nominal extent. Roger II had to spend almost ten years pacifying all the territory. Powerful barons and many cities in Apulia, supported by Pope Innocent II, continuously revolted. Lothar, the German emperor, invaded the kingdom in response to the pope's request in 1136. The pope himself also made an expedition in 1139, but was captured by Roger, son of Roger II. As a result, he was forced to rescind the excommunication of Roger II and to confirm his status as king of Sicily, duke of Apulia, and prince of Capua.

The kingdom as a political entity

By the end of the summer in 1140 Roger II restored peace and order in the kingdom, and gained almost complete control over the whole territory, which now consisted of the county of Calabria and Sicily, the duchies of Apulia and Naples, and the principalities of Taranto and Capua. The gain of land north of Calabria had multiplied his territory and population. Sicily and southern Italy were put under one ruler and to all intents constituted one political entity. The extent of the kingdom became the basic framework for the history of this region thereafter, and it remained long in people's mind as the *regno* (kingdom) par excellence. Modern scholarship tends also to take the existence of the kingdom as a framework within which to describe the society of medieval southern Italy and Sicily.

No matter how important the creation of this political entity was, however, the kingdom was not a uniform one, but a complex of different regions with different traditions. Roger II used the administrative units of the old polities as his largest governmental districts, and for that reason he kept the duchy of Apulia, the principality of Taranto, and the principality of Capua as administrative divisions of the kingdom. He appointed his sons as dukes and princes as if the old polities continued to exist under the authority of the king. The principality of Capua offers a good example. It fell into the hands of Roger II in 1135, and was given to his third son Anfusus. Its unity was preserved for a certain period of time within the kingdom; documents were dated by the regnal year of Anfusus, and he had his own chamberlain, who seems to have been active in the administration of the principality as late as 1149. The kingdom was thus a mosaic of different political units unified under Roger II.

Within the boundaries of the newborn kingdom lived people with different cultural traditions: Arab-Islamic, Greek-Orthodox Christian, Latin Catholic Christian, and Jewish. These people did not live together, but lived in different regions and districts. The southern and western parts of Sicily were mostly inhabited by Muslims, and the north-eastern part by Greeks. The majority of the inhabitants of Calabria and a part of Apulia were Greeks. To the north of Calabria lived mainly south Italians of Latin Catholic tradition. Almost all of the lay landlords were Latin, above all Norman, and so were many of the high clerics. The coexistence of people with different cultural backgrounds within the kingdom was a simple result of the unification of political entities belonging to different cultures.

After the pacification of the peninsula in 1140, however, the kingdom was gradually transformed into a state more cohesively and systematically governed by new administrative apparatuses. Roger II's intent is well reflected in the so-called 'Assizes of Ariano', the laws he promulgated just after the pacification. The first article included in the Vatican manuscript proclaimed that because of the variety of people subject to the Norman rule, their usages, customs, and laws should not be abrogated unless they are clearly contradictory to the newly promulgated laws. This clearly shows the ruler's will to respect the existing laws and customs among different people on the one hand, but on the other it also makes clear that his edicts had priority over them. Roger II tried to control the people in much the same condition as they had been, but definitely under his strong and sole authority.

Kingship and the royal court

At the centre of the kingdom there were always Christian Norman kings, and the governmental centre of the kingdom was the royal palace in Palermo. The royal court of the kingdom became fixed at the royal palace in Palermo. The character of sovereignty changed according to the form of central power, as did the power structure of the court. Day-to-day power was not always held by a king, but sometimes held by a head minister or a group of the *familiares regis*. These three forms of central power appeared in turn at the royal court of Sicily. When a king himself did not exercise power, the court became the stage for an intense power struggle and for a cunning battle for hegemony. Confrontations among different groups, such as bureaucrats, clerics, and feudal lords, between natives and foreigners, and among different cultural groups, complicated the situation further.

During a large part of the reign of Roger II, the king himself exercised power. In the royal court, Roger II had many able officials, most of whom he inherited from his parents, as well as Norman aristocrats and Christian clerics. These officials bore various titles of Roman, Frankish, Byzantine, and Arabic origins, such as *cancellarius, camerarius, kaprilingas, protonotarius (protonotarios), notarius (notarios), logothetes, amiratus,* etc. The high officials who bore the title of *amiratus,* which is of Arabic origin, were powerful magnates in the court with the king's full confidence. They commanded the army and were concerned with the administration of the kingdom. Most of them were Greek. A powerful head minister, George, who also bore the title of *amiratus,* was a typical example of such a Greek. Although supported by these able ministers, officials, and feudal vassals, Roger II solved various problems personally, and dealt with important matters himself. Thus, Roger II himself exercised power for a prolonged period, and he was the real centre of administration for a large part of his reign.

His son William I (1154–66) was completely different. Once the unstable situation after the death of Roger II subsided, William I entrusted the government to the head minister Maio, and decided to live an easy life in a secluded palace. The king stepped down from the centre stage of politics, and the chief minister Maio held full control over the kingdom. After the death of Maio in 1160, William I appointed the archdeacon of Catania, the count of Marsico, and the bishop-elect of Syracuse to be *familiares regis,* and entrusted them with the government. From this time, the *familiares regis* came to have special significance in the kingdom. *Familiaris regis* was a well-defined title to indicate a member of the royal inner council during the reigns of William I and his son William II (1166–89). Although the holders of this title swelled to ten people at one stage, they were usually between three and five. As the decision-makers on policy and other important matters, they were the most powerful people in the kingdom.

William II did not exercise power either. In the early period of his minority, his mother Margaret entrusted the government to, first, Peter, an ex-Muslim eunuch, then, Stephen, a son of the count of Perche in France. Both of them fled the kingdom in disturbances. Stability was restored when Walter, one of the *familiares regis* and the dean of Agrigento, was consecrated archbishop of Palermo. He changed the composition of the inner council, and established a triumvirate consisting of himself, Gentile the bishop of Agrigento, and the notary Matthew. This triumvirate continued for about fifteen

years with changes in membership, and was modified by the addition
of the archbishop of Monreale. This archbishopric was created in 1183
and its first archbishop William joined the *familiares regis*. The government of the kingdom by the four *familiares regis* lasted until the
death of William II.

Norman administration

With regard to administrative organizations, we should underline the
importance of chronological developments, because so many previous scholars have treated offices belonging to different periods as if
they were contemporaneous, and have thereby created a confused
image of the Norman administration. In order to examine the structure of the Norman administration, we must clearly specify the
time period, which should be limited within a sufficiently narrow
time-frame.

Roger II introduced the first important administrative changes
after his pacification of the peninsula in 1140. He installed local
chamberlains and local justiciars systematically all over the kingdom.
Then he created a new office with the Arabic title of *dîwân at-taḥerqîq
al-maʿmûr*. This office was created around the remaining Arab
documents, which included information on land and its inhabitants,
in order to keep and to revise these useful documents. It soon came to
be called *duana de secretis* in Latin. Under Maio, royal officials
advanced in specialization and hierarchization; this change was especially marked in the organization of chamberlains and justiciars in
the central government. A chamberlain working in the central government came to be called 'chamberlain of the royal palace' (*camerarius regalis palatii*), while another title of 'master chamberlain of the
royal palace' (*magister camerarius regii palatii*) appeared a little later.
This master chamberlain of the royal palace came to take a significant
role in the central administration. The presence of justiciars in the
central government also displayed the increased level of specialization and hierarchization under Maio. At the beginning of William II's
reign, a new office called *duana baronum* was created for the government of the peninsula. This new office was located in Salerno, perhaps in the castle of Terracena, and had competence over the whole

peninsula except for Calabria, carrying out various administrative duties needed there.

After the creation of the *duana baronum*, we can see the structure of the Norman administration at its most developed stage. In this period, the royal inner council of *familiares regis* held the highest authority in the government and made decisions on important issues of the kingdom or on matters concerning the king's interests. The master chamberlain of the royal palace and his two subordinate chamberlains of the royal palace directed the executive and adminis-trative functions of the central government. Most of the holders of these offices were Muslims or ex-Muslims. For special duties concern-ing the administration of land, however, there was the special office called *dîwân at-taḥqîq al-maʿmûr* in Arabic (or *duana de secretis* in Latin, or *mega sekreton, sekreton* in Greek), which was located at the royal palace in Palermo and under the direction of one of the two chamberlains of the royal palace. It had high officials called *magistri duane de secretis* in Latin, *aṣḥâb dîwân at-taḥqîq al-maʿmûr* in Arabic, *hoi epi tou megalou sekretou (hoi epi tou sekretou)*, or *archontes tou sekretou* in Greek, most of whom were also Muslims or ex-Muslims.[1] Their primary duty was land administration within Sicily (later pos-sibly Calabria too), but they were among the most powerful officials of the kingdom. For the government of the peninsula a branch office called the *duana baronum* in Latin (or *sekreton tôn apokopôn* in Greek) had been created at Salerno to meet a variety of local adminis-trative needs. It had high officials called *magistri duane baronum* in Latin or *hoi epi tou sekretou tôn apokopôn* in Greek, who were also among the most powerful officials of the kingdom. Local officials such as local chamberlains, local justiciars, magistrates of towns (*catepani* or *stratêgoi*), and *baiuli*, worked for the king's interest under the direction of these high officials.

One of the most important characteristics is the administrative difference between Sicily together with Calabria, and the rest of the peninsula. In Sicily and Calabria the king had more immediate con-trol of inhabitants and lands by means of registers of lands and vil-leins. Vassals and churches were not have such strong obstacles to the royal administration. Here existed a more valid and stable adminis-tration. In peninsular administration, however, the vassals were

---

[1] οἱ ἐπὶ τοὺ μεγάλου σεκρέτου (οἱ ἐπὶ τοῦ σεκρέτου); ἄρχοντες τοῦ σεκρέτου.

indispensable. The king could control and govern the inhabitants and the land only through vassals. The administrative organization of the kingdom was based on the existing administrative institutions of the former rulers, or was created to control the different existing offices. The time lag in absorbing different regions, each of which had its own political and historical integrity, made it difficult to organize a homogeneous administrative system over the whole kingdom, and, as a result, led to the coexistence of different administrative systems. Although some scholars have seen in this kingdom an advanced degree of centralization of government, and even the origin of modern states, its administrative system was in fact a mixture of different systems.

The kings' ambitions and diplomacy

Through the decade-long pacification, Roger II consolidated his authority within the kingdom and expanded its power base. This inner solidarity made possible his remarkable naval expansion into Africa and Greece. His fleet repeatedly attacked northern Africa and finally established mastery in the area between Tripoli and Bône. He also made an expedition against the Byzantine Empire, taking Corfu and Neapolis. By his death in 1154, Roger II had gained dominance over important commercial routes in the central Mediterranean, which was to be lost under William I.

William I, after expelling the invasions of the papal and German armies at the beginning of his reign, increased his influence over the papacy, and, at the death of Hadrian IV, succeeded in establishing his candidate as Pope Alexander III (1159–81). In 1158 he concluded a peace with the Byzantine emperor and remained on good terms thereafter. During the reign of William II the kingdom maintained good and peaceful relationships with many foreign states. A treaty with Genoa in 1156 provided Sicily with an assured market for its grain and cotton. Pope Alexander III was its best ally. After a failed attempt by the German emperor to gain control of both northern and southern Italy in the 1160s, the Peace of Venice of 1177 established a truce with the German Empire for fifteen years; and the marriage of Constance, aunt of William II, to Henry, son of Emperor Frederick

Barbarossa, further improved the relationship between the two monarchies. The kingdom made alliances with Genoa and with Venice, and even retained a peaceful relationship with the normally troublesome Byzantine Empire for quite a while. Furthermore, the marriage of King William II to Joanna, daughter of King Henry II of England, in 1176, consolidated the close connection between the two most powerful Norman kingdoms in twelfth-century Europe. While keeping on good terms with foreign powers, William II also showed great military adventurousness. Taking advantage of the dispute over a successor to Emperor Manuel, he attacked the Byzantine Empire in 1185. The Norman fleet took Durazzo and Thessalonica in the same year, and marched on Constantinople, resulting in a war that lasted for several years. He also sent expeditions against the Muslims, especially those in Egypt. The Norman fleet attacked Damietta in 1169, Alexandria in 1174, and Tinnîs twice between 1175 and 1178; and he attacked Majorca to the west as well in 1181/2. William II also sent his fleet to join the Third Crusade in 1189. But he died before knowledge of the successes of his *amiratus* Margarito in the East reached him.

Transition

William II died childless at the age of 36 in 1189. His aunt Constance, a daughter of Roger II, was the legitimate heiress to the crown of Sicily, but her marriage with Henry VI, king of Germany, caused fear among Sicilian magnates of Sicily losing its independence to the German Empire. Eventually, Tancred, count of Lecce and illegitimate son of Duke Roger, and therefore grandson of Roger II, was elected king in 1190. But his reign was filled with difficulties from the beginning. He had to fight against his opponents and enemies. An opposition party revolted in the peninsula, while the Muslims rose in Sicily. King Richard the Lion-Heart of England arrived in Messina with his crusading army and created havoc. In 1191 Henry VI, now emperor, invaded the kingdom and established his authority in Salerno. Although Tancred succeeded in reconquering the peninsula, the kingdom had lost its integrity and the cohesiveness preserved under his predecessors. It was on the way to dismemberment and disorder. Tancred died in 1194, leaving his child William III as successor.

Henry VI, having again put the peninsula under his authority, marched on Palermo, removed the child-king William III from power, and had himself crowned king of Sicily on Christmas Day 1194, one day before his wife, who had only reached Jesi in central Italy, gave birth to an heir, the future Frederick II. The coronation of Henry marks a change in the royal dynasty of the kingdom from the Hauteville Norman house to the German Hohenstaufen, although Norman blood was transmitted to Frederick II through his mother Constance. But no less important was the creation of the Italo-German political zone in which political elements closely interacted. Thereafter, the history of southern Italy cannot be fully understood without considering German factors. Henry VI soon returned to Germany, leaving the government to Constance. The kingdom was after all a private foreign domain for him, no matter how wealthy it was. He died in 1197, followed by Constance in 1198. Although Constance had chosen the pope as guardian of her son, the kingdom was submerged in political confusion. The king's authority withered, and warlords came to fight one another for lands and hegemony. The kingdom lost its integrity, and was no longer a single political entity.

Frederick II

After the death of Henry VI the kingship of Sicily was inherited by his son Frederick II. He was crowned at Palermo at the age of 3 in his mother's arms in May 1198. When his mother died in the same year, he was officially put under the guardianship of Pope Innocent III. In fact, however, he was just left in Palermo, and was raised there. During his minority the kingdom became immersed in ever deeper disorder. In Germany the succession to Henry VI caused serious confrontation between two parties, and produced two kings, Philip (Frederick's uncle) and Otto IV the Welf. After the assassination of Philip in 1208, Otto IV was re-elected as sole king of Germany and was crowned emperor in Rome in 1209.

In 1208 Frederick II came of age at 14, and undertook a difficult task, the restoration of order and royal control in the kingdom. During his minority, disorder had prevailed throughout the kingdom. Many barons had become independent, and usurped their neighbouring lands including the royal demesne. Castles had been built here and there without royal permission. Many cities had also rid themselves of royal control. In 1209 Frederick II gathered his army and subdued rebellious barons by force. But there was a long way to go to fulfill this task. In the following few years, his life and fortune drastically changed. In 1210 the pope excommunicated Emperor Otto IV who had marched into Italy and invaded the kingdom of Sicily, and in 1211 the supporters of the Hohenstaufen in Germany elected Frederick II as king of Germany. Otto IV, who had already marched deep into the southern end of the peninsula, turned back to Germany, and Frederick II also left Sicily for Germany. Frederick II occupied Constance without much difficulty and was crowned at Mainz in 1212. Thereafter he was engaged in subduing the opposing barons and restoring order in Germany for twelve years. It was in 1220 that he finally came back to Sicily.

Restoration of royal authority

When he returned to the kingdom of Sicily, Frederick II was not simply a king of Sicily. He had already established himself as the ruler of Germany, leaving his young son Henry (VII) as king in Germany.[2] He had even had himself crowned as emperor at Rome on his way home. With these titles and power, he resumed the difficult task, interrupted during his absence, of restoring order and royal control in the kingdom. His strong will to do so is well shown in the 'Assizes of Capua', which were promulgated in December 1220, just after his return to the kingdom. In the prologue, he proclaimed that he would restore the state of the kingdom to the good condition of the reign of William II, ordered that those castles unjustly built during the period of disorder should be destroyed or delivered to royal authority, and that those charters and privileges issued during this period should be examined and confirmed by the royal chancery. Without doubt, the king's top priority was to restore royal authority within the kingdom. Thereafter, he energetically fought against powerful independent

[2] Henry is known as Henry (VII) to avoid confusion with Henry VII of Luxembourg, emperor early in the fourteenth century.

barons in the peninsula, and subjected them to royal authority. He crushed the rebellious Muslims in Sicily, and transferred a large part of the Muslim population in Sicily to Lucera in the peninsula.

After working hard at the consolidation of royal authority in Sicily and southern Italy, Frederick II took up the cross for the crusade in 1228. He had taken the crusade vow at his coronation in Germany, but the unstable condition of the kingdom obliged him to put off his departure, to the intense ire of the pope; excommunicated by Pope Gregory IX because of the constant delays, he finally left the kingdom for Cyprus and the Latin kingdom of Jerusalem in June 1228. He had taken as his second wife the heiress to Jerusalem, so he went there as crusader, as emperor, but also as king of Jerusalem in right of Isabella. He succeeded in obtaining Jerusalem by negotiation with al-Kâmil, sultan of Egypt, and celebrated his diplomatic victory with a crown-wearing in the Church of the Holy Sepulchre in March 1229. This remarkable success without shedding blood was not appreciated by the pope, however. On the contrary, the papal army invaded the kingdom of Sicily in what was a papal holy war against a crusader, an odd event by any standards. Frederick II immediately came back home and expelled the papal army. He made a generous peace treaty with the humiliated pope at San Germano in June 1230.

Thereafter he devoted himself again to consolidating the kingdom. In October of the same year, he summoned 'old good people' from various regions of the kingdom and made enquiries about local laws and customs. Then, he presented the edicts of his constitutions at the royal court of Melfi in June 1231, and promulgated them in the following September. A large part of them are concerned with crimes and legal procedures, which suggests that their main purpose was to attain and keep peace and order in the kingdom. From this time to his death in 1250 he continued to issue additional new laws (*novellae*) in order to consolidate the kingdom, although distracted by the wars against the Lombard Leagues and the papacy; and his successors continued this practice.

The Norman inheritance

To what extent the Norman administrative system functioned during the period of disorder in the late twelfth and early thirteenth centuries is a question over which scholars' opinions differ widely. Some see the evidence for continuity in the existence of Norman titles and administrative districts in documents, while others think the Norman administration came to a standstill in the political confusion after the deaths of Henry VI and Constance. But, as many scholars have pointed out, there is certainly a conspicuous similarity and common character between the Norman kingdom and that of Frederick II, including the idea of kingship, cultural activities at court, and administrative organization.

When restoring royal authority, Frederick II obviously had an image of the kingdom of his Norman predecessors in his mind. He intended to revive the governmental system of his Norman ancestors, and to bring about a rebirth of the strong authority of the Norman kings. Such an intent is clearly shown in the assizes of Capua of 1220. In the assizes of Capua, he proclaimed his wish to restore the institutions of the Norman period, and ordered that his justiciars' duties should be the same under William II, and that the divisions of duties between his justiciars and *baiuli* (bailiffs) should be the same as in the Norman period. His will is also reflected in the Constitutions of Melfi of 1231, which included the edicts of his Norman predecessors. His key officials in the administration were in fact justiciars, chamberlains, *baiuli* as in the Norman period. And, like his Norman predecessors, he tried to exclude the powerful lay magnates from the government, and created a corps of professional bureaucrats. One innovation in this respect was the foundation of the university of Naples, as a training centre for future bureaucrats. A number of bureaucratic families emerged, many of them drawn from the Amalfi peninsula and the lands around Naples, and some of these, for instance the Rufolo family, would continue to serve later kings as well even after the violent change of dynasty that was to occur.

A changed kingdom

Still, the kingdom could not be the same, no matter how hard Frederick II tried to revive the kingdom of his Norman predecessors. Indeed, the inner condition of Sicily and southern Italy had changed too deeply; there was a conspicuous change in its demography. The

Muslim population decreased rapidly in Sicily from the late twelfth century to the early thirteenth century. The Saracens continuously revolted during this period, and Frederick II decided to transfer them from Sicily to Lucera, an inland town of the peninsula. Thus Lucera became the colony of Muslims in the kingdom, and remained so until 1300. Most of them lived a peasant life separated from outside Christian society, while some served the king as soldiers or courtiers. The coexistence of Muslims and Christians, one of the more striking features of the Norman kingdom, came to an end. Muslim agricultural skills were lost from Sicily, and a large part of the land for fruit, vegetables, indigo, henna, and so on, was converted to grain producing land, though attempts were made to remedy this by bringing Jewish cultivators from north Africa who had the same skills, but not the same religion, as the departed Saracens.

The kingdom's centre of gravity also changed. Palermo was no longer the sole unrivalled capital. Frederick II moved around the kingdom, and resided much more often in the peninsula than his Norman predecessors, who usually stayed in Palermo or Messina. Foggia, an inland town in Apulia, and Naples, a huge port city in Campania, were attaining the status of a capital in the peninsula. Some officials gained more power, while others lost their influence. For example, justiciars became more and more active and important in his administration, but the master chamberlains of the royal palace, as well as the office of *duana de secretis*, seemed to have lost their influence. In his government, we find few of the Muslim or Greek officials, who had been so conspicuous and influential under the Norman kings. The assizes of Capua, while showing the king's strong will to restore Norman institutions, prohibited the custom of the Norman period that permitted senior ecclesiastics and local nobles to take charge of judicial matters. The Constitutions of Melfi, while including many edicts of the Norman kings, at the same time denied the effectiveness of his predecessors' laws that were not included.

Frederick II's position as the ruler of the kingdom was totally different from that of the Norman predecessors. He was in a far more complicated situation than the Norman kings. As Holy Roman Emperor he was at the centre of European politics and had a difficult relationship with the more and more assertive papacy. He was not simply a ruler of just one kingdom as his Norman predecessors were, but a ruler of two large political entities, the kingdoms of Sicily and

Germany. Unlike the Norman kings who could concentrate their energy and concern on southern Italy, he had to rule two different kingdoms with completely different traditions and peoples, one a decentralized kingdom with powerful nobles and cities, the other a bureaucratic kingdom in the Mediterranean tradition of Byzantium and Islam. It can easily be imagined how difficult it was for one person to govern the two kingdoms separated by the strong natural obstacle of the Alps. Frederick II made his son Henry (VII) king of Germany and entrusted him with rule in Germany, with the intention that he himself would concentrate on the kingdom of Sicily. However, this did not work out well, because Henry alienated the great German princes by trying to create his own power base. He had to remove his rebellious son in 1235, and put another son, Conrad IV, on the German throne in 1237. All this involved coaxing, rather than coercing, the German princes, since it was they who elected the German king, and they had grave doubts about the merits of effectively permitting hereditary succession. Based in southern Italy his eyes had to watch troubles and problems beyond the Alps. No matter how important the kingdom of Sicily was to him, it was after all a mere part of his dominion. Added to this were his worries about the situation in northern Italy, where Lombard rebels, increasingly encouraged by the papacy, drew him into the bitter rivalries of Milan, Cremona, and other towns, and this culminated in the hysterical denunciation of Frederick at the Council of Lyons (1245) when Innocent IV declared him deposed as king and emperor.

The dismemberment of Frederick II's dominion

Frederick II died from illness in the castle of Fiorentino on 13 December 1250, with many issues unresolved, notably the relationship between pope and emperor and the problem of Lombardy. Any successor would have difficulties in ruling his inheritance. The large dominion extending from Sicily to the Baltic Sea, and even as far as the Middle East, was too large to be unified in any meaningful sense, and almost impossible to be ruled by a single ruler, given the natural obstacles such as the Mediterranean and the Alps. His successor would also have to deal with the hostile papacy. Even that energetic and intellectual monarch Frederick II had great difficulties ruling his vast dominion in the face of papal hostility. It was Conrad, his son and king of Germany, whom Frederick II chose as his successor. Conrad succeeded to the German throne and the kingship of Sicily, while Manfred, an illegitimate son, took the position of regent for Italy and Sicily. When his father died, Conrad was at war with William of Holland, who was the leader of the anti-Hohenstaufen party in Germany. His campaign in Germany turned out to be a stalemate, but Hohenstaufen influence rapidly withered there. He returned to Italy in 1252, but struggled to secure his inheritance, and died in 1254, leaving a 2-year-old son, Conrad V or Conradin.

This put an end to the large political complex of Germany and Italy which had been formed by the crowning of King Henry VI of Germany as ruler of Sicily and strengthened further by Frederick II. Germany and southern Italy, separated into different political entities, began to take different courses. Germany experienced double elections for a new king after the death of William of Holland in 1256 and thereafter a troubled interregnum until 1273, and became a land submerged in political confusion, falling victim to further decentralization. The kingdom of Sicily also fell into a state of war. After the death of Conrad, Pope Innocent IV tried to control the kingdom, while Pietro Ruffo, who had been a faithful follower of Frederick II and Conrad, tried to establish his own dominion based on Messina. Manfred defeated the papal army at Foggia in 1254, but could not restore order within the kingdom. His coronation as the king of Sicily in Palermo in 1258 did not improve the situation to any significant degree.

Charles of Anjou and the two kingdoms

In its hostility to the Hohenstaufen, the papacy searched for an able pro-papal candidate for the throne of Sicily, and, under the French pontiff Urban IV (1261–4), chose Charles, count of Anjou and Provence and brother of King Louis IX of France. Charles was crowned as king of Naples and Sicily in January 1266, in Rome, and initiated his campaign against Manfred with a force of French, Provençal, and Italian knights. He killed Manfred at the battle of Benevento, and took control of a large northern slice of the kingdom. He defeated Conradin, the sole descendant of Frederick II in the legitimate male line, at Tagliacozzo and mercilessly executed him in 1268. He made Naples his effective capital, and began to rule the kingdom with great energy, succeeding in his efforts to restore order in Sicily and southern Italy.

The Angevin kingdom, which appeared as a political entity from the dust of political confusion, was in a sense a revival of the old Hohenstaufen kingdom. Although the crown was transferred to the French royal house from the German Hohenstaufen, the basic framework of the kingdom seemed to remain the same. Its boundaries did not change much, nor did its inhabitants. Even its governmental system did not appear to show much difference from the former one. It is not clear whether this system survived the political confusion or was revived by Charles, but most historians agree to a conspicuous continuity from Hohenstaufen to Angevin government. Charles brought French elements to the government, but its basic structure remained the same as the Hohenstaufen or Norman. Some of Charles's officials are known to have served Frederick II and Manfred. It is also known that Charles preserved Hohenstaufen taxation, including the notorious *collecta*, despite promises to the pope not to levy it. His son Charles II had the Norman register of military service known as the 'Catalogue of Barons' copied, just as the Hohenstaufen had done before, and inserted it into the Angevin registers of official acts, which symbolically shows how strongly the Norman and Hohenstaufen structure of land distribution remained alive. Charles continued to entertain close relations with the foreign merchants, aiming to sell Sicilian and Apulian grain to the Florentines and the Venetians among others; and the relationship with the leading banks in Florence, which provided his court with credit and luxury textiles in return for tax concessions on grain exports became a mainstay of Angevin finances for the next eighty years.

No matter how conspicuously continuous it appears, however, the Angevin kingdom was certainly not the same as the Hohenstaufen one. Its inner condition had changed, and its surrounding situation was different. Although the majority of the population remained almost the same before and after the political confusion, there were a great number of immigrants from the peninsula to Sicily in the thirteenth century. When Charles took the throne, Sicily was no longer an island of Muslims and Greeks; it had been transformed into an island of Latin Christians. In addition the Muslim population was about to disappear from the kingdom. In fact, their last survivors in Lucera, who had been transported from Sicily by Frederick II, were to be sold as slaves in 1300 under Charles II. Thus, the kingdom was no longer a state in which Muslims, Greeks, and Latins coexisted, but an almost solely Christian Latin one.

After the pacification of the kingdom, many foreigners, especially French and Provençal settlers, came to southern Italy. Some of them worked for the central government, while others received lands and became landlords. They constituted the new ruling class. This created a fault line between the foreign ruling class, backed by the foreign king, and the ruled natives. However, the native aristocrats, who were struggling to gain positions at the centre of power, were given a chance to replace the ruling foreigners. Furthermore, Charles chose Naples, not Palermo, as the capital of the kingdom, which meant a shift of gravity from Sicily to Campania; he only once visited Sicily, on his way to a crusade against Tunis. Although Norman and Hohenstaufen elements survived strongly in local administration, as did their governmental methods, the governmental structure subtly changed. Sicily became a province. Sicilians lost their central status, and their political and cultural influence at the royal court withered. The king may well have regarded Sicily simply as a source of profit from the grain trade and other natural assets.

The relationship between the king and the kingdom also changed greatly. At his coronation in 1266 Charles was 40 years old and was already count of Anjou and of Provence. He had married the heiress of the county of Provence in January 1246, and thus had come to rule this wealthy county. In August of the same year he had received Anjou and Maine from his brother Louis IX, and these always remained important fiefs to whose government he gave close attention even from afar. For Charles, no matter how important it was, the kingdom of Sicily was but one part of his dominion. Under the Hohenstaufen there had been a large and dense Italo-German zone in which various political elements closely interacted. In place of that, Charles created an Italo-Angevin zone that consisted of Anjou, Provence, southern Italy, and Sicily. He was king of Sicily, but also king of Albania and

Jerusalem, count of Provence, Forcalquier, Anjou, Maine, and Tonnerre, overlord of Tunis, and sometime Senator of Rome. His concern was not limited to the affairs of the kingdom, and his ambitions went far beyond that, crossing over the Mediterranean. His agenda included the Tunis Crusade of 1270, attacks against the schismatic Greeks in Constantinople, the acquisition of lands in Burgundy and Flanders, the crusade to the East, and interests in Greece, the Balkans, and Sardinia. His dominion was too large to control, as was his ambition.

The Sicilian Vespers and arrival of the king of Aragon

On 30 March 1282 a revolt broke out at the Church of Santo Spirito in Palermo. A personal quarrel between a Palermitan and a French soldier was its apparent principal cause. The revolt quickly spread throughout the island, and many French soldiers were killed. The Sicilians asked Pope Martin IV to give them autonomy under his auspices, but the pope rejected this request and excommunicated all the inhabitants of Sicily. In August, representatives of the towns and nobility of Sicily held an assembly, and decided to look for a protector outside the kingdom. They chose Peter III, king of Aragon. He was the husband of Constance, daughter of Manfred, who herself had been proclaimed queen of Sicily at the royal court of Aragon after the death of Manfred. Having accepted their offer, Peter landed at Trapani in late summer, and was crowned king of Sicily following his election by a parliament held at the ancient Norman church of San Cataldo in Palermo; he was already awaiting the invitation, having sailed to north Africa on a self-proclaimed crusade against the Moors, high in the expectation that Sicily rather than Africa would prove to be his final destination.

This revolt, the so-called Sicilian Vespers, has been characterized by historians in various ways. One of the most lasting questions is whether it was a revolt against the French ruler or against the traditional oppressive rule adopted by the Normans, the Hohenstaufens, and the Angevins. Some scholars attribute its cause to the failure of Charles's government, and insist that the rebels' purpose was to eliminate French and Provençal officials from the court as well as French landlords. Others attribute it to economic burdens, especially that of the notorious *collecta*, first levied by Frederick II. It has been recently pointed out that many of the Amalfitan officials targeted by the rebels belonged to the families that had served Frederick II and Manfred. Some scholars even see a sense of national identity as Sicilians in this revolt, which was largely confined to the island part of the kingdom, although others question this interpretation.

The most important point of this revolt is, however, the fact that Charles could not subdue the revolt properly and quickly. This failure caused the breakaway of Sicily from his kingdom, and made Sicily a different political entity. The profound and long-lasting result was the coexistence of two rival kingdoms in southern Italy. It long remained the most fundamental political feature of southern Italy thereafter. The two political entities, each of which had its own close relationship with outside powers, that is, the houses of Barcelona and Anjou-Provence, opposed each other and brought southern Italy into a state of endemic warfare, damaging to the local economies and a constant distraction to popes planning crusades, north Italian cities in search of protectors, and so on.

The two kingdoms of Sicily and Naples

The war started in 1282 between the Angevins and the Aragonese (the house of Barcelona), and lasted until 1302. However, after a break it was renewed on and off, continuing for about two centuries, and is justly called the 'Two Hundred Years' War' by David Abulafia. Meanwhile, Charles died in 1285, and was succeeded by his son Charles II. In the same year the French king began an anti-Aragonese crusade. In 1290 Charles II ceded Anjou and Maine to Charles of Valois. The Anjou family continued to rule the kingdom of Naples until 1435, while a branch of the house of Barcelona ruled Sicily until the start of the fifteenth century, when the island was reintegrated into the Aragonese–Catalan political federation.

As stated earlier there was a governmental difference between Sicily together with Calabria and the peninsula under the Norman kings. This difference, based on political frameworks and traditions predating the Norman conquest, was consolidated in the process of the conquest and the centralization of administration. At first glance these two fundamental administrative frameworks appear to have been separated into the two political entities. Some scholars seem to think the Sicilian Vespers activated an inner dividing line and separated the kingdom, but we should not stress these regional differences too much. The regional lines of division existed in layers. We cannot totally deny the unity of the kingdom, either, for one and a half centuries had already passed since the creation of the Norman kingdom, and the kingdom already had common historical experiences including the idea of the kingdom, laws, customs, institutions, and cultures. What happened here was not an inevitable result of history caused by regional differences, but a simple incident that changed the destination of the history of southern Italy. Taking the opportunity of the revolt, the Aragonese king used military force to realize his wife's claim of succession to the throne. Thus, the two political forces based in Naples and Palermo, both of which claimed their own legitimacy to the throne, collided with each other and divided the peninsula and Sicily.

These two kingdoms, both sharing the Norman and Hohenstaufen tradition, came to coexist in southern Italy for an extended period. Both of them were situated in the geographical framework of Italy, but they belonged to different political zones embracing larger geographical areas. The kingdom of Sicily came to be a part of the Aragonese zone, while the kingdom of Naples continued to be a part of the Angevin. At the Straits of Messina the two houses of Aragon and Anjou confronted each other and they continued to do so for about two centuries.

3

Papal Italy

Brenda Bolton

Introduction

Between the mid-eleventh and mid-fourteenth centuries—that is,
from the reformed papacy to the Avignonese legation of Cardinal
Albórnoz (1353–7)—papal Italy, although its frontiers were always
fluid, became a defined and consolidated entity. At its widest extent, it
stretched from Ceprano and the river Liri in the south to Radicofani
in the north, and eastwards through the centre of the peninsula,
crossing the Apennines to reach the Adriatic coast. Within these
boundaries lay a complex assemblage of landed properties over which
the popes claimed certain ancient rights and precedents, ruling them
through an effective machinery of administration and justice at the
local level. However, in parallel with the creation of a recognizable
structure of papal government, an unprecedented expansion of papal
authority was taking place throughout Christendom, largely but not
exclusively associated with Gregory VII, Innocent III, and Boniface
VIII. The popes' attempts to justify their temporal rule in central Italy
tended to concentrate on the purely legal title deeds to papal territory,
the Donation of Constantine being only the first among many such
imperial and royal grants and confirmations of temporal jurisdiction
from Pepin (754) to Rudolf of Habsburg (1273). At the coronation of
Henry VII in 1309, Clement V required the new emperor to confirm
by oath that he would indeed abide by all previous legal privileges. In
fact, early justifications of papal temporal rule were generally
accepted and it was not until the beginning of the fourteenth century
that Pierre Dubois articulated the first serious doubts as to whether
popes had the right to have control over territory in central Italy.[1]

---

[1] Petrus de Bosco, *Summaria brevis*, ed. H. Kämpf (Leipzig, 1936), pp. 12–13;
D. Waley, *The Papal State in the Thirteenth Century* (London, 1961), pp. 301–2.

The possessions claimed by the popes derived from the former ancient duchies of Rome and Perugia, and the Lombard duchies of Spoleto and Benevento, forming the nucleus of the Patrimony of St Peter. The *Ludovicianum* of 817, concluded between Louis the Pious and Paschal I, listed the full inventory of land granted by Pepin and Charlemagne. Its provisions were vital in reviving papal claims in the late twelfth century when Cencio, then papal *camerarius*, included the text in his *Liber Censuum*. It confirmed the northern frontier as the ancient limits of suburbicarian or Roman Tuscany, that is, Tuscia Romana, as far as Radicofani, and laid claim to certain dioceses and territories such as Bieda, Sutri, Nepi, Orte, Amelia, Bomarzo, and Narni, which together formed an area with its own definite characteristics. Among the most complex of these regions was the former Roman Sabina, with a less well-defined boundary eastwards to the Apennines. This included the diocese of Rieti but omitted the imperial abbey of Farfa, which had been granted a variety of immunities in 755. In the south, a region very different from the north, lay the diocese of Tivoli, with Campania and Marittima bounded by the river Liri. The *Ludovicianum* also included claims to other areas such as the Exarchate of Ravenna and the eight counties of the Pentapolis, including the cities of Ancona, Osimo, Senigallia, and Fano on the Adriatic coast. Regarding Rome itself, the Emperor Lothar's *Constitutio Romana* of 824 was significant in that two *missi*, one papal and one imperial, were to share judicial functions over the City and its environs. Henceforth, the Romans, but not the popes, were bound to swear allegiance to the Frankish emperor, thus establishing a significant basis for future imperial claims.

As the empire of the Carolingians disintegrated, so the territorial authority of the popes was much diminished. From the early tenth to the mid-eleventh centuries, Rome suffered a weak but continuous German presence, while the surrounding area was subjected to the factional rule of noble families. Nevertheless, papal aspirations to the *terra Sancti Petri* during this period remained remarkably consistent, and were brought back into play from the late eleventh century onwards to reconstruct the legal basis of papal overlordship. A previously failed claim, unsuccessfully pursued by popes since the eighth century, came to realization in 1052 when the former Lombard duchy of Benevento was officially transferred to the papacy. Leo IX

(1049–54) and the reforming popes who succeeded him, led the way in crushing noble families such as the Tuscolani, the counts of Galeria, and the Crescentii Ottaviani who had both dominated the papacy and controlled the region for the previous fifty years. Newer family factions, such as the Frangipani and the Pierleoni (of Jewish descent), emerged instead to provide valuable support for Leo, who successfully claimed back for the Church the important suburbicarian bishoprics of Subiaco and Tivoli. He thus gradually began to clear the way for his successors to stabilize and consolidate the papal position.

Amongst these, Nicholas II (1059–61) was highly significant. In his short pontificate, he attempted to resolve those tensions facing the pope as universal leader of the Church and as heir to the Patrimony of St Peter. Forced to secure Rome against a rival candidate supported by the factional aristocracy of the City, his own election was sanctioned retrospectively by the far-reaching provisions of the Easter synod of 1059. At Melfi in the same year, Nicholas completely reversed previous papal attitudes by establishing sovereignty over the new Norman principalities and, in so doing, helped to secure and define the southern frontiers of the Patrimony. The princes were required to take personal oaths of fealty and security to the pope and to pay an annual payment or *pensio* to the Roman Church for the lands they held 'of St Peter'. Papal policy henceforth, from 1059 to 1156, was to limit what it saw as the Norman threat to designated lands in the south—Apulia, Capua, and Sicily—so as to protect the Patrimony. Therefore, they recognized the Norman princes as defenders of St Peter and vassals of the Holy See, holding their lands not by hereditary succession but instead, as Paschal II declared, 'by the grace of St Peter and of us'. While the problem was by no means finally solved, the southern flank of the Patrimony was to remain relatively stable for many years.

The pontificates of Nicholas II and Gregory VII (1073–85) marked a local and highly significant territorial recovery. It was essential to have the support of those local inhabitants of the Patrimony loyal to the Church and hence the establishment of *castra specialia*, special fortified strongholds, was pursued with vigour. Nicholas II set out the conditions on which he would repopulate the deserted village of Roccantica in the Sabina, each settler paying a graduated *pensio* and the *fodrum* or hearth tax. In return, the pope took the *castrum* under his special protection, and made a similar agreement with the inhabitants of nearby *castrum Lori*. Gregory's agreement with Albininum on the Via Flaminia near Narni provided for the garrisoning of this strategic *castrum*. The pope reserved the right to build a residence or fortified tower within it and to place his *milites* there 'for the use and service of St Peter'. While the popes of the late eleventh century concentrated on creating or securing *castra* in the Sabina, their twelfth-century successors established a chequerboard of strongholds from north to south of the Patrimony, the process slowing down only after the death of Hadrian IV.

The gradual stabilization of their position in relation to the emperors, together with this significant recovery of papal territory, saw the popes interpreting their rights in a more strictly feudal sense. Following the Anacletan Schism (1130–8), the period of the 1140s and 1150s actually witnessed a gradual diminution of conflict in Tuscia Romana, Sabina, and Marittima. While the City of Rome was set apart from the Patrimony by the commune, which pressed for the *Renovatio Senatus* between 1144 and 1145, the Roman revolt, far from weakening the papacy, actually helped to reinforce its ties with an important element among the local nobility of the Patrimony. In 1188, after more than forty years of virtual papal exclusion, Clement III finally succeeded in consolidating his hold on Rome. He significantly reconstructed the Sacred College and increased the number of cardinals. Of the twenty-five created, twelve were from Rome and the Patrimony, strengthening its strongly Roman character for a whole generation. Under Celestine III, papal influence was again restricted, not only within the City but also throughout Sabina and Marittima. When Innocent III, taking up the initiatives of predecessors such as Nicholas II, Eugenius III, and Hadrian IV, recovered the duchy of Spoleto and the March of Ancona, a wider Patrimony—even a Papal State—was at last beginning to take geographical shape. The question of exercising and maintaining authority, however, remained.

The pope and the emperors

In the first half of the thirteenth century, an anonymous Roman cleric wrote:

This power should be believed to belong not to emperors, who obtain only the title of Roman Emperor, but to the bishops who are dwellers in the City. Let those, therefore, blush and be confounded, who strive to release the Roman Church and the City, which God has ever loved, honoured and exalted, and to separate them from the unity of the blessed Peter and his representative.[2]

This informed cleric, speaking from personal knowledge, feared that the frequent tensions between papal and imperial power were threatening the peace of the City of Rome and the unity of all Christendom, particularly papal Italy. Gregory VII's total identification with St Peter as expressed in his commission in the New Testament exalted his own personal and official role. He invariably spoke and thought of himself as Peter's vicar and wrote in letters of papal lands as *terra sancti Petri*. The Salian emperors did not adopt the phrase, preferring instead to speak of papal *regalia* and *possessiones*. The emperors styled themselves *Rex Romanorum et semper Augustus*, best translated as 'King of the Romans and ever Emperor', in order to express continuity with the past; but this title and position could only be conferred on them in St Peter's through unction and coronation by the pope. The popes continually tried to extract promises from the emperors or emperors-elect, their traditional defenders, that they would not invade or occupy the Patrimony: but with little success. From Gregory VII's bitter deposition of Henry IV to the invasion and eventual defeat of Manfred in 1266, which marked the end of Hohenstaufen attempts to dominate the peninsula, significant crises regularly occurred in papal relations with the ruling German dynasties. When, soon after Manfred's death, Charles of Anjou arrived in Rome, it must have seemed to the popes that, following the departure of one imperial figure, another had to all intents been installed in their capital.

---

[2] Biblioteca Apostolica Vaticana, MS Lat. 10999, fo. 150r.

From the last decades of the eleventh century, the popes attempted to define the nature of their authority in relation to imperial power by instituting ceremonies intended to demonstrate the duality of the papal office. As royal priest and imperial bishop, the pope was involved in both spiritual functions and secular lordship. As he held the supreme position on earth, so too he claimed to control temporal powers by spiritual coercion. Two ceremonial usages referred to by Gregory VII in his memorandum, the *Dictatus papae* (1075), aimed at enhancing the power and majesty of the papal office, were the appropriation of the imperial insignia and the requirement that princes should kiss only the feet of the pope. The *Constitutum Constantini*, or Donation of Constantine, purporting to be an edict of the first Christian emperor, but in reality probably a late eighth-century forgery, emerged after centuries of obscurity, to become a substantial weapon in the conflict with the empire. The Donation handed over to Pope Sylvester and his successors, not only the symbols of rulership, orb, sceptre, and purple robe, worn as 'a sign of imperial status', but also the Lateran Palace. Gregory's second ceremony, the kissing of the pope's feet, was an imitation of the Byzantine imperial ceremony of *proskynesis*. These and other ceremonies, which reinforced the nature of papal at the expense of imperial authority, were represented in frescoes at prominent sites within Rome where they would receive maximum exposure to visitors and pilgrims alike.

At the Lateran Palace, in the new Audience Chamber created by Calixtus II, a chronological series of frescoes showed the relevant imperial anti-popes being trampled underfoot as the reformed popes triumphed over their rivals. Thus, Alexander II was depicted as crushing the anti-pope Cadulus, Urban II stood over Guiberto of Ravenna (Clement III), Paschal II over Albert, Maginulf and Theodoric, and, finally, Calixtus himself who stood over Burdinus (Gregory VIII), merely the 'creature' of the emperor Henry V. The emperor was also represented, jointly holding a scroll with Calixtus II, on which were inscribed the first words of his concession to the papacy in the Concordat of Worms of 1123.

The popes held one advantage in their right to confer the imperial crown upon the German king at Rome. After 1138, Innocent II rebuilt two rooms in the Lateran Palace, decorating one of them with scenes from the coronation of Lothar III and an explanatory inscription. In one scene, the bare-headed emperor swears an oath before the open door of a church. In another, Innocent is seated on the papal throne, while Lothar, his head still bare, bows towards the pope. These frescoes, known only through the chance survival of a sixteenth-century sketch, were open to interpretation in the broadest sense.[3] As the pope conferred temporal power on the emperor through the act of coronation, so, what he disposed, he could also withhold.

Such political themes in a visual medium were repeated in the following century. In 1244, when Innocent IV left Rome for Lyon, he appointed Stephen, cardinal priest of Santa Maria in Trastevere, as *vicarius Urbis*, papal representative in Rome. For the next two years, the forces of Frederick II dominated the whole Patrimony, both north and south of Rome; and it was feared that the emperor might march on the City itself. At some point, Stephen established himself at Santi Quattro Coronati, a fortified church, on the *via papalis* between the Lateran and the Colosseum. The Chapel of San Silvestro, which he constructed and decorated, was consecrated by Rainier, bishop of Ostia, after Easter 1246. The decorative cycle of frescoes depicts scenes from the legend of Sylvester as taken from Eusebius of Caesarea's *Life*. The final scene on the north wall, in which Constantine takes the reins of Sylvester's horse and performs the office of *strator* or groom, is derived from the *Constitutum Constantini* alone.

By the thirteenth century, papal claims to supreme authority were increasingly based on the Donation of Constantine. In his sermon for the Feast of St Sylvester, Innocent III argued that Constantine had unambiguously surrendered the Western Empire to the pope and his successors, claiming that the mitre, symbol of papal authority, took priority over the crown, the symbol of imperial authority, which the pope had been offered and had refused. According to the pope, this amounted to the 'natural seniority of the spiritual power against the temporal'.[4] In the mid-1230s, Gregory IX used the Donation to support both the papacy's territorial claims and the pope's right to crown emperors. But the most extreme interpretation was that of Innocent IV's bull, *Eger cui lenia*, of 1246. Following the claims of Innocent III and Gregory IX, that Constantine had endowed the papacy with royal as well as papal authority, Innocent announced that,

---

[3] P. Linehan, *The Spanish Church and the Papacy in the Thirteenth Century* (Cambridge, 1971), pp. 8–9, for the embarrassment of Estevô, bishop of Braga.

[4] *Patrologia Latina*, 217, cols. 481–4, 482A, 'quia pontificalis auctoritas et prior est, et dignior et diffusior quam imperialis'.

before his conversion, Constantine had ruled illegally. Hence, in issuing the Donation, he was only returning to the pope what had rightfully belonged to the papacy all along.

Most significant of all the scenes is that of Constantine performing the office of *strator* and marshal, a ceremony used on two particular occasions: when the emperor first met the pope and at the imperial coronation. Lothar III had performed the ceremony in March 1131 when he met Innocent II at Liège, and his coronation fresco at the Lateran Palace must have served to confirm imperial fears. In 1155 at Sutri, Frederick Barbarossa had delayed the performance of the *officium stratoris* for two days, lest this could be interpreted as a feudal act. Subsequently, however, Otto IV had performed the same office without protest outside the City in 1209 and Frederick II may have done likewise at his coronation in 1220.

The papal recovery

The papal reform movement of the mid-eleventh century had been crucial in ensuring that a small nucleus of patrimonial lands was transformed into an administrative and institutional reality. A new urgency to defend the freedom of the Church, the *libertas Ecclesiae*, encouraged the papacy to set its own house in order by claiming undivided sovereignty over the Patrimony of St Peter. While papal rule over the former duchy of Rome remained unchallenged in the twelfth century, serious points of conflict with the empire had arisen along the northern frontier of Tuscia Romana or occasionally, from the reign of Frederick Barbarossa, in relation to the levying of *fodrum*, the imperial hearth or hospitality tax. Gregory VII had set in motion the claim that the *sacerdotium* might use those attributes of sovereignty up to that time reserved for the *regnum*. The ideas of *imitatio imperii* were incorporated into the liturgy for papal coronations; while the papal banner, the *vexillum Sancti Petri*, was used to signify the recovery of papal territory, as at the *castra* of Acquapuzza in 1158 or Fumone in 1216.

The Curia emerged with a machinery of government adapted to serve the needs of a papal 'monarchy'. New institutions appeared: the *camera* or central organ of finance; the papal chancery or *cancellaria*,

and the *capella* or group of clerics established to supersede the liturgical functions of the cardinals. The Curia thus became an organ of
government charged with a wide variety of tasks, lifting it above
conflicts in the localities and preparing it for the expansion of papal
authority not only in papal Italy but also over all Christendom. The
College of Cardinals assumed a special significance, for it was through
their activities as papal agents and advisers that the pope established a
permanent presence in the Patrimony. Further, their role was vital as
the majority of cardinals were recruited from the region, ensuring
that their local knowledge and contacts worked to the benefit of the
papacy. Although the Curia had opened its recruitment, there
remained a variable majority of cardinals from the region around
Rome throughout the period. Even more marked was the reinforce-
ment of this tendency under the series of Roman popes at the end of
the twelfth century. Clement III, Celestine III, and Innocent III were
all Romans and the influence of this local element increased in the
administrative field during their pontificates. Likewise, Gregory IX,
Alexander IV, and Boniface VIII all continued what has been called
'this beneficial colonisation of Christianity', reflected in a majority of
chancellors, notaries, and scribes whose origins lay in the south of the
Patrimony, or even beyond the river Liri.[5]

The accession of Innocent III in 1198 marked the high point of this
evolution in papal government. As the first university educated pope,
originating from the Patrimony, a man of experience in curial affairs,
he became the model for other later curialist popes. The positive
'recovery' or *recuperatio* of papal territory has been linked to the
premature death in 1197 of the emperor, Henry VI, and to Innocent's
specific policy. In 1198, it was impossible to recover those parts of the
Patrimony lost to imperial forces—and there were many of them—
without the exercise of temporal power. Innocent III was supremely
conscious of the effort to be expended, and of the grave danger that
his endeavours might be reduced to little more than those of a local
temporal lord. Certainly it is from his pontificate, provided with the
first surviving set of almost complete registers, a substantial papal
biography, and a series of chronicle and eyewitness accounts that
much significant evidence has survived to indicate his methods. In

---

[5] B. Barbiche, 'Les "Scriptores" de la Chancellerie apostolique sous le pontificat de
Boniface VIII (1295–1303)', *Bibliothèque de l'École des Chartes*, 128 (1970), 115–87.

the spirit of Gregory I, he added to his activities the duty of pastoral care or solicitude but feared the weight and responsibility of his position in regard to temporal involvement, citing the biblical phrase, 'he who touches pitch shall be defiled by it'.[6] According to his biographer, the more he wished to free himself from temporal concerns, the more he became immersed. His attitude was demonstrated in a highly relevant letter of 1198 to Richard I of England in which he made clear that he saw the Patrimony as a single political unity, similar in that sense to the other kingdoms of Christendom, but also stressed its uniqueness in the sense that this one derived from none other than God himself, *ab ipso Domino*.

Innocent, the first pope since Gregory I to be both theologian and author, was uniquely placed to enunciate the justification in his dealings with the Patrimony. His theological arguments were formed against the background of the recent Hohenstaufen domination of the region, and were expressed in his use of the biblical phrase, 'my yoke is easy and my burden light', to imply a higher conception of that temporal power exercised by the pope. He set out his views most extensively in a series of letters to the cities of the Tuscan League and the duchy of Spoleto, hoping to establish the framework of papal government by securing the co-operation of the cities. Papal Italy had been chosen as the cornerstone of the Christian religion and the seat of its power. It had, therefore, to be organized.

Institutions

Innocent III's programme of reform for papal Italy relied on a governmental structure of provinces ruled over by rectors. Campania and Marittima was already a province. To this, he added Tuscia Romana (the Patrimony of St Peter in Tuscany), the duchy of Spoleto and the March of Ancona. Sabina, almost entirely consisting of papal domain, was generally not administered separately, and, later on, was governed from Tuscia Romana. The tiny region of Massa Trabaria, north of Città di Castello, had a rector in 1205 but later came under the jurisdiction of the March. Innocent failed in his attempt to

[6] Ecclesiastes 13: 1.

acquire the Romagna, which did not fall within papal territory until 1278. Under Boniface VIII, the county of Urbino seems to have had its own rector. Benevento constituted a small papal enclave deep in the Sicilian kingdom.

While Gregory I seems to have appointed only clerical rectors, the twelfth-century popes seem to have used a mixture of both clerical and lay. The *comes Campanie* or rector of Campania, was the official charged with preparing the journeys of the pope around the Patrimony. The rector first appeared during the pontificate of Eugenius III when Peter of Ceprano arbitrated in an inheritance dispute. Under Anastasius IV, John of Santi Giovanni e Paolo was invested with the functions of rector, obtaining the surrender to the Church of vacant fiefs in three *castra* in Campania. Anastasius's successor, Hadrian IV, also used cardinals as rectors, retaining John in his office and appointing another cardinal, Simon of Santa Maria in Domnica. Hadrian's two named rectors are exceptional. Few are known before the pontificate of Innocent III but that they are known at all reveals the stability of the office of rector, indispensable at this decisive period in the evolution of a coherent local territorial policy. Innocent III gave both form and purpose to the institution, formalizing the office in 1207 at Viterbo. His use of clerical rectors was similar to that of Gregory I, but he also appointed laymen to these positions. The office of rector helped to give a province its identity, hence personal qualities of integrity were of real importance. Innocent used his own family members on three occasions when the pressure of work and the need for trust were paramount, praising them for the purity of their faith and the seriousness of their judgement. Should the rectors also be cardinals, then they had also to work closely with the diocesan bishops. At times of crisis, the provincial system might be suspended or merged together in one figure. In the 1240s, when Frederick II threatened the whole area, Cardinal Rainier ruled the Patrimony, the duchy, and the March for five years as 'papal vicar'. In any prolonged papal absence, the rectors were empowered to gather an army in order to avoid a considerable delay. Both Innocent III and Honorius III used legates alternately with rectors and usually limited their tour of duty to a year. Later in the thirteenth century, the duration of rectorates was between one and four years.

Boniface VIII, concerned to halt the abuses current among papal rectors, issued three separate and valuable constitutions, for Campania and Marittima, for Tuscia Romana, and for the March. In *Romana mater ecclesia* of 1295 to Campania and Marittima, he attempted to avoid rivalry between communal courts and those of the rector, by granting the first court to take cognizance of a case the right to resolve it. He also aimed to prevent abuses by local officials, particularly in respect of crimes committed on the highways, by enforcing the protection of the roads, or *custodia stratarum*. *Licet merum*, issued early in 1300 for Tuscia Romana, attempted to define the relationship between the communes and the provincial authority, but granted judicial authority to those towns with the customary right to choose their own officials. The *podestà*, consuls, or rectors could henceforth be appointed to exercise full rectorial jurisdiction, *merum et mixtum imperium*, save in certain reserved cases. Here, too, the *custodia stratarum*, or obligation to defend the highway was enforced, but towns were to be punished only for genuine negligence. The export of food supplies beyond the frontiers of the Patrimony was forbidden, but exceptions were made for Rome and the Curia. In regard to the March of Ancona, Boniface's constitution of 1303, *Celestis patrisfamilias*, did not grant full jurisdiction to the towns of the region but was more concerned with the settlement of specific grievances and the prohibition of statutes issued by the rectors. His legislation excluded the Romagna and the duchy of Spoleto, but its importance is clear from the fact that later the communes were reluctant to give up these constitutions, known as *Bonifacianes* after him. While he clearly considered the government of the Patrimony a matter of significance, he handed out rectorships to his Caetani family and Orsini friends as if they were sinecures.

North and south

Real differences existed between the regions to the north and south of Rome. In Tuscia Romana, the economic and political development of the second half of the twelfth century had accentuated the relations and links with nearby Tuscany. In particular, Viterbo, with its affinity to communal organization and its spirit of independence, had associated itself, entering into a league formed by several Tuscan cities at the end of 1197, after the death of Henry VI. Innocent III sought to profit from the situation, also claiming Tuscany as part of the papal dominion by virtue of ancient donations, but taking care to prevent the integration of Tuscia Romana with Tuscany. One problem for Innocent III was to absorb a relatively urban society into his restored patrimony; but a greater difficulty was the open opposition from the two largest cities of the region which favoured communal autonomy. Viterbo and Orvieto had very different relations with him during the period.

In spite of the relative success of Hadrian IV's pontificate, Viterbo's experience of papal rule was slight. In the twelfth century, Rome was the enemy and Viterbo remained for the most part under the imperial forces of Christian of Mainz and later Philip of Swabia. With the death in 1197 of Henry VI, the situation altered radically. The Viterbans rebelled on news of the emperor's death and decided to join with the cities of the Tuscan league. Innocent III's clear intention was to add to the lands already recognized as the papal patrimony, Tuscia, the duchy of Spoleto, and the March of Ancona, thus subordinating central Italy to effective papal government. Innocent succeeded first in affirming his control of Rome by forcing the election of a new Senator and requiring a feudal oath from Peter de Vico, the Prefect. Relations with Rome began badly and Viterbo was placed under interdict. The events of 1199–1201 revealed the fragility of the nascent papal state. Innocent's policy was victorious, but almost always thanks to help from an ally whose interests were not identical to his own.

While the towns of the Papal States provided the popes with one set of problems, the land provided them with another most serious issue. By the end of the twelfth century, with the small independent settlements of the Patrimony owing direct allegiance to no one save the pope, and an increasing population, the impact of the distinction between cultivated and uncultivated land became ever more marked. Pressure on available land and resources transformed vast tracts of forest, previously granted as pious donations, into bundles of rights and jurisdictions. Local populations fiercely contested the generous concessions to monasteries and religious houses made by a succession of popes and by which the papacy had gained solid support. From the early thirteenth century, these communities insisted on exercising their customary rights over timber and pasture, undeterred by blandishments or threats. The struggle was played out most visibly to the south of Rome, a region where feudal relationships were strong. There, the protagonists were the inhabitants of several *castra* and the monasteries with the popes awkwardly in the middle.

Trisulti, in the diocese of Alatri, provides the best-documented case for almost the whole of the thirteenth century. Formerly a Benedictine house, Trisulti had been granted the forest of Eici by the inhabitants of the nearby *castra* of Collepardo, Guarcino, and Vico around the year 1000. In 1204, Innocent III refounded it as the first Charterhouse to be settled in the Patrimony, endowing the monks, in their search for a desert wilderness, with this particular forest. The Carthusians, however, refused absolutely to tolerate the cutting of wood or grazing of animals in the forest by the Collepardes and Vicani who had previously enjoyed such rights. From 1206 to the end of the century, the popes struggled to protect the interests of the Carthusians of Trisulti and local inhabitants alike. Trespass, illegal seizure of wood, even violence by the local people—the popes met them all with fines, threats of excommunication, and, eventually, with offers of other land. The unequivocal language of papal grants to the Carthusians of Trisulti continued to provoke such violence that, in 1254, Innocent IV and the monks were obliged to call on the nearby *castrum* of Alatri to defend them against the men of Collepardo. Not until 1280 did the Collepardes finally recognize the monks' right to the forest of Eici and, even then, the peace was uneasy.

The Carthusians were not the only monks to cause the papacy anxiety. In the course of the thirteenth century, Casamari and Fossanova, the two most important Cistercian houses of the southern Patrimony, also vigorously defended their interests against nearby communities. Gregory IX attempted to forge a compromise agreement between Fossanova and Piperno in 1227 to allow monks and citizens alike to share rights over wood cutting, hunting, and grazing. This was just one of many such sensitive initiatives which the popes found themselves involved in as a result of their earlier grants and privileges to favoured monasteries.

Papal itineration

The heightened mobility and more visible presence of the pope as he left Rome to itinerate about his territory with his entourage of cardinals, curial officials, petitioners, tradesmen, pilgrims, visitors, and followers was one obvious change that took place in the period from 1100 to 1304. Between these dates, the popes spent approximately 122 years outside the City and only 82 years in Rome. While some popes were subjected to enforced absences, the itinerant lifestyle gradually became more a matter of choice than of necessity. As the control of powerful families who had previously reduced the papal sphere of action to a few small temporary refuges or strongholds began to grow weaker, so the perambulations of the popes came rather to resemble those of a sovereign than of an outcast. The tented summer encampment so favoured by the papal household was first recorded in 1079 when, together with the Curia, Gregory VII left the heat of the City to travel to the cooler banks of the river Liri at Ceprano, there to live under canvas. In 1202, in the most famous of papal summer visits, Innocent III stayed by the Lake of Nero at Subiaco, as did Alexander IV in 1260. Later, in 1298, Boniface VIII would spend some time in his encampment at Rieti.

An anonymous thirteenth-century Roman cleric comes straight to the point.

> Let the Roman bishops learn to love the Roman City and stay in it, because popes living outside Rome seem to have the name of their dignity half complete—although in reality, they are lords everywhere! Let the Romans indeed busy themselves to revere him in the fear of Christ, and with all affection to honour him because, as a woman without a husband, so does the City of Rome without a pope seem to be![7]

Although this should be extended to include with Rome the whole Patrimony, the cleric's reluctance to accept the absence of the pope may have been shared by others who felt, as he seems to have done, that their pontiffs often deserted them at times of crisis. Citizens, however, were to grow accustomed to periodic outbursts of violence. Their City had been 'sacked' by the Normans in 1084, occupied thereafter by imperial forces and anti-popes until the 1120s, and dominated by commune and Senate from 1143 to 1188. In the early thirteenth century, Rome had to brace itself for the further upheavals of the so-called 'Tower Wars' while, in the middle of the century, the protracted

---

[7] Biblioteca Apostolica Vaticana, MS Lat. 10999, fo. 150r.

absence in France of Innocent IV gave free reign to Brancaleone degli Andalò.

Once the popes began to move frequently, they required more permanent resting places for themselves and their officials than the ephemeral shelter provided by tents or pavilions, although it should be stressed that it was by papal choice that they stayed in these rather than in nearby fortified houses. By 1154, a summer palace, a *palatium*, had been raised at Segni, in addition to Eugenius III's construction of a new and better-fortified palace at St Peter's. A whole series of summer palaces—Ferentino, Veroli, Alatri, Anagni, and Rieti—began to spring up across the southern Patrimony and the Sabina, and more substantial winter quarters at Albano, used by Hadrian IV in 1158. Once permanent establishments were built, popes were able to hold full consistories of their cardinals and, as at Segni in 1173 and 1181, even to perform the respective canonizations of Becket and Bruno of Segni.

This was no mere rest cure or holiday for the popes. In the second half of the twelfth century, they profited from their periods of itineration to visit religious houses, to ensure that necessary reforms were applied, to encourage bishops to hold diocesan synods, to put pressure on local lords to renounce alienations and even to establish hospices. A host of papal privileges to new religious foundations would follow each visit. The political consequences of the papal presence were no less important. Each stay offered the opportunity for the pope to render justice in person, often playing off local lay and ecclesiastical lords against each other. The seasonal movements of the pope and the Curia to salubrious cities in a 'véritable transhumance du personnel administratif'[8] had important consequences for papal government and its impact on the localities. It contributed powerfully to form around the apostolic ruler a cohesive group of advisers and executives who tended to become somewhat detached from the Roman context. Further, the popes were able to initiate preliminary efforts to put in place local administrations in areas recently incorporated into their territory.

The informative eyewitness account of William, abbot of Andres, a petitioner to the Curia, provides invaluable information about Innocent III's stay in Viterbo from the end of May to mid-October 1207.

---

[8] P. Toubert, *Les Structures du Latium médiéval*, 2 vols. (Rome, 1973), vol. ii, p. 1054.

On arrival, William reported that he 'found Rome there' and the pope staying in that city 'as if it were his own'. According to William, Innocent, 'the canny shepherd', having escaped the heat of the Roman summer, had chosen to maintain his followers and reside in Viterbo, not only on account of the tranquillity and climate of this rich city with its baths and grain supplies, but also because of the enormous number of pilgrims coming every day to the Curia. An additional 40,000 persons stayed there for a whole month, swelling the indigenous population of Viterbo to several times its usual size. Unable to find lodgings himself, he wrote ruefully that 'no commodity necessary for the human body or for the needs of horses had ever been sold at such a high price'. In preparation for the pope's arrival, officials were sent on ahead to prepare the accommodation and to ensure that the roads were safe for travel. The cities were expected to provide free hospitality for the higher curial officials, while excessive rents and prices were to be controlled. Innocent began a trend that was taken up with enthusiasm by his successors. Between 1226 and 1303, no pope ever spent the whole summer in Rome. Only after 1309 when Clement V finally took up 'temporary' residence in Avignon, did the popes unintentionally remove themselves from their territories, leaving them vulnerable to the depredations of Angevin rulers and factional nobility alike.

Development and support for the faith

Although all regions of Christendom merited equal treatment in the eyes of the popes, nevertheless they felt that they had inherited a special duty of paternal solicitude towards the City and the Patrimony. From the mid-eleventh century, they were able to apply and to test out important principles of reform within this privileged field of action. They aimed, thereby, to enhance and support the faith of their subjects whom they regarded as being within one special family, the family of St Peter.

The traditional agents promoting the faith were the bishops of the Patrimony, who were immediately subject to the pope as archbishop of the region. There were more than twenty of them, all bound to swear an oath of recognition to the pope, promising obedience and due reverence and, in return, being rewarded by his special vigilance and protection. The papacy appointed as bishops its most able clerics and the best of these had their imitators, biographers, and even hagiographers. Toubert has demonstrated that the *Lives* of the local bishops, Peter of Anagni (1062–1105), Berardo of Marsi (*c.*1110–30), and Bruno of Segni (1079–1123), all composed soon after their subjects' deaths, were prototypes of the dossiers required for later canonization processes. They were models of the 'new' bishop, aristocratic, mature, and educated in the cloister. Significantly, all had spent time at the Curia before being elevated to their sees where, during extended episcopal careers, they set about reforming clerical morals, enhancing the faith of the people through teaching and preaching, restoring the material base of their dioceses, performing charitable works, and acting to keep the peace. The details in these *Lives* indicate that in the Patrimony, a region directly subject to papal authority, a rudimentary canonization process was already precocious and effective at the beginning of the twelfth century.

The effect of papal itineration and the increased likelihood that the Curia was present in one or other of the cities of the Patrimony during the summer months meant that the popes could keep a constant eye on vacant dioceses and 'recommend' local candidates for nomination. Bishops, too, could be assessed for their suitability for elevation to curial positions as and when the popes encountered them on their travels around their territory. As the idea developed of a popular consensus for the free election of bishops, so liturgy came to play a vital part in the whole process of celebration. Episcopal *laudes* and other forms of celebratory rituals with which the faithful were encouraged to welcome their new bishop came to have a practical as well as a ceremonial use. One effect of the papal reform movement was a predilection for ceremonies at which several local bishops could gather to concelebrate and together revive the spirit of the primitive church. One such occasion occurred in 1196 when the bishop of Ferentino consecrated the high altar of the collegiate church of S. Maria del Fiume, raised by the pious gift of the counts of Ceccano. A member of the comital family, Jordan, cardinal of Santa Pudenziana and formerly abbot of Fossanova, was present, accompanied by the bishops of Alatri, Anagni, Segni, Terracina, and Veroli. There were several practical results of these concelebrations. The invited bishops brought relics of the saints, taken from their respective local churches, and by establishing indulgences increased the prestige of the new sanctuaries. At Veroli in 1210, Bishop Odo (and after him his successor Leto), went to extraordinary lengths to ensure the authenticity of the newly discovered relics of Mary Salome. At all stages, Innocent III himself was kept informed by appropriate members of the clergy and extreme caution taken with the 'scientific' proof of what was claimed.

The consecrating of new altars, and the reconsecration of others over which there remained some doubt as to their past history, was an encouragement to the faithful of the Patrimony and came to be one of the outward and visible signs that a church had been brought back into the fold. If no lesser person than the pope himself could perform such a consecration, then the effect on the faithful would be even more dramatic. Hence, Innocent III's progresses around the Patrimony usually resulted in the consecration of altars or rich gifts of altar cloths and vestments—at Rieti, Spoleto, Perugia, and Todi in 1198, at Viterbo and Sutri in 1207. He was also instrumental in the promotion of the *Acheropoita*, the venerable image of Christ in the *Sancta Sanctorum* or papal chapel at the Lateran, and the reproduction throughout Tuscia Romana of this particularly Roman image.

Rome, at the heart of Christendom, was the focus for all the faithful. The relics of the apostles, Peter and Paul, the City's powerful and influential protectors, directed pilgrims coming *ad limina* to the great basilicas dedicated to their names. Objects of special veneration were the *confessio* in St Peter's, and the relic collection at the Lateran containing the heads of both saints. Their head reliquaries were processed around Rome at particular moments of crisis, as on 22 February 1239, the Feast of St Peter's Chair in Antioch, when Gregory IX appealed to the Romans to protect the City from Frederick II.

Defending the faith: heresy

In Tuscia Romana, heresy was already infiltrating the region before 1198, while an effectively organized Patarine 'church of the Valle Spoletana' was in existence further to the north. Viterbo, strongly imperial and heretical, represented a more serious problem than Orvieto. Both cities received the full force of Innocent's displeasure.

The faithful 'rector', Pietro Parenzo, was dispatched to Orvieto to extirpate heresy, and was murdered two months later. In March 1199, the pope directed new and repressive measures against Viterbo in *Vergentis in Senium*. The bull's provisions were universally applicable to other rulers, but stressed the confiscation of goods that was to take place in the lands subject to papal jurisdiction. Heretics, their supporters, and followers were to be excluded from public office, losing all legal capacity. Their goods were to be confiscated and heirs were to be disinherited. This suggests that the pope was determined to strike at the heart of the society that nurtured heresy. In 1200, the pope threatened Viterbo that it would lose its episcopal see should the city continue to support heretics. In June 1205, Innocent addressed two further letters to the Viterbese, one of these the harshest ever to emanate from the papal chancery. The pope was complaining that a heresiarch had been elected as the city's *camerarius*, while other excommunicates and believers had been appointed as consuls. Viterbo and Orvieto were part of the same problem and Innocent complained to their two bishops jointly.

From the end of May until October 1207, in a move with significant consequences for his temporal rule over the northern parts of the Patrimony, Innocent III stayed at Viterbo. This prolonged visit enabled him to assess the situation. At the *parliamentum* held in September, the strongest measures yet, such as obligatory oaths, the imposition of penalties, and the demolition of houses, were enacted, all aimed at eliminating heretics from the area. He annulled not only by spiritual but also by temporal authority unfair measures promulgated by the laity against churches or ecclesiastical persons, notwithstanding any oath 'which is said to take priority'. He encouraged his subjects to peace and concord, one with another, claiming that anyone scorning this course of action, should be restrained by the mandate of the ruler of the apostolic patrimony. Finally, he confirmed the honour of diocesan status first granted by his predecessor, distinguishing it with the title of city.

It is surely correct to underline the link between Innocent III's policy to recover territory in the first years of his pontificate and the approval given by the pope to the new and highly original religious movements which were born in Umbria, a particularly contested area. The view that Francis represented an alternative to heresy has been advanced but, for the pope, Umbria was not just a 'papal antechamber'.[9] It was a region in which he was determined to install a papal government. Between 1198 and 1210, Innocent faced many problems from the independent communes there. In particular, Assisi resisted the surrender of their fortress to the papacy in 1198 and elected an excommunicate as *podestà*. In June 1204, Innocent told them that they might freely elect their rector but must seek confirmation from the Holy See.

The Jubilee

On 22 February 1300, the Feast of St Peter's Chair in Antioch, Boniface VIII proclaimed a Holy Year of Jubilee. His reason for so doing has been described as 'one of the great mysteries of medieval enthusiasm', but he knew, from his time spent in England (1265–8), of the Jubilee of Canterbury of 1220. The immediate cause of the celebration seems to have been a popular demand for remission of penance to mark the end of the century. Pilgrims flocked to Rome and saw some of the treasures that made Rome the artistic capital of Christendom. Particularly between 1278 and 1303, popes from Nicholas III to Boniface VIII patronized mosaicists, sculptors, and artists such the Cosmati, Arnolfo di Cambio, Pietro Cavallini, Jacopo Torriti, and Giotto.

Conclusion

By the first decade of the fourteenth century and with the popes in Avignon, the Papal State had become a protectorate of the Angevin rulers. At the same time, the temporal finances of the papacy seem to have fluctuated but were to improve later during the Avignon period. As Angevin influence broke down, so in the 1330s violence increased and papal authority could not 'make itself heard above the clash of swords'. A papal legate was sent but the power of the Roman nobility, combined with a famine in 1347, made the regime of Cola di Rienzo, a

---

[9] R. Manselli, *L'eresia del male* (Naples, 1963), p. 257.

'rector' of Rome and ruler of a vast swathe of lands between Corneto and Terracina, more acceptable to Avignon.

Between 1100 and 1350, the attempt of the papacy to rule central Italy can rarely be seen in isolation from other events. The popes exercised sovereignty over a territory whose origin and nature were essentially temporal—no different from those of secular rulers. However, the spiritual nature of the office of pope tended to obscure the fact of the state over which they claimed to rule. In the late eleventh and twelfth centuries, the papal decision to resist imperial domination of the Italian peninsula was the natural outcome of a tradition, leading to the Church's acceptance of land and use of force to secure territorial authority. At the same time, the popes justified their policy of establishing *castra* or fortified strongholds by stressing the idea of papal benevolence under the special protection of St Peter. The thirteenth century saw the establishment of papal overlordship, first in the duchy of Spoleto, then in the March of Ancona, and, later, with the assistance of the Angevins, the acquisition of the Romagna. For this territorial conquest, the popes, most notably Innocent III, developed a more spiritual justification.

By the third quarter of the thirteenth century, papal Italy extended beyond the mountain range of the Apennines as far as the Adriatic coast just north of the river Adige. When, in 1278, the Romagna was acquired in full sovereignty and the province integrated into the Patrimony, the military and financial power of the popes was further enhanced. By 1300, all the essential machinery of administration and institutions of government had been put in place, its strength demonstrated by the ability to survive the tensions of the Avignon papacy. Only then did Pierre Dubois venture to suggest that tensions might exist for a pope who was militarily capable concerning his suitability to hold spiritual office. Dubois's solution was for the king of France, as Senator of Rome, to hold the Papal State as a fief, paying the pope a sum equal to the revenues. By the middle of the fourteenth century, most of the communes were too weak to oppose the famous 'Constitutions', which Cardinal Gil Albórnoz attempted to implement throughout these territories.

4

The rise of the *signori*

Trevor Dean

The Italian communes of the thirteenth century have been celebrated both for their re-creation of the institutions and methods of ancient democracy, and for their anticipation of the achievements of modern states in defining and achieving secular political goals.[1] At a time when western Europe was dominated by monarchies, political participation in the Italian communes was widened beyond the families of a narrow elite. Appointment to the communes' executive boards and committees was based not on wealth or rank or seniority but on election or the drawing of lots. Above all, the influence of powerful individuals and families was restricted through devices such as secret ballotting, short terms of office, and limits on repeated office-holding. All this produced a 'broader democratic base . . . than in any known regime before the French Revolution'. At the same time, concepts and symbols of sovereignty, freedom, and autonomy were appropriated and asserted; and along with assertion went a real expansion in the powers of government and public administration in areas such as legislation, the exercise of justice, taxation, coinage, public space, the regulation of essential services, and the power to mobilize or commandeer men, money, and materials for warfare and defence. The communes thus produced 'an elaborate constitution, a strong administration and the nucleus of a permanent bureaucracy'.

[1] For what follows, see P. J. Jones, *The Italian City-State: From Commune to Signoria* (Oxford 1997), ch. 4. The quotations come from pp. 370 and 403.

These achievements were soon, however, under threat. 'Democracy' did not bring peace, and the baleful power of division and faction grew stronger. Despite their pretensions, communal governments lacked resources, and in practice relied on communities, social groups, and private initiative across the whole range of public business, from policing to revenue collection. 'Bureaucracy' is a misnomer for the untrained, incompetent, and often corrupt holders of offices in the communes. Frequent rotation of governmental and administrative personnel brought confusion rather than participation and impartiality. Citizens, anyway, showed a preference for avoiding rather than shouldering public duties, and for attacking rather than obeying agents of the communal state. More importantly, the pretensions of communal governments were made impossible by four powerful forces: class and wealth sought and won privileged, preferential, profitable treatment at the hands of government in areas such as justice, taxation, and military obligation; the practices of clientage and patronage sought to turn state offices and resources to private gain; family clans provided a rival focus of loyalty and sought to occupy and dominate the state itself; and finally feudal lordships— *seigneuries* of castles, lands, dependent tenants, and jurisdiction— persisted, untamed, across much of northern Italy, and were able to use the cities' penchant for unceasing warfare to strengthen their positions in both town and country.

The response to this failure of the communal city-state was political change. From the middle decades of the thirteenth century, political life in northern Italy began to be dominated by a new breed of political and military leaders, generally known as tyrants, despots, or (better) *signori*. At a time of intense military activity and pressure during and after the reign of Emperor Frederick II, such men provided internally divided cities and their incomplete communal states with the beginnings of a more stable political order. In an accelerating development, as imperial authority withered in northern Italy, monarchical authority was re-created at the local level, in the persons first of Frederick's former political and military lieutenants (Uberto da Pallavicino, Ezzelino da Romano), then of local faction chiefs (Azzo d'Este in Ferrara, Martino della Torre in Milan, Mastino della Scala in Verona). Though their power often remained informal, they passed that power to their heirs, who formalized their position through popular 'elections' and technical transfers of arbitrary power

(Ferrara 1264, Mantua 1299, and so on). In the course of time, some of these lordships developed into the principalities and regional states of fourteenth- and fifteenth-century Italy: the Visconti in Milan, the Gonzaga in Mantua, the Estensi in Ferrara, the Montefeltro in Urbino. By 1300, most cities of northern Italy were under signorial rule; those that were not soon followed (Padua, Parma), while attempts to create city-lordships were also made in Tuscany.

So much for the broad development. Within each city, there was much variation and uncertainty. Let us take as illustrative the case of Parma.[2] For five years at the beginning of the fourteenth century (1303–8), the nobleman Giberto da Correggio held the position of lord of this city. The origin, course, and eventual collapse of his lordship offer many typical features of the north Italian *signorie*. The first of these is an origin among rival armed factions in the city. The ruling elite of Parma had for long been divided into two factions— one supporting the empire, the other the Church—but this simple opposition had more recently been complicated by the appearance of a 'bishop's party', which in the political events of the 1290s and 1300s became allied to the 'imperial party'. In 1295 rumours of a stockpiling of weapons in the bishop's palace led to the expulsion of the bishop by his opponents and the ransacking of a monastery. In this crisis, a troop of men came from Giberto da Correggio's own estates to support him. In addition, outside forces—the city's allies, its political exiles and enemies—intervened. The city of Parma received military aid from its neighbours and allies, the cities of Milan, Bologna, and Piacenza; while the exiles, ensconced in castles in the territory, were reinforced by the city's enemies. The following year saw some military operations by the city against the exiles. A peace was negotiated in 1297; but, as it did not allow the exiles to return, they conspired against it, and in the next two years were by stages overcome, killed, captured, or put to flight. Pacification necessarily involved a solution to the exile question. By 1303, however, tensions were rising in the city over the possible recall of some or all of the exiles. Giberto da Correggio led the successful pressure for all to be readmitted and rehabilitated. On the very day that they returned, Giberto was the focus of an apparently spontaneous acclamation: a large crowd of his

---

[2] 'Chronicon parmense', ed. G. Bonazzi, *Rerum italicarum scriptores*, 2nd edn., vol. ix, pt. 9 (Città di Castello, 1902–4), pp. 71–106.

friends and the returned exiles began to shout 'Long live lord Giberto'. They occupied the main piazza, and bore Giberto in triumph into the communal palace, the seat of government. At a makeshift 'council' meeting, Giberto was proclaimed 'lord, defender and protector of the commune and *Popolo*, and conservator of peace'. He was invested with the twin symbols of the commune's authority and strength: the banner of St Mary and the *carroccio*, the great wooden wagon that bore the banner into battle. On the following day, a more formal session of the city council met to ratify this appointment, and every member swore to defend Giberto's position as lord.

However, not everyone acquiesced. One of the other leading families, the Rossi, left the city and retired to their estates, effectively refusing to acknowledge Giberto's authority. Within two years they were making armed preparations aimed against him, and were receiving military aid from his enemies, principally from Azzo d'Este, lord of the city of Ferrara. Disturbances in Parma continued. Giberto's cousin was killed, in Giberto's own bedchamber, by a member of the Senaza family; in retribution, members of that family were exiled. A conspiracy to depose Giberto was exposed in 1305, its leader being captured and imprisoned. Giberto attempted to parry the hostile intervention of the lord of Ferrara by undermining the latter's control of the nearby cities of Modena and Reggio: when the latter rebelled against Ferrara in 1306, Giberto was involved in the new settlement, and his brother was appointed as *podestà* of the commune (chief executive). At this point, Giberto was looking both to consolidate and to expand his power. He was briefly made lord of the neighbouring city of Piacenza, but lacked the internal support to make a success of this opportunity. He aimed to make political capital out of his daughters' marriages, giving one of them to the lord of Verona, another to the lord of Mantua. However, internal plots against Giberto continued in 1307, leading to fresh waves of exiles, while the city's attacks on the Rossi castles were unsuccessful and costly in lives. The finale took place over three days in March 1308. In a tense situation rumour and report came to play an active role in the drama. A trivial incident—a brawl in Giberto's palace in which he was wounded in the hand—set off wider fighting between the factions in the city, in which men were killed and houses set ablaze. For the moment, Giberto, with the civic authorities and soldiery, held the piazza—the symbolic political heart of the city—and tried to reimpose peace. Drawn in by reports of fighting, some of the exiles returned, found a way into the city, and engaged Giberto in a great battle on the main square. Deserted by many of his supporters, Giberto eventually fled, finding an escape route along the city ditch. An orgy of looting ensued, until calm was restored; the following day, rejoicing and dancing replaced looting.

Compressed into five years we here see typical features of many *signorie*: an origin in factional strife, with the lord associated with pacification; attempts to consolidate or expand the lordship thwarted by an erosion of internal support and by an incapacity to prevent external subvention of exiled enemies; and collapse of power in the course of armed confrontation in the main square. Other significant elements include the role of rural retainers drafted in to support the lord's urban politics, and the use of marriage to create or solidify political alliance. However, in each city the pattern of events, the bases of support, the political context, and outcomes were different. The aim of this chapter is to explore those differences. The history of four different northern Italian lordships—in Milan, Piacenza, Verona, and Ferrara—will be recounted in order to suggest comparisons and contrasts, to reveal differing backgrounds, contexts, and outcomes; but this should be seen for what it is—a simplifying strategy aiming to deal in a short space with a very complex historical development. For a time, northern Italian politics resembled nothing so much as a sort of permanent revolution, in which unstable communes gave way to lordships, which expanded, failed, and disappeared, giving way in turn to stronger lordships or revived communes. Historiography characteristically deals with forms of political power that survived, with victors rather than losers: this chapter, while devoting most space to the successful, long-lasting *signorie* of the Visconti, Estensi, and della Scala, also looks at unsuccessful short-lived cases, such as the Correggio in Parma and the Scotti in Piacenza.

The passage of power from commune to *signore* could come about in a variety of ways. In some cases the transition was bloodless and almost unchronicled, as at Ravenna in 1275 or Treviso in 1283. In other cases the change was the result either of a slow build-up of lordly power (the Bonacolsi in Mantua) or of repeated, self-destructive outbreaks of internal disorder, as in Modena and Reggio in the 1280s, or Treviso in the 1320s, where one poetic commentator observed that his fellow citizens 'every day fight a new war'. Some leaders took advantage of political and military crises to discredit their opponents and to marshal consent behind their emerging dominance, for example Alberto Scotti in Piacenza in 1290. Elsewhere, the revolution could be bloody and partisan. When the then lord of Milan, Napoleone della Torre, was installed as lord of Lodi in 1270, his factional supporters toured the town killing, robbing, and terrorizing their disarmed opponents. Accession to power could also take the form of military conquest: when Napoleone was in turn dislodged as lord of Milan in 1277, it followed a surprise night attack by Ottone Visconti and his forces, and the capture of most of Napoleone's family. These variations were not chance happenings, but were related to the existing social and political structures within cities.

One of the key variations between cities lay in the strength and activity of the *Popolo*, a combination of artisans and traders excluded from communal government. These groups came together to form their own 'commune within the commune', with its own leader, its own assemblies and statutes, its own premises, churches, banners, and militias. Their aim was to challenge and to absorb the commune. The interests of the *Popolo* and the interests of the nobility have often been seen as antithetical: the former organized collectively through neighbourhood associations and guilds, the latter through clans and factions; the former sought to defend and expand the rights and powers of the city-state in areas of food supply, justice, and taxation, the latter to limit them; the former represented solidarity and civil concord, the latter division and lawlessness. And from the clash between these two groups, it has sometimes been asserted, the *signori* arose: they were either generated from within the *Popolo* as an instrument in the struggle against the aristocracy, or spearheaded an aristocratic reaction to overcome the *Popolo*. There is some truth, but also much misrepresentation in this assertion, as we shall see.

Piacenza

Though the political history of Italian towns in the thirteenth century was described at the time in terms of conflict between the knightly class (*milites*) and the populace (*Popolo*), Pierre Racine argues that in Piacenza this cannot be reduced to conflict between the landed

aristocracy and guildsmen.[3] The first reason is that the social structure was more varied, with overlapping groups ranging from the
ancient aristocratic lineages, through layers of the business class—
from large international traders to local food suppliers—to the
manufacturing groups in the textile industry. The second reason is
that the leaders of the *Popolo* were in fact aristocrats, and there were
both knights who adhered to the *Popolo* and *populares* who supported the knights. What we have here, Racine surmises, is not class
division, but aristocratic clienteles: civil conflict remained first and
foremost a play of rivalry between aristocratic families. Third, the
relation of the guilds to the *Popolo* in Piacenza is not clear: they were
not constituent parts of it, and some guilds (merchants, judges)
adhered to the knights. Last, trading activity was not an unambigu-
ous mark of distinction between knights and *populares*: some
knightly families were turning to trade, yet provided leaders of the
knightly faction, whereas other families involved in trade adhered to
the *Popolo*. So, what looks at first sight like a class division, between
landed and urban interests, between aristocratic and mercantile,
turns out on closer inspection to repeat the factional struggles, family
rivalries, and personal vendettas of the aristocracy. The *Popolo* provided one group of aristocratic families with the means to claim
the government of the commune from another group of aristocratic
families.

Each faction, popular and knightly, sought to control and absorb
the commune, and provided the support for a succession of attempts
to seize personal power. Such attempts bred networks of factions
across northern Italy, as the knights or *Popolo* of one city supported
the knights or *Popolo* of another. The first attempt in Piacenza came
in the 1230s, as Guglielmo Landi tried to move from his large rural
power base to control of the city, with the support of the city of
Cremona. The second came in 1253 when Uberto Pallavicino took
Piacenza into his regional conglomeration of cities, of which he was
variously lord or *podestà* (a combination of chief executive, judge,
and military commander). Uberto was a member of a large aristocratic clan with properties across the borders of Piacenza, Parma, and
Cremona. He was a previous leader of the *Popolo* of Piacenza, and

[3] What follows is based on P. Racine, *Plaisance du Xe à la fin du XIIIe siècle*, 3 vols.
(Lille, 1979–80).

had received an imperial delegation of power as 'imperial vicar in Lombardy'. His hold on Piacenza, however, was short lived. According to Racine, deep divisions within the landed elite meant that the knightly faction did not rally to him, while an economic crisis in the later 1250s led to him being expelled by the *Popolo* (led by other aristocrats). Changes in the balance of power among the local aristocrats gave Uberto a second term of power in Piacenza (1262–6), but it was increasingly aristocratic families engaged in business who took control over the direction of politics. It was they who led Piacenza into a ten-year protectorate under the king of Naples, Charles I of Anjou, from 1271 to 1281; and it was from their number that a native lord eventually emerged. Alberto Scotti came from a business family associated with the *Popolo*, which, however, was also active from the mid-thirteenth century in buying land and urban property. Later in the century they were bankers to the pope and international traders. Alberto Scotti's company was the most powerful in Piacenza, and it was from the 'society of merchants' that he derived his personal power. When his primacy began in 1291, he was appointed 'rector of the society of merchants and defender of the commune and *Popolo*'. What distinguishes his power is its informality: he held no office in the commune (such as *podestà*); he was granted no special powers by the commune (such as lord); and he held no delegated function from the emperor (such as a vicariate). His power lasted longer than any so far in Piacenza (until 1304), and he certainly tried to pass his power on to his son; but his political and military intervention in Milan overextended the range of his narrow power base and he was eventually forced out of Piacenza by a coalition of his enemies.

Verona

The emergence of the della Scala lordship in Verona shares some similarities with Alberto Scotti's in Piacenza.[4] Like the Scotti family,

---

[4] What follows is based on G. M. Varanini, 'Istituzioni, società e politica nel Veneto dal comune alla signoria (secolo XIII–1329)', in A. Castagnetti and G. M. Varanini (eds.), *Il Veneto nel medioevo: dai comuni cittadini al predominio scaligero nella Marca* (Verona, 1991); and id., 'Istituzioni, politica e società nel Veneto (1329–1403)', in A. Castagnetti and G. M. Varanini (eds.), *Il Veneto nel medioevo: le signorie trecentesche*

the della Scala were not members of the existing local aristocracy: they owned no castle, no large estate. The power of the first della Scala lord, Mastino (1268–77) was informal and based on the *Popolo* and the society of merchants. Mastino appears as 'Captain of the *Popolo*' in the early 1260s, and then as *podestà* of the merchants. Other than these positions, Mastino, again like Alberto Scotti, held no official post, though he was titled 'lord' by at least one chronicler. The difference with Piacenza lay in the clearer displacement of the knightly class. Mastino's rise to ascendancy in 1277 coincided with the expulsion of many knights of the 'count's party' (the faction of the titular count of Verona, from the illustrious San Bonifacio family). Those knightly families who were not expelled seem to have entered a period of decline, excluded from the communal councils, unable to afford to maintain horses and armour, their urban towers no longer foci for political mobilization. Consequently, the della Scala lordship coincided with a substantial replacement of the civic elite, as new families, more often associated with the della Scala, rose to prominence. By the mid-1270s, the della Scala regime was established—Mastino was lord, his sons Guido and Alberto were respectively bishop and *podestà* of the merchants—and Mastino's assassination in 1277 did not halt the further consolidation under Alberto. Control over ecclesiastical institutions and resources expanded. Marriages with leading families of northern Italy (the Este and Pallavicino) helped settle the della Scala into the broader ruling class. Then, under Alberto's son and successor, Cangrande (1311–29) a period of territorial expansion began, focused first of all on Vicenza, but leading rapidly to the subjugation of the whole region to Cangrande: first, he obtained an imperial vicariate for Vicenza (1311–12); then he achieved the military conquest of Feltre and Belluno (1321–3), dominion over Padua (1328), and the conquest of Treviso (1329). Internally, the eclipse of communal institutions in Verona was very evident in these years: the *podestà*, instead of being replaced annually, remained in office for fifteen years; the lord alone announced revisions to statute law; and membership of the communal

(Verona, 1995); E. Rossini, 'La signoria scaligera dopo Cangrande', in *Verona e il suo territorio*, vol. iii, pt. 1 (Verona, 1975); with material also from A. Di Salvo, 'Il signore della Scala: percezioni e rielaborazioni della figura di Cangrande I nelle testimonianze del secolo XIV', *Rivista storica italiana*, 108 (1996), and L. Green, 'The image of tyranny in early fourteenth-century Italian historical writing', *Renaissance Studies*, 7 (1993).

council was controlled. Increasingly, the court came to displace the commune: this provided avenues for social advancement for soldiers and officials, as new families, from Verona and from outside, came to form a new elite.

The rapidity of Cangrande's conquests, combined with his premature death, fostered the growth of myths around his memory: prophecies were, retrospectively, associated with him; he appeared as a man of destiny, unstoppable while he lived. To contemporaries and later writers, Cangrande stood out for a range of exceptional qualities: his capacity for swift and decisive military action; his magnanimity towards captured opponents ('Cangrande was no savage avenger', said one chronicler); his restless, unsparing pursuit of the objective of enlarging his dominion; and his near-regal self-presentation in public ceremonies, such as triumphal entry into conquered cities or magnificent courtly occasions.

Cangrande's expansionist policy was continued, but now fatally, under his nephew Mastino II: he enlarged the della Scala dominion beyond the Veneto region by taking Brescia in Lombardy (1332), Parma in the Po valley (1336), and even Lucca in Tuscany (1336). As Varanini has pointed out, the usual description of Mastino II, based on contemporary chronicles, stresses his rash ambition and arrogance. For many chronicle-writers, hostile to 'tyranny', Mastino, like Cangrande, fitted the stereotype of the tyrant who overreached and destroyed himself. However, on closer inspection, taking account of other sources, Varanini sees 'clear and deliberate efforts to give consistency to della Scala rule', by a combination of respect for existing institutions and intervention in the areas of taxation and military resources. Under Mastino II, there was a certain amount of administrative centralization in Verona: some functions were reserved to officials resident there; subject cities had to maintain an envoy there; measures first adopted by Verona were later applied to the other subject cities. However, this was balanced by some recognition of the existing structures of government in subject cities, though these structures were exploited, so as to provide resources for della Scala wars, and reformed (new statutes were issued; communal councils were reduced in membership and functions).

Della Scala expansion was, however, brought to an end in a three-year war against Florence and Venice. The ostensible cause of this war lay in a series of disputes between Venice and the della Scala relating

to the interests of Venetian traders, landowners, and clients following
the growth of the della Scala state in the 1320s, especially the conquest
of Treviso; but the truer cause, it seems, lay in Venice's refusal to
accept so powerful a lord as a neighbour and its concern that key
commercial routes across northern Italy were now in the control of a
small group of *signori* allied among themselves. In this crisis, Mastino's
composite state fractured: aristocratic families in border areas abandoned the della Scala and submitted to other rulers; at the instigation
of Venice, families in Vicenza mobilized against the della Scala; and in
Padua the da Carrara family emerged as leaders who had the backing
of Venice. Treviso was lost to Venice, and the della Scala hold on
Lucca and Parma was fatally weakened. Once peace was restored, the
della Scala lordship was reduced once again to Verona and Vicenza,
though it survived another half-century before falling victim to
another coalition, of Venice and Milan.

Milan

It has been suggested that the long war of the pope and the Lombard
League against Emperor Frederick II and his north Italian allies—
sealed in victory following his death in 1250—had two effects on
political development in Milan.[5] It modified the practices of government, accustoming the political class to the more dictatorial style of
the papal legate, who resided there directing operations against the
emperor; and it accentuated tensions between the *Popolo* and the
nobles, especially over issues of taxation and eligibility for canonries
in the cathedral chapter. Popular tumult against the archbishop and
clergy, supported by the nobles, broke out in 1252. But the nobility
was not a solid block, and it divided in the mid-1250s, as the della

    [5] What follows is based on *Storia di Milano*, iv. *Dalle lotte contro il Barbarossa al
primo signore (1152–1310)* (Milan, 1954), pp. 271–363; F. Somaini, 'Processi costitutivi,
dinamiche politiche e strutture istituzionali dello stato visconteo-sforzesco', in
G. Andenna, R. Bordone, F. Somaini, and M. Vallerani (eds.), *Comuni e signorie del-
l'Italia settentrionale: la Lombardia* (Turin, 1998); F. Cognasso, 'Le basi giuridiche della
signoria di Matteo Visconti in Milano', *Bollettino storico-bibliografico subalpino*, 53
(1955); id., 'Note e documenti sulla formazione dello stato visconteo', *Bollettino della
Società pavese di storia patria*, 23 (1923); 'Annales mediolanenses', in *Rerum italicarum
scriptores*, ed. L. A. Muratori, xvi (Milan, 1730).

Torre family were deserted by the other noble families. This led the della Torre to adhere to the *Popolo*, whose leaders they became. This realignment was the occasion for riots and murders, and the perceived ambition of the archbishop led to further disturbances in following years. Eventually, in 1257, Martino della Torre expelled the bishop and the noble faction and executed the commune's tax supremo who, according to the local chronicles, had used 'every means to extort money', and 'particularly hated the *Popolo*' (his body was dragged to burial in the city ditch: a sign of popular justice against a designated public enemy). In order, according to the chronicler, to 'rub out' the noble party more easily, Martino conferred the position of captain-general on Uberto Pallavicino, the main military leader in Lombardy, and Uberto led successful action against the Milanese exiles, many of whom were captured and imprisoned. At this point (1260), the della Torre were looking to extend their power by acquiring the archbishopric—the previous bishop had died in 1257—but though Martino's cousin Raimondo had the votes of some canons, the pope intervened, alienated by the della Torre association with the anti-papal Uberto Pallavicino, and appointed Ottone Visconti instead (1262). In response, Martino and Uberto occupied the bishop's properties and prevented Ottone from entering the city.

Martino died in 1263, and his power passed to his brother Filippo, who used the title 'perpetual lord of the *Popolo* of Milan'. As well as inheriting from his brother the lordships of Novara and Lodi, Filippo also acquired those of Bergamo, Brescia, and Vercelli. He terminated the alliance with Uberto Pallavicino, aligning instead with the pope's champion, Charles of Anjou. He achieved little else before his death in 1265, being succeeded by Napo, brother of Raimondo (now bishop of Como). Despite a favourable international context—the della Torre led northern Italian support for Charles of Anjou's papal campaign to conquer the kingdom of Sicily—multiple problems arose for Napo: protest from the pope over exclusion of the bishop and other 'oppressions' of the Church; shock at the excessive revenge taken against Milanese exiles following their murder of Napo's brother; riots against the heavy taxation required to support mercenary soldiers; discontent and rebellion among the subject towns (Lodi, Como, Novara), partly fomented by the Milanese exiles; and the continued disturbing presence not far from Milan of Ottone Visconti, who issued an interdict against the city in 1274. As Ottone joined forces with the exiles, becoming their leader, they made further inroads into della Torre power, and in January 1277 attacked Napo in Desio, capturing him and most of his family. They were sent to prison in Como and held, so the chronicler says, 'like dogs'; Napo died there in the following year.

It is important to register the role of revenge in the Visconti attack on the della Torre in Desio.[6] According to a sort of newsletter preserved in the Piacentine chronicle, Francesco della Torre was wounded in the attack, thrown from his horse, then trampled and beheaded; Andriotto della Torre was also beheaded. Both heads were presented to Count Riccardo di Langosco as trophies of revenge for the killing by the della Torre of his kinsman, count Goffredo. Goffredo was a nobleman from Pavia whom the Milanese exiles had appointed as their military leader in 1275; he had been captured by the della Torre and, contrary to accepted chivalric laws of war, sentenced to death. Mistreatment of prisoners was an important source of aristocratic desire for revenge. We should note how more successful lords, such as Cangrande della Scala, cultivated magnanimity towards those vanquished and captured in battle.

Once readmitted to Milan, the noble coalition exacted numerous concessions, revising the balance of power with the *Popolo*: the della Torre and their supporters were exiled and their properties were confiscated; the organization of the *Popolo* was reformed; anti-noble laws were reviewed; the cathedral chapter was closed once more to non-nobles; tax assessments were revised; and some of the functions of the communal Council of 800 were transferred to a smaller committee of twelve (the Office of the Twelve Provisors). At first, to deal with fresh attacks by the della Torre, Ottone had to call in the military aid of the marquis of Monferrato, who was granted lordship of Milan for ten years, but the marquis's attempts to draw the Milanese nobles to himself, to advance his own political ambitions, as well perhaps as the need to avoid jeopardizing Milan's relations with the papacy, led Ottone in 1282 to terminate the marquis's lordship, expelling his officials and his supporters among the Milanese nobility. Further action against the nobles—destruction of a castle, expulsions—followed in

---

[6] 'Annales placentini gibellini', *Monumenta Germaniae historica, Scriptores*, xviii (Hanover, 1863), p. 565; 'Gualvanei Flammae Manipulus florum sive Historia Mediolanensis', in *Rerum italicarum scriptores*, ed. L. A. Muratori, xi (Milan, 1737), p. 701.

1287, and in the same year Matteo Visconti was appointed captain of the *Popolo*, allowing Ottone to withdraw from political life (he died in 1295). In 1288 a popular assembly granted Matteo the authority to revise the statutes, and he was confirmed in the post of captain of the *Popolo* for a further five years. In the 1290s he obtained similar positions in Como and Novara. Despite Matteo's efforts to consolidate his position through family marriages (to members of the Este and della Scala), and through associating his son Galeazzo in his position in Milan, opposition to Matteo built up in the 1290s, and in 1301 there were revolts in Novara and Vercelli, as well as plots against Matteo in Milan, where a large group of nobles was now conspiring against him. The della Torre also reappeared in Lombardy, as Alberto Scotti—remarkably still active politically as he approached the age of 80—put together an alliance aiming to reinstall them in Milan. In the face of this coalition, Matteo surrendered without a fight and accepted exile.

By 1311, however, Matteo was back: he took advantage of the new emperor's peace-making expedition to return to Milan, though the peace that was made between Visconti and della Torre was described as a 'sham' by the local chronicler. The outcome of Matteo's manœuvre was that the della Torre were exiled once more, this time definitively, and Matteo re-created his power in Lombardy: he became lord of Milan (a general council in 1313 elected him 'general rector of the commune' for life), and of other cities; Galeazzo Visconti was lord of Piacenza; and there were pro-Visconti regimes in Como, Novara, and Pavia. The Visconti 'state' at this point was, according to Cognasso, a federation or agglomeration of cities governed by Matteo. As such it was reliant on three supports: on a member of the Visconti family acting as *podestà* in each city, on the maintenance of a network of marriages with the important families of Lombardy, and on the retention of large numbers of supporters in each city, starting with the leading families and their clienteles. Cognasso's verdict was that this was insufficient to resist strong disintegrating forces when they arose in the 1320s. The federation therefore collapsed under the weight of a papal offensive when the Visconti were accused and sentenced for heresy and necromancy, and a crusade was launched against them. Matteo died in 1322 in the middle of defending himself against this papal onslaught. His son Galeazzo became lord, and barely held on to Milan against a combination of external military challenge and internal noble unrest. Despite losing the lordship for a few months, Galeazzo survived and recovered, and his son Azzone succeeded him in 1327. Having obtained peace and pardon from the pope (1331–2), he then embarked on a renewed policy of expansion, taking Bergamo and Vercelli in 1333, Cremona in 1335, and Como, Lodi, Piacenza, and Brescia in 1336. On his death in 1337 his uncles Giovanni and Luchino were elected as lords. By 1340 most of the cities of Lombardy were under the Visconti, and subsequent decades brought them power in Bologna (1350), Genoa (1353), Reggio (1371), and in cities in the Veneto and in Tuscany in the late fourteenth century.

The Visconti lordship thus originated not in the *Popolo*, but in the aristocracy, which aligned with the archbishop in their struggle against the della Torre lordship based on effective leadership of the *Popolo*. However, as in Piacenza, the lines of division were not clear cut, as part of the *Popolo*—the merchants and *Popolo grasso* (wealthier commoners)—allied to the archbishop and the exiled nobles. Again, unlike both Piacenza and Verona, the Visconti were members of the feudal aristocracy, with large estates and a presence in the cathedral chapter of Milan. One fourteenth-century chronicler, an advocate for the Visconti, claims that, of all the Milanese nobility, they were always one of the noblest and oldest families (though the branch of the family from which the Visconti lords descended was one of the less well endowed). The Visconti came to power as the aristocratic leaders of an aristocratic faction, and for some years Ottone remained dependent on his allies. The year 1287, therefore, is claimed to mark a crucial turning-point for the Visconti regime, in that it freed itself from that dependency. Henceforth the Visconti were not anti-noble, but were able to mediate between social and political groups. It is no coincidence that the same year saw the first appointment of Matteo as Captain of the *Popolo*, or that in the 1290s the *Popolo* temporarily recovered some of its role in armed defence of the city.

Ferrara

The origin of the *signoria* in Ferrara was different, again, in both social context and the course of events.[7] As in Milan, the lords— members of the d'Este family—were members of the feudal aristocracy, but there were two features that distinguished them from the Visconti: first, they were not originally part of the local urban elite, but had moved to Ferrara to inherit lands and followers from a leading Ferrarese family; secondly, there was little or no tension between nobles and *Popolo* in Ferrara. The ancestral lands of the Este family were situated south of the city of Padua, around the castle of Este, and their political ambitions in the first half of the thirteenth century spread from these estates across most of the Veneto and into eastern Lombardy (specifically to Mantua). However, in the mid-thirteenth century, a combination of the development of their acquired political base in Ferrara and of the emergence of local lords in the cities of the Veneto led to a redirection of Estensi ambitions to Ferrara, its surrounding territory, and neighbouring cities. In the first half of the thirteenth century they contested a leading position in Ferrara with the local Torelli family. At this period, the contest was characterized by the typical aristocratic methods of feudal-vassalic clienteles and the pursuit of vendetta, combined with periodic expulsions and exiles. In 1240 the Torelli were ousted, and it is significant that their subsequent attempts to return had none of the efficacy or power of their della Torre counterparts in Milan. The Estensi managed to assure themselves of the loyalties of both nobles and people. Henceforth the Estensi were free of challenges from other families, and the major threat to their lordship came from conflicts among themselves. Occasional physical attacks on the Este lord—in 1273 and 1288—seem to have lacked wider support among the nobility and urban society; indeed in 1288 the people tried to lynch the assailant in an outburst of spontaneous loyalist sentiment.

---

[7] See T. Dean, *Land and Power in Late Medieval Ferrara: The Rule of the Este, 1250–1350* (Cambridge, 1987); 'Chronicon estense', ed. G. Bertoni and E. P. Vicini, *Rerum italicarum scriptores*, 2nd edn., vol. xv, pt. 3 (Città di Castello and Bologna, 1908–); 'Chronica parva ferrariensis', in *Rerum italicarum scriptores*, ed. L. A. Muratori, viii (Milan, 1726).

The power of Azzo d'Este remained informal, but at his death in 1264 his grandson Obizzo II was elected lord of the city, in one of the first such elections. Unusually, a record of this event is preserved in two documents: a chronicle narrative and a statute law. According to the former of these sources, Azzo's funeral aroused lamentation and tears even among his enemies, but when everyone returned from the funeral to the main square, they found that an armed group of citizens had taken up position and a general assembly was being summoned by bells and criers. The leaders of several neighbouring cities spoke to the crowd. So too did one member of the Ferrarese elite. His message was essentially 'The king is dead; long live the king'. In other words he preached dynastic continuity, presenting the 17-year-old Obizzo d'Este, Azzo's grandson, as a suitable successor. And the crowd shouted out its agreement, 'especially,' the chronicler sardonically notes, 'those who possessed the property of exiles, or had become rich in privileges'. A representative of the commune then conferred lordship on Obizzo. The statute law lists with legal precision the content of this signorial power:

Obizzo . . . should be the governor, rector, and general and perpetual lord of the city of Ferrara and its district, in all matters to be provided, corrected and reformed there, at his arbitrary will. And he should govern the jurisdiction, power and dominion . . . of the city, and have the power to add, do, order, provide and dispose as he pleases and as seems beneficial to him, and generally he can do and dispose in all things as perpetual lord of the city, at his pleasure.

'More power was thus given to this new lord than everlasting God possesses', the chronicler wryly comments. The power was also hereditary.[8]

As with lords in Milan, Piacenza, and Verona, factional connections with aristocrats in other cities, combined with ambition and a need for security, soon led to enlargement of the *signoria* beyond the single city. The Estensi cultivated the leading family of Modena, the Rangoni, from the 1250s, through marriage, appointments, and joint actions; and in 1288 the Rangoni were among a group of Modenese civic leaders who surrendered lordship of their city to Obizzo. They were followed two years later by the neighbouring city of Reggio. The

---

[8] 'Chronica parva ferrariensis', cols. 487–8; *Statuta Ferrariae anno MCCLXXXVII*, ed. W. Montorsi (Ferrara, 1955), pp. 5–7.

Estensi thus achieved a territorial amalgamation that survived, with some brief interruptions, until 1598. However, the law of self-destructive overreach also applied to the Estensi in the early fourteenth century. Azzo VIII, who had succeeded Obizzo II in 1293, was notorious for his ambition: to one contemporary commentator, it seemed that he wanted to become 'lord of Lombardy'. He was at war with Parma and Bologna in the 1290s; he intervened in Lombardy against Matteo Visconti in 1302; he contracted an expensive marriage to the daughter of the king of Naples in 1305, which provoked the hostility of his own brother; and finally he meddled in the factional conflict in Parma, arousing the opposition of Giberto da Correggio, who subsequently led a coalition of northern cities against Azzo which cost him the lordships of Modena and Reggio. When Azzo died in 1308, his kinsmen lacked the capacity to hold Ferrara, which they lost to Venice until 1317.

Some common themes

Building consent in such conditions was not a straightforward task. Lords often ran the risk of conspiracies aimed at their persons. Mastino della Scala, lord of Verona, was assassinated in 1277 by a large group of conspirators. In Ferrara in 1273 a single disgruntled nobleman attacked the lord Obizzo II d'Este on the main square, but failed to kill him. In Milan the overthrow of Matteo Visconti in 1302 was assisted by growing noble agitation, and Visconti rule for years to come was periodically disturbed by noble plots (1322, 1340). For many lords, one solution to the problem of aristocratic opposition was to accentuate the chivalric and courtly aspects of their power. Some lords, such as the Este in Ferrara or the da Camino in Treviso already inhabited such a world: they were barons of familial antiquity, whose households were frequented by poets; their virtues were praised and their deaths were lamented in verse by troubadours from the early thirteenth century onwards. Such lords held courts, festivals, and tournaments, celebrated the occasions on which they received or granted knighthood, and cultivated their reputation for liberality and martial valour. For example, Obizzo II d'Este lost an eye in an accident while tourneying for a lady's love. His predecessor, Azzo, was described as 'supremely magnificent' and as endowed with a 'most beautiful body'. Bodily beauty was the natural concomitant of chivalric virtue. Gherardo da Camino was defined as a 'noble baron' in one source, and as a 'noble knight', 'a totally well-meaning man, humane, courtly, liberal', in another. Uberto da Pallavicino impoverished himself through his large curial spending, just as Azzo d'Este ran into debt owing to his need for large spending at the Christmas and Easter festivals, traditional moments of courtly formality. The chroniclers of such lords' deeds pay great attention to the lavish meals, the splendid tournaments, and ceremonies that they staged. By such practices, these lords give us an early example of the role of the court and palace in 'taming' the aristocracy.

Those lords who did not already inhabit this courtly chivalric world soon learnt to appropriate its style and values. The della Scala are a key example of this tendency towards ennoblement. Curiality, as Varanini has put it, was part of Cangrande's identity as lord: honouring the lords of the region and noble exiles from outside, showing his prestige and liberality, were essential elements of his style of rule. Towards the end of his life there is also visible a new emphasis on the ritual and formal aspects of palace organization. A poem written after his death celebrates him as a chivalric exemplar: a valiant, noble baron, loyal, of unparalleled prowess, generous and courtly, devoted to the Virgin Mary.

Contemporary opinion on the *signori*, however, was often hostile. Take the denunciation by Stefanardo da Vicomercato of the della Torre lordship in Milan:

Public welfare is oppressed; common profits are turned to private uses. The lands of the clergy are invaded. Depriving their co-citizens, the lords' fierce will has no bounds. They build tall towers at others' expense. Supported by the strength of the *plebs*, they plunder riches. They want the gains for themselves alone, yet cause losses to everyone else. They reject partners in power, dominate alone, usurp honours alone. Their old supporters in town rage with fury; others they force to leave their ancestral homes; others still they enclose in dark prisons. A breed of cruel destruction.[9]

---

[9] 'Fratris Stephanardi de Vicomercato Liber de gestis in civitate Mediolani', ed. G. Calligaris, *Rerum italicarum scriptores*, 2nd edn., vol. ix, pt 1 (Citta di Castello, 1910) pp. 38–9.

Similar themes, of unbridled will, of a concentration of power and appropriation of wealth, of using the populace against the nobility, are voiced in other complaints too. In the early fourteenth century, a pro-della Torre poem lambasted Matteo Visconti for setting the plebs against the nobles, for secretly sowing discord, for rejoicing at disputes among the powerful, for subordinating all the factions by using their reciprocal hatreds. Similarly, the Paduan chronicler Mussato expressed a negative judgement on Cangrande della Scala: he was 'violent and intractable, restraining no impulses, rushing to whatever anger provoked him, inexorable, preferring to seem fiercer in his behaviour and gestures than his severity had actual power to perform'.[10] However, within time, the *signori* had their defenders and advocates too. Chroniclers eventually turned courtier, cataloguing in awe the comings, goings, and doings of their dynastic lords. Most prominent among propagandists for the *signori*, perhaps, was Galvano Fiamma. He attributed to the Visconti lords of Milan, Giovanni and Luchino, a series of beneficial reforms: the establishment of internal security for both residents and travellers, pacification both between aristocratic clans and between classes, an end to economic disruption caused by frequent warfare. Fiamma also claimed that tax imposts under the Visconti were low and infrequent, that revenues were husbanded rather than squandered, that criminals were punished rather than pardoned, and that official extortion had been curtailed.[11] At the same time, Fiamma painted a sympathetic portrait of Luchino Visconti that is worth quoting in full:

Luchino was and is a man exceptionally handsome in body and face, well-proportioned in all parts, healthy and sound. He took to wife the noble lady Violante, daughter of the marquis of Saluzzo, by whom he had a daughter . . . Luchino was knighted while still a boy and was made lord of Pavia: there he built a very strong castle and successfully exercised his lordship of the city for a long time. Then he was made lord of Milan, Brescia, Como, Bergamo, Lodi, Piacenza, Novara, Vercelli and Cremona. He added the city of Asti to his lordship, where he ordered a strong castle to be built . . . He assembled an army of knights, footsoldiers and archers, and he dealt blows to the regions of

---

[10] Di Salvo, 'Il signore della Scala', p. 44.

[11] Gualvanei de la Flamma, 'Opusculum de rebus gestis ab Azone, Luchino et Johanne Vicecomitibus', ed. C. Castiglioni, in *Rerum italicarum scriptores*, 2nd edn., vol. xii, pt. 4, (Bologna, 1938), pp. 43–5. Full translation in T. Dean, *The Towns of Italy in the Late Middle Ages* (Manchester, 2000), pp. 235–8.

Italy; he never ceased from warfare and, fortunate in war, he was feared beyond measure by his enemies. He largely suppressed the game of dice. He severely punished adulterers. He had the city streets paved. At times of famine he had over 40,000 paupers fed at public expense. He forced Pavia to obey him and compelled them to raze their walls to the ground with their own hands. He had outstanding habits ... No one has ever served justice and peace better. He was of constant heart and true to his word, for, whatever he promised, he delivered. In the best way possible he preserved the revenues and properties of the [civic] commune, and abstained from levying tribute ... Every day he carefully heard the cases of poor women and treated thirty paupers to the best food at the table in his palace. He devoutly heard or said mass and the office of the Blessed Virgin Mary every day. On prohibited days and Saturdays he ate nothing but Lenten food. He was, moreover, magnificent in his horsemanship and horse-trappings, in his hawks, falcons, sparrowhawks, and large dogs, in his knights, squires, lute-players, jesters and his exceedingly large entourage. He built many castles and palaces in city and *contado* and across Lombardy ...

This portrait combines many of the themes we have previously mentioned: the stress on warfare and martial valour, on chivalric activities and values (knighthood, horsemanship, fidelity, care for women and the poor), on religious rectitude and devotion, on courtliness (bodily beauty, large entourage), and on public works and welfare (paving, poor relief, action against gambling, and adultery). At the same time, the role of military power—which detractors might present as illegitimate oppression—is all too evident: his concern with castle-building, his fearful military reputation, his rough treatment of the city of Pavia. That Luchino was feared reminds us of Machiavelli's discussion of the commonplace theoretical question, 'whether a lord should aim to be loved or feared' (*The Prince*, ch. XVII). Machiavelli's answer was characteristically forked, distinguishing between moral and political values: one would like to be both loved and feared, he suggests, but as it is difficult to combine them, it is much safer to be feared than loved. It was a common critique of *signori* that they were feared by their subjects, indeed that they aimed to instil fear; but Fiamma answers such critics by pointing to the ways in which at least one lord sought to combine love and fear.

PART II

SOCIAL CHANGE AND THE
COMMERCIAL REVOLUTION

Trade and navigation

Marco Tangheroni

Italian maritime expansion in the western Mediterranean

The flag of the Italian navy carries the symbols of Venice, Amalfi, Genoa, and Pisa, in homage to the 'four maritime republics'. This reference to past glories is not without foundation, but it should not be allowed to efface the significant differences in the histories of these republics, both in terms of character and chronology. In the early medieval period Amalfi and Venice had been part of the Byzantine Empire, and even though they gradually asserted more and more independence, they also maintained close links with Constantinople. The merchants of Amalfi played a role in the commercial routes of the Arabs, constituting a sort of Christian port in the Islamic world, to which Sicily also belonged, having been conquered in the ninth century. Merchants from both Amalfi and Venice visited the markets of Pavia, ensuring a supply of precious oriental goods. Pisa and Genoa, by contrast, had been part of Lombard Italy from the first half of the seventh century, and later of the Carolingian Regnum italicum. Even though there are indications of a certain continuity in the maritime life of Pisa, it was not until the second half of the tenth century that there was any trace of representatives from Pisa or Genoa beyond the northern Tyrrhenian Sea. Amalfi was already powerful in the eleventh century, when it was described by contemporaries as a rich and cosmopolitan city, and its merchants and ships were seen as far away as Constantinople and the ports of Egypt. But in the twelfth century Amalfi rapidly lost its importance. This was partly because of its absorption into the Norman kingdom of Sicily and attacks launched from Pisa, but above all because the context of Mediterranean trade was changing. Other important southern ports on the Tyrrhenian side of the Italian peninsula included Gaeta, while a number of Calabrian ports played an important role in the medium-range export of wines, oil, and fruit.

The Christian reconquest of Sicily was largely the result of a gradual loss of control of the western Mediterranean by Arab navies. But it also provided a stimulus for renewed attacks from Genoa and Pisa. Ships and merchants from the two cities took advantage of the situation to seize control of nearly all maritime routes between Sicily and the Italian peninsula and north Africa. Beginning in the early eleventh century Genoa and even more so Pisa were responsible for reasserting Christian hegemony over commercial shipping in the western Mediterranean. The two cities intervened in Sardinia, where they crushed the attempt by Mujahid of Denia to create an advanced maritime dominion between 1015 and 1016. Ships from Pisa sacked the ports of Bône in 1034, and Palermo, which was still Muslim, in 1064. In 1087 a Christian coalition defeated the well-armed al-Mahdia, mobilizing an expedition that foreshadowed the Crusades. Finally, between 1113 and 1115, after the First Crusade, in which a Genoese squadron and a large fleet from Pisa, led by the city's archbishop, participated, Pisa organized a powerful expedition against Majorca, and won important commercial privileges from Count Ramon Berenguer III of Barcelona. The expedition from Pisa included marquises, counts, princes, Romans, Florentines, Sardinians, and innumerable other groups—testimony to the attraction of maritime expeditions both to inhabitants of inland cities, and to members of the feudal upper classes. The Balearic Islands, however, quickly reverted to Islamic rule.

For its part, Genoa concluded a treaty with Ramon Berenguer III, after merchandise bound for Genoa was captured by the Catalans. This treaty regulated the rights of Ligurian ships, which were required to pay entry fees in order to enter the ports dominated by the Catalan count. Genoa kept up its operations against Muslims rather longer than Pisa. Between 1146 and 1148 it attacked Minorca, and in alliance with Alfonso VII of Castile captured Almeria, and then helped to conquer the Catalan city of Tortosa, whose position at the mouth of the Ebro river made it strategically important. After the mid-twelfth century, however, neither Genoa nor Pisa took part in further military action against Muslims. When they were invited to join a planned Sardo-Catalan coalition against Majorca, they declined, possibly because they had already won free access to, and favourable conditions at, the African ports. A variety of agreements provided merchants from both cities with legal autonomy, property rights in case of shipwreck, individual rather than collective responsibility in case of attack by pirates, payment guarantees, and the right to re-export unsold merchandise without customs duties. Moreover, they had established settlements in Islamic ports, with houses, warehouses, a church, an oven, and a cemetery. The greatest European mathematician of the medieval period, Leonardo Fibonacci, grew up in Bougie (now Bejaia), where he was educated by Muslims.

As well as the eleventh-century documents of the Cairo Genizah, Genoese notarial registers (which have survived from the middle of the twelfth century) and international treaties reveal the importance assumed by the maritime and commercial routes which linked Liguria and Tuscany with the lands of the Maghrib. These ranged from Morocco, which was open to trade with Christians from 1160, to other political entities that correspond roughly with today's Algeria and Tunisia (known as Ifriqiyah) but whose boundaries were in constant flux because of dynastic changes and ethnic and tribal conflicts. The African coasts were also within easy reach of the ports of Sardinia and Sicily. In the thirteenth century the Venetians were also present in growing numbers, as were the Catalans.

Sicilian grain reached the ports of northern Africa. Here the Italian merchants bought many local products, such as ceramics, textiles (though the African textile industry went into crisis at the end of the eleventh century), rugs, sheepskins, wool, salt, and oil, as well as near eastern products such as spices and silks. They exported products for dyeing, manufactured goods (mainly metal, including arms, notwithstanding papal prohibitions), and, from the twelfth century onwards, fabrics.

As Italians gradually replaced African merchants as intermediaries in trade with the Muslim areas, and with the prevalence in those areas of an economy based on intensive agriculture and artisan production, the commercial relationship between Italian cities and North Africa became unequal. The monetary aspect of this relationship added further complications. Although there has been much historical debate, and it is certain that the caravan routes from sub-Saharan Africa shifted towards Egypt, 'Sudanese' gold remained important in the Maghreb. The relative abundance of gold, and the relative lack of silver in Ifriqyah meant that the gold to silver ratio was superior to that in Italian towns, where gold was scarce. It is far from easy to measure Italian exports of silver and imports of gold, but it is certain that Ligurian notaries mentioned gold in various forms more and more frequently. In 1252, at almost exactly the same time, Genoa and Florence both started minting a stable gold currency. The Florentine florin would conquer the world of European finance (it has been called the 'dollar of the Middle Ages'), before being partially substituted by the Venetian ducat. It would be too simple to explain the increasing availability of gold as a consequence of the monetary imbalance between Africa and Europe, but it cannot be completely disregarded either. Genoa and Pisa were in competition in southern France, each mutually seeking to exclude the other from the principal ports of Provence, such as Nice, Marseilles, and Arles, through a series of complex agreements that cannot be recorded in detail here. As Genoa came to dominate the Ligurian Riviera and increased its influence in the area, one of the consequences was greater openness to Europe beyond the Alps.

Over the same period, the large islands of the western Mediterranean also grew in importance. It was not by chance that control of Sardinia was one of the main issues of contention in the almost permanent conflict between Genoa and Pisa. We shall see this played out in more detail in another chapter, but it is important to remember the significance of Majorca. The island had already been important when it was under Muslim control, thanks to its position close to Catalonia, southern France, and northern Africa, but once it was conquered by the king of Aragon in 1229 it became the great emporium of the Mediterranean.

Italian maritime expansion in the eastern Mediterranean

By the eleventh century, the Venetians were already the almost uncontested lords of the Adriatic Sea, and had consolidated their presence in Constantinople and in the whole of the Orient, where the older relationship of dependence had been transformed into one of alliance, with associated fiscal and commercial privileges. Thus, when Venetian ships supported the Byzantine Empire against the Normans, who had attacked Durazzo in 1082, Venice obtained an area in the imperial capital right on the banks of the Golden Horn, with houses, shops, warehouses, and a bakery. The merchants and ships of the lagoon city progressively acquired an important role in the routes and internal traffic of the empire's maritime dominions. At the same time they were transporting agricultural products from Greece and Alexandria. In the second half of the century merchants from Genoa (and possibly also from Pisa) made inroads into Egypt, some even using ships from Amalfi. It was the First Crusade that gave Italian shipping a greater interest in the East; as Pistarino has noted, the writings of the Genoese chronicler Caffaro reveal that the crusade 'was the main turning point in the history of Mediterranean commerce and of the Mediterranean itself'. The crusade was mainly a land-based undertaking, as is evident from the itineraries followed by most of the contingents, but a small fleet from Genoa, and, after the taking of Jerusalem, a large fleet from Pisa, consisting of 120 ships and led by the archbishop of the city, Daimberto, proved decisive in the conquest of the coastal centres. After an initial prudent delay (due to ambiguity in the relationship between the crusaders and the Byzantine Empire), Venice then sent an even larger fleet into eastern waters. This was an occasion to confront, and, in later decades, to resolve, the difficult problem of the transport of horses by sea over great distances. The technical skills of Venetian shipbuilders were also applied to the problem of constructing siege weapons. Though not always coordinated, the Christian fleet was nevertheless assured of naval supremacy over its Egyptian rivals.

Thanks to their ships, Venice, Genoa, and Pisa obtained significant gains from these undertakings. In the short term they realized high profits from their share of the spoils of war. They obtained increasing privileges from the kings of Jerusalem and from the lords of the feudal states of Syria and Palestine in the Holy City and in the principal coastal centres they had helped to conquer, such as Antioch, Jaffa, Arsuf, Caesarea, Haifa, Acre, Laodicea, Tripoli, Beirut, and Tyre. The generous terms of these commercial concessions increased in proportion to the fierceness of Muslim reaction, particularly after the victory of Hattin and the reconquest of Jerusalem by Saladin. These privileges took the form of two sorts of concessions: on the one hand, the right to establish settlements in various cities that were sometimes, at least on paper, of extraordinary size; on the other hand, favourable conditions for the commercial activities of their citizens. On some occasions the Italians established such a degree of autonomy that even in the judicial sphere they were able to set up what were effectively colonies. Finally, the importance of transporting pilgrims and crusaders should not be forgotten.

However significant the commercial interests and financial investments connected with Palestine and Syria may have been, it seems that in the twelfth century the connections with Egypt were even more important. This was so notwithstanding papal prohibitions, on pain of excommunication, against the export of strategically important goods to the Muslim world. A Venetian envoy to Innocent III tried in vain to have this prohibition revoked, on the basis that the lagoon city 'was not involved in agriculture, but was focused on navigation and commerce'. An Egyptian customs record of the 1170s relating to the ports of Alexandria, Damietta, and Tinnis provides information on the types of goods that were traded by the Italian merchants: above all they exported wood and iron, and imported linen, cotton, skins, glass, sugar, and alum, and also grain and salt. Naturally this source does not specify which of the products acquired in Egypt were to be carried to the west, and which were to be traded along the way, in the markets of Syria and Palestine and the Eastern Empire, along the lines of a triangular trade that was growing fast. The document also indicates that as well as Venetians and Genoese there were also merchants from Sicily and Sardinia (these were probably Pisan merchants settled in Sardinia). Merchants from Pisa itself were notably absent, possibly because of missing pages in the tract, but also possibly because they were in disgrace.

On more than one occasion the progress made by Italian merchants was threatened by Christian aggression, as for example when a Norman expedition went up the Nile or when Christian ships were involved in particularly serious piracy, or when ships from Pisa took part in an attack on Alexandria led by Amaury I, king of Jerusalem (1168). On these occasions merchants from the cities judged responsible were imprisoned and their property was confiscated, but generally ambassadorial pleading re-established smooth relations quite rapidly. In 1173, an agreement was made between Saladin and the merchants of Pisa—who had bases at Alexandria and Cairo—and the following year these same merchants helped defend Alexandria against an attack by William II, the king of Sicily. For their part, the Egyptians were highly dependent on the wood, iron, and pitch that only the Christian merchants were able to supply in reasonable quantities. The Egyptians were inclined to favour their presence, therefore, while seeking at the same time to regulate it. Saladin made this explicit in a letter to the Caliph of Baghdad written in 1182.

The third pole of attraction in the east was Constantinople, and to a lesser extent, the other maritime centres of the Byzantine Empire. These were most important for Venice, whose historic links, solid trading position, and important privileges of the eleventh century have already been mentioned. In the twelfth century the predominant position of Venice remained more or less unchanged, even though some difficulties led Venice to establish agreements with the Normans in Sicily, the traditional enemies of Venice as well as of the Byzantine Empire. There was no lack of punitive provisions against the Venetians either. The worst case was the imprisonment of all Venetian merchants in the empire, which provoked a counter-attack in Venice that culminated in the assassination of the doge. The event confirmed the importance of the relationship with Constantinople for the Venetians. On the other hand, in an attempt to limit the Venetian monopoly, the emperors had begun to give concessions to merchants from Pisa and Genoa, which resulted in the establishment of important new quarters in the capital, even though they never equalled the importance of the Venetian presence and never obtained the same fiscally favourable conditions.

Western shipping had a substantial monopoly over international traffic in Constantinople, but westerners also obtained an increasing share of internal commerce from Byzantine shipping, at least in those areas related to international goods. Spurred by the religious division between Latins and Greeks, the heavy presence of westerners, considered invasive and domineering, encouraged feelings of xenophobia in the native population of Constantinople, which strongly influenced the internal politics of the empire in the last decades of the century, resulting in bloody anti-Latin uprisings. Notwithstanding this violent rupture, commerce with Constantinople remained economically significant for the Italian maritime powers, including the more complex triangular trade with the Holy Land and the Muslim world. Luxury goods remained important, particularly silks and spices, and a range of artisanal goods that arrived in the Mediterranean ports from the empire, the Muslim Near East, and even further afield. Nevertheless, there was a notable increase in trade in less profitable goods, such as grain and oil, for the Byzantine trade of Venice and its rivals encompassed not just Constantinople but the Greek mainland and islands and Albania, including territories easily accessible from the Adriatic.

Italian cities and the Mediterranean, 1200–1350

After the partial failure of the crusade led by Frederick Barbarossa and by the kings of France and England, Innocent III called up Christians to a new expedition. The starting-point was Venice, where a large number of crusaders gathered, although still not enough to fill the great fleet that had been prepared. Unable to pay the arranged sum, they accepted the Venetian proposal to conquer Zara (1202), then move towards Constantinople to which they would lay siege. In the meantime, an anti-western *coup d'état* had deposed Alexios IV, who had made extravagant promises to the crusaders. The city was subsequently conquered by the crusaders and sacked violently for three days (April 1202). The conquerors thus created an eastern Latin empire, placing Baldwin of Flanders on the throne. Venice kept for itself three of the city's quarters (including the port and arsenal), as well as certain key ports on the Ionian and Aegean seas, including Crete, which Genoese pirates based in Malta had already tried to grab.

This island was valuable in its own right, and Venetian agricultural settlements developed even on its soil; but it was important above all as a port on the way to Syria and Egypt. In this way Venice, which successfully foiled most attempts by its own citizens to create their own personal domains, established a distinctive type of maritime empire, governed by its functionaries. This meant that Venice was guaranteed naval supremacy in the north-eastern Mediterranean, at Constantinople, and in Romania, the name then given to the Byzantine lands.

The Genoese, however, who in the last decades of the twelfth century had increased their presence in Constantinople, began to oppose the Venetians, above all through systematic recourse to hit-and-run raids. While the nascent Latin empire showed grave signs of weakness, there survived small Greek settlements which nurtured claims to the Byzantine Empire. The threat in Italy represented by Frederick II forced Genoa and Venice to accept a status quo based on the recognition of Genoese interests in Syria and Venetian interests in Constantinople and the Aegean. But the tensions were to reignite after the middle of the century.

Between 1256 and 1258, the Venetians, allied with the strong Pisan colony, defeated the Genoese at Acre, managing to expel them from the city. The Genoese, while they reorganized in Syria, offered support to the Greek dynasty of Nicaea. They signed the Treaty of Nymphaion with Michael VIII Palaiologos, who had already been victorious in Macedonia, promising him the necessary maritime support for the reconquest of Constantinople and the restoration of the Greek empire (1261). This agreement (though strongly opposed by the pope and the Guelf nobility of Genoa), opened extraordinary prospects for the Genoese in the east, beyond the guarantee of a dominant position in Constantinople, where they solemnly destroyed the palace which was the seat of Venetian authority, carrying the stones back to Genoa to construct a public building. They then launched themselves to exercise control over commerce in the Black Sea.

In the years immediately following this, while Michael VIII sought to temper the strength of the Genoese colony in Constantinople, Venice fought to recover its dominance of the high seas, dispatching a large fleet and fighting victorious battles in Greek and Sicilian waters. The picture in the Mediterranean was complicated by the descent into Italy of Charles I of Anjou, his victory over Manfred, and his conquest of the kingdom of Sicily, which included Naples and all of southern Italy. Venice, which had sided with Charles, supported the Guelf alliance in Italy while Genoa took a pro-Ghibelline line. It made new agreements with Michael VIII, obtaining the right to establish a strong colony at Pera, on the Asian side of the Golden Horn, right in front of Constantinople (1268): for more than two centuries this colony was the centre of the Genoese maritime economy and political presence in 'Romania'. The Genoese also controlled Caffa, on the northern coast of the Black Sea, Chios, a centre for the export of mastic, and Phocaea, famous for its alum, a vital ingredient in the textile industry. Only in 1270, during the crusade led by Louis IX in Tunisia, was a settlement made between the two cities.

Meanwhile, in the western Mediterranean, where Venice had few interests, the struggle for supremacy between Genoa and Pisa continued. Although the Ligurian city had already established dominance over Corsica, control of Sardinia was still very much contested. As we shall see in another chapter of this volume, the Genoese, in the same years that they were defeated at Acre, also saw the failure of their plans for Sardinia, as the merchants of Pisa gained the upper hand. Even so, Pisa was not able to protect the Sardinian coasts from incessant attacks by the Genoese. The continuing menace prompted Pisa to opt for a decisive conflict, and on 6 August 1284 the two cities' fleets met each other at what became known as the Battle of Meloria, off Porto Pisano. After a hard fight, victory finally went to the Genoese, thanks to their numerical superiority and the skill of their commanders. Pisa lost 3,000 men and 9,000 were taken prisoner; Elba fell into Genoese hands.

This was a heavy blow for the Tuscan city, and it proved decisive in terms of dominance over the western Mediterranean. Genoa's growing superiority had begun to be obvious some decades before this battle, particularly because its arms manufacturers and merchants had greater financial power and greater reach, both within and beyond the Mediterranean. As early as 1277, a fleet of Genoese galleys established a maritime link with Flanders and then England, links that towards the end of the century became regular annual events. Politically, while Genoa had precociously affirmed authority over the two rivieras, and incorporated all important Ligurian centres within her expansion, Pisa had become progressively more isolated. Since the time of Frederick I Pisa had been tenaciously Ghibelline, and therefore hostile to important Tuscan cities such as Florence and Lucca, both of which were expanding commercially and demographically. Between 1200 and 1300 the approximate population of Florence probably grew from 20,000 to 100,000, while Pisa moved from about 30,000 to about 40,000. In economic terms, Genoa's hinterland in the Po valley was very strong and very well connected to financial and commercial networks beyond the Alps. Pisa only held a stronger position than Genoa in Tunisia and Sardinia.

Meanwhile, other political forces began to acquire significance in the western Mediterranean, among them Venice, which, from the early 1300s had also begun to organize fleets to visit the northern seas. In 1282, the insurrection of the Sicilian Vespers, in which Sicily rebelled against Charles of Anjou, who had begun to pursue ambitious policies of expansion in the Mediterranean, gave an opportunity for the intervention of Peter III of Aragon, who claimed the inheritance of Manfred, whose daughter he had married. There followed a general Mediterranean war, in which France passed on to the offensive, invading Catalonia and allying itself with the Catalan kingdom of Majorca, which was ruled by a cadet dynasty of the house of Barcelona. The military supremacy of the Aragonese fleet revealed the existence of a new maritime power: acting largely in concert, the count-kings of Barcelona and the Catalan mercantile bourgeoisie began to lay the foundations of a 'commonwealth' which would later include Sicily, Sardinia, and, in the fifteenth century, Naples and southern Italy. For many years Sicily had been an important economic arena for northern Italians, as its central position in the Mediterranean gave easy access to Africa and the Levant. The island was also attractive for its own urban markets, and for the production of agricultural goods, above all cereals.

In 1295 Pope Boniface VIII concluded the Treaty of Anagni, which created the kingdom of Sardinia and Corsica, which he gave in fief to the king of Aragon, James II, in the hope that the Aragonese would evacuate Sicily in return. In Sicily, on the other hand, James II's brother Frederick ascended the throne, and the island became an independent kingdom, though still within the Catalan–Aragonese orbit. In Sardinia, after decades of fruitless diplomatic initiatives aiming to give the fiefdom meaning by ejecting the Pisan settlements, James decided to settle the matter militarily. Pisa, though still capable of a fight, was defeated over the course of two wars fought on and around the island (1323–6). From then on, having lost Sardinia, the ruling class of Pisa abandoned maritime commerce and dedicated itself to other pursuits. Pisa nevertheless remained a commercial and port city of primary importance. Using the port of Pisa, the presence of Florentines was sufficient to make Florence itself into a maritime power, though not a naval power. Genoa, which had participated in the war over Sardinia, soon entered into conflict with the new maritime power of Aragon, in 1330 and 1336.

In the eastern Mediterranean, on the other hand, the struggle for supremacy between Genoa and Venice continued. Venice was characterized by greater state intervention in the economy, including maritime commerce. The Venetian merchant navy generally travelled in convoys that were organized right down to dates of departure and return. Genoa, though capable of co-ordinated war effort, tended to be more individualistic, both in maritime commerce (in which voyages by single ships predominated), and in political expansion. Perhaps it is as well not to overdraw the differences, but in some ways these characteristics define Genoese and Venetian history. The chronicler Martino da Canale said proudly that while Venetians could continue their voyages as always, the Genoese were forced to cross the seas covertly, like pirates. In truth though, Venice achieved full control of the eastern seas, even though its superior political stability would prevail over the unstable situation in Genoa, which in the end was subject to the loss of its independence.

In the last decade of the thirteenth century the Genoese fleet inflicted two heavy defeats on Venice, first at Laiazzo (Ayas), off Asia Minor (1294), and then at Curzola, in the Adriatic (1298), but it did not have the force, or the courage, to attack the lagoon city directly. They reached a peace agreement based on the status quo in 1299, but Venice and Genoa would return to confront each other in the middle of the following century, this time seeing Venice allied with Aragon–Catalonia. In a long and bloody battle in the Bosphorus in 1353, the Venetian–Catalan fleet had to withdraw; the following year, in Sardinian waters near Alghero, a Catalan fleet reinforced by Venetian ships claimed a triumphant victory. Likewise, in the Aegean, nearly the entire Genoese fleet was captured. Milanese interests, as well as those of Giovanni Visconti, to whose overlordship Genoa had been entrusted, led to a peace based on compromise.

The overall pattern of maritime and commercial routes was undergoing considerable change. Constantinople maintained its full functions as a major commercial city notwithstanding wars and crises. For Italian merchants the most important goods remained wool from Turkey, linen from Egypt, alum, and wax. They exported French, Flemish, and Italian cloth, Calabrian oil, and wine from southern Italy, Sicily, and Crete. Acre had been the great entrepôt of Syria-Palestine: it was the destination for cereals and oil from southern Italy, French and Flemish cloth, and linen and cotton from Tunisia. When Acre fell in 1291, and with the diminishing Christian political presence in the Holy Land, Laiazzo became an important port until it, too, became Muslim in 1339. The greatest emporium remained Cyprus, crossroads for a large number of maritime routes. The author of a celebrated manual for merchants in the first half of the fourteenth century, Francesco Pegolotti, noted that Nicosia received goods from Turkey, Rhodes, Armenia, and Syria, and that the Italians established on the island exported towards Romania and the east. Modern studies conducted on notarial registers of the island have confirmed these observations and shown the great variety of goods exchanged: as Geo Pistarino has written, these included 'grain, oil, wine, rice, fruit, fish, sugar, salt, wax, soap, wool, linen, silk, clothing and fabric, skins and furs, leather, pearls, coral, gold, silver, copper, tin, aluminium, wood, glass, earthenware; and above all spices; spices of every type'. The Genoese had been the most active in Cyprus until the thirteenth century but, after the fall of Acre, the Venetians strengthened their hold on the island. The kingdom of Cyprus thus became another object in the contest between the two cities. There were, on the other hand, merchants from many parts of Europe: Pisa, Florence, Ancona, Provence, Marseilles, Narbonne, and Catalonia.

In the Muslim world, while the advancing Turks eliminated the traditional entrepôts of Syria and Palestine, Alexandria grew in importance. This was the classic meeting point of east and west, even the far east, because Alexandria received, either by land or via the Red Sea, merchandise from India and China which was then re-exported to Syria or Constantinople, or to the maritime cities of the eastern Mediterranean. In Alexandria Italians acquired paper, sugar, silver, and other typical artisanal products of Egypt. However, Italian imports of western products, including cloth, were increasingly able to compete with oriental goods

Technical and institutional aspects of Italian maritime commerce

The expansion of Italian maritime cities in the Mediterranean detailed so far would not have been possible without parallel advances in the shipbuilding techniques and navigational arts of their fleets. Italian mariners incorporated and extended the knowledge and innovations of Byzantine and Muslim fleets, and to some extent those of the northern navies. This influence is attested through the Arabic and Greek origins of various terms connected with navigation. Islamic shipping played a mediating role bringing westwards techniques and knowledge acquired in the Indian Ocean.

There were two main innovations in the shipping techniques of Italian cities, and more generally Mediterranean fleets. The first was the galley propelled by oars as well as sails, and the second was the ship, propelled only by sail. The first innovation was of Byzantine origin (the word 'galley' has Greek origins), and was long and narrow, to favour speed. Because of this shape, and the space taken up by the rowers and their provisions, the galley did not have a great payload capacity. In addition to military use, it was primarily used for the transport of goods that had a high value-to-volume ratio, where speed and security were crucial. The rowers, arranged in rows of two and later of three per bench, on only one deck (unlike the great warships of antiquity), each with one single oar, were, and remained until the end of the medieval period, free labourers, attracted by good wages and the possibility of participating in personal commerce of their own. The differing salaries according to position on the ship confirm that rowing was a job that required experience, not just physical strength. The 'classic' galley of the thirteenth century measured about 40 metres in length and 5 metres across the beam, that is, with a length–beam ratio of 8:1. Vessels of the same type, but smaller, narrower, and faster, called *sagittae*, or *saette* in Italian, were made especially for rapid raids. Galleys were constructed in arsenals that were increasingly large and specialized, owned by the state.

Sailing ships were much broader, with a length-to-beam ratio of about 2.5:1. Payload mattered more than speed, which in any case was dependent on wind conditions. In a sea without dependable winds, such as the Mediterranean, sometimes ships were becalmed, such that the length of a journey was always unpredictable. Over the course of the thirteenth century, sailing ships, which continued to be built by private shipbuilders, continuously increased in size. This tendency is clear in Venice, where at the beginning of the century the Senate had been concerned to fix a minimum size for ships, but by the end of the century felt the need to impose maximum size limits. Some of these ships provoked descriptions such as 'sea-borne castles'. An example is the Venetian ship *Roccaforte*: 38 metres in length and 14 metres across, it was 9.3 metres high at the centre of the hull, and 14 metres high at the forward and rear forecastles. It had a displacement of 1,200 tons when loaded, but we know that there were others that weighed 2,000 tons. Naturally only a few dozen ships were over 1,000 tons, the majority of them being in the medium range, and only Venetian and Genoese shipwrights were able to build the larger ships. The merchant fleets of minor centres, often of quite modest dimensions, played an important role in the system, as did the small coastal vessels connected with long-range transport. A third type of sailing ship made its appearance on the Mediterranean at the beginning of the thirteenth century: the *cocca*. Of Atlantic origin, the *cocca* was relatively small, but considered more secure because it was easier to handle, and more economical because it required fewer sailors. As an example, normal sailing ships of the period required one sailor per 5 tons of cargo, but the *cocca* required only one sailor per 10 tons.

The progressive improvement of shipbuilding techniques—though not yet fully understood because of the limited remains of ships from the period found and studied so far—allowed the construction of larger vessels. Above all, the construction of more complex rigging systems, using the lateen (triangular) sail, increased the manœuvrability of ships by permitting greater exploitation of the winds. Handling was also improved with the introduction of the single tiller positioned at the rear, in place of the two rudders at the side of the ship. First known on the ships of the North Sea in the middle of the thirteenth century, the system reached northern Spain at the end of the century, and entered the Mediterranean at the beginning of the fourteenth century.

The new rudder also permitted the use of the magnetic needle. Its uses had been known for some time, but when it was used in association with a wind-vane it became a true compass. The variation between the magnetic and geographic poles was not yet understood, but in the Mediterranean it is not of great significance. The application of trigonometry in the fourteenth century would permit the calculation of a route as a rectilinear resultant of a zig-zag course, but astronomical navigation was not yet in use in the period under consideration. Thus methods of estimation and the personal experience of the navigator remained crucial. Navigators did have charts at their disposal from the end of the twelfth century, as well as descriptions of ports and routes. Cartographic schools existed at Pisa and Genoa as well as Majorca and in Catalonia.

Technological progress was closely tied to economic motives. The construction of ships with larger capacity allowed the economic transport of bulky low-value goods, such as salt and grain. The decreased dependence on the coastline for navigation led to an increased willingness to cross the Mediterranean, even in the winter, at least from the second half of the twelfth century. On the other hand, this technical progress was always stimulated by the growing and diverse demands of commerce.

The investment finance necessary for the construction and armament of ships, the purchase of merchandise, and the recruitment of crews, who were partially paid in advance, was generally provided by a new institution, visible from the eleventh century onwards, and known as the *commenda* (or *colleganza* in Venice). The *commenda* brought together the capital necessary for a maritime voyage from various sources, putting it at the disposal of a captain. At the end of the voyage the profits were divided, remunerating the captain with a pre-established quota. In cases where the captain also contributed his own capital, the shares were divided somewhat differently. In Genoa and Pisa this variation was known as the *società di mare*.

The *commenda* allowed collection of the necessary capital investment, and it would be an error to be misled by the modesty of the sums indicated in the extant notarial records: the number of investors was high, and those who had large sums to invest preferred to divide them across many ventures in order to reduce risk. In Venice, for example, at least according to Lane, a typical example would represent the investment of something like 100 people, who entrusted varying sums to more than a dozen travelling merchants, some of whom made up the crew. The expedition's leader was given full liberty to act according to his discretion; even the destination was often indicated generically as a region, or even as *ad partes transmarinas*, and only rarely, usually for nearby destinations, was a particular port indicated. The effectiveness of the *commenda* in meeting the needs of maritime commerce is confirmed by the strength of the institution during the second half of the thirteenth century, by which time landed commerce was dominated by the more lasting and better articulated business association known as the Company.

The principle of spreading risk took account of the notion of the 'fortune of the sea'—the risk of failure of individual voyages, whether by shipwreck or attack by pirates. This notion lay behind the institution of the 'maritime loan', in which the risk was shared by the lender, as with the *commenda*, who had the right to ask for higher rates of return than those applying to other types of loan. Unlike the *commenda*, however, with the maritime loan the interest rate was fixed in advance, and for this reason it fell under the general condemnation of every form of interest-bearing loan by canon law during the thirteenth century.

The principle of the 'fortune of the seas' also gave rise to the beginnings of insurance practices, which began not by chance in port cities. In Genoa there are records of rudimentary forms of insurance dating back to the last decades of the thirteenth century. Insurance institutions per se, not connected to institutions of credit, are recorded in Florence from the first decades of the fourteenth century. From the point of view of the insurer, usually engaged in other mercantile and financial businesses, the risk was reasonable to the extent that, covering a large number of voyages contemporaneously, one wreck would only amount to a small percentage of the damage indemnified. The insurer did not immobilize his capital for a period of several months, while through the practice of reinsurance, which soon spread, the risk was divided and reduced even further. The conditions which gave rise to insurance companies in Tuscany were various: levels of trust which led merchants to abandon recourse to notaries to make arrangements directly among themselves; the possibility of drafting simple policies; the existence of large companies that were able to effect coverage of a large number of events; their capacity to gather all the information necessary to evaluate risk. As has been observed, the invention of insurance testifies to the existence of an institution born of the propensity for complex analysis, or, in other words, the study of the various components of their own activities on the part of the great Italian medieval merchants.

Maritime commerce and the Italian economy

In this chapter we have concentrated on medium- and long-range maritime commerce among the various great Italian maritime cities. This commerce brought together a large number of coastal centres along the peninsula both large and small: the minor cities of the Ligurian Riviera, Piombino, and Talamone on the Tuscan coast, Corneto and Civitavecchia in the Patrimony of St Peter, Gaeta, Naples, and the Calabrian ports, the great port cities of Sicily such as Palermo and Messina, the important maritime cities of Apulia, and so on. The study and understanding of these complex commercial networks, and above all their interrelationships, is not easy, and has only begun to be fully understood in a number of limited cases.

The problems could really only be hinted at in these pages. The same is true for the relationship between the economic growth of the Po valley and that of Tuscany—the 'Italies' that are generally referred to by the phrase 'Italian primacy' in the medieval period—with maritime commerce in the Mediterranean and beyond. It is evident that it is not possible to understand Venice's extraordinary development without considering its links with the hinterland and with Europe beyond the Alps; nor is it possible to understand Genoa's growth without knowing about its close relationship with Piedmont and Lombardy, above all Milan, and with France and Flanders. Nor is it possible to explain the expansion of Pisa without keeping in mind the importance of its own hinterland and the navigability of the Arno almost to Florence. The problem, however, is more complex when it comes to weighing up the contribution of maritime commerce to the development of the Italian economy as a whole; or to examining the growing presence of Italian merchants beyond the Alps (the *Lombardi*).

Brief consideration should also be given to the emergence of banking in the twelfth to fourteenth centuries. As Edwin Hunt has shown, even at its peak around 1300 the great Peruzzi bank of Florence was deeply engaged in commerce, particularly the trade in grain and textiles, and it would be wrong to characterize the great companies of early fourteenth-century Florence and elsewhere as banks specializing in the money business.[1] Still, Piacenza, Genoa (notably before the banking crisis of 1252), Siena, and latterly Florence helped fuel the expansion of trade by extending credit to businessmen, and one of the earliest documents in the Florentine vernacular is a fragment of a banker's records from 1211, indicating intense business across the Apeninnes. Links between bankers such as the Bardi and the Peruzzi of Florence and foreign rulers such as the kings of Naples or the Avignon popes helped stimulate maritime and overland trade. This was achieved in the face of persistent doubts in ecclesiastical and royal circles concerning the ethics of moneylending, sometimes therefore necessitating elaborate procedures to circumvent accusations of usury.

The most recent historiography tends to revise, in some cases radically, the models of the past which attributed excessive and exclusive importance to commerce, and in particular long-range commerce, as the motor of economic development—an external variable that would suddenly intervene from outside to modify a static system. Recent work underlines the dynamic aspects within the system that favoured the circulation of goods: the management, not insensitive to the idea of profit, of the great feudal domains, and their acquisition of products from distant parts, the expansion of local markets, a certain continuity in urban demand, the persistent growth, in northern Italy and Rome, of a merchant class, and the importance of river trade.

However, while taking account of the most reliable of these historiographical tendencies (that is, without accepting extreme postulates of the equivalence of the commerce of the eighth and ninth centuries with the commerce and merchants of the twelfth and thirteenth centuries), we must remember that maritime activity in its early phases guaranteed extremely high profits in relation to the human and financial resources it employed. It is important to speak of maritime 'activity' and not just commerce because the latter was merely a component: raids, piracy, and large organized expeditions realized high and rapid profits. These profits (incomparably greater

---

[1] E. S. Hunt, *The Medieval Super-Companies: a Study of the Peruzzi Company of Florence* (Cambridge, 1994).

than short-distance or land-based commerce) increased the capacity of maritime cities to attract further investment, and this in turn led to the possibility of increasing military strength.

With the increase in commercial activity and the partial reduction in warlike activities, profits tended to fall, and to a certain extent diminished the rates of profit of individual enterprises. Merchants responded on the one hand by increasing their geographic range by 1200, and diversifying and broadening their merchandise, extending their activities to bulkier, lower-value products, and increasing the volume of traffic. On the other hand, they attempted to shore up profits with other responses, sometimes juridical in nature, aimed at reducing risk. The creation of an elaborate code of international commercial law, inherited from Byzantine law and enriched with Catalan traditions, was one of the great achievements of the Italian maritime cities.

In the Italian hinterland, the economy grew and diversified with the development of inland cities, some of which, such as Milan and Florence, grew particularly rich and powerful. The system of production, prompted by the possibility of export, became increasingly sophisticated, both in the primary and secondary sectors. The woollen cloth industry of Florence became particularly successful by 1300. The growth of the economy in virtually all of Italy and the better part of Europe is striking not only for its strong initial phase, but also, and perhaps above all, for its centuries-long duration. The Mediterranean (and later Atlantic) commerce of the Italian maritime cities, which contributed powerfully to the initial take-off, guaranteed a noteworthy, and probably essential, contribution to this process.

6

Material life

Patricia Skinner

The rich documentation available from Italy in the period between about 1050 and 1300 provides often detailed evidence of the material life of its inhabitants. Indeed, the 'commercial revolution' which Robert Lopez argued to have taken place in precisely this period enabled those with sufficient wealth to enjoy material goods from almost all of the known world, but it also led to a major diversification of wares. What was essential was joined by what was desirable, and the consumer society came into being in a way previously unknown. Trade in long-distant luxuries came to be dominated by Italian merchants, and thus the elite society of medieval Italy, particularly that clustered in the burgeoning urban centres, had access to new ornaments, clothes, and flavours for their food which they often record for posterity. Their increasing wealth was directed towards display in housing, apparel, arms, and other possessions, to the extent that by the end of our period Italian city-states were moving towards legislation to clamp down on such ostentation. However, the phrase 'material life' cannot be applied exclusively to such consumerism. A wider definition is used in this chapter, to encompass five main areas: buildings and living conditions, personal possessions including clothing and the utensils of everyday life, tools and equipment for work, foodstuffs and other ephemeral items, and, finally, the luxury goods which only a very tiny minority could afford, but which survive precisely because of their high value.

Buildings and living conditions

The most striking aspect of Italian housing during this period is its increasing height. Beyond the well-known and still extant towers of the nobility in cities such as Rome, Bologna, Verona, and San Gimignano, to cite the best preserved, we also have abundant evidence in the charters of the period of multi-storey housing belonging to quite modest landowners. In the face of increasing pressure on space in the urban environment, we see the development of buildings in which different floors or rooms might be occupied by more than one family. The small trading city of Amalfi is a case in point, with houses reaching three or four storeys by the twelfth century, and often elaborate arrangements being made to prevent undue disturbance between residents of each floor engaging in cloth manufacture, sultana-making, and grinding of food or grain.

The emergence of the tower house represented a major change and reflects the turbulent political atmosphere in most cities from the eleventh century onwards, when aristocratic rivalry produced a demand for fortified residences within and outside towns. We know now from recent archaeological excavations, particularly in Rome, that domestic architecture for the well-off in the preceding centuries had consisted mainly of a stone- or brick-built *domus* of only two storeys, with the upper floor used for residential space and the lower for storage or stabling. Extant towers and portions of medieval houses show the use of stone or brick for the ground floors, but it is entirely possible that upper storeys were constructed of wood, with staircases up the outside. What evidence we have from descriptions shows that roofs were tiled or covered in shingles or planks, and provision was made for drainage of rainwater, not always successfully. Houses might incorporate a kitchen area (although local, communal ovens were still not unknown) and a cellar or storage place on the ground or subterranean level, and living quarters, including solars and bedrooms, on the upper floors. Such houses are well documented in medieval charter evidence, although archaeological investigation is only just beginning to reveal the material remains of such buildings. The houses of the poor, by contrast, are still little known, but more refined excavation techniques are revealing small, wooden structures of tiny size and probably only one storey. Earlier leases made in the city of Salerno to tenants, who might not have been wealthy enough to buy houses themselves, also reveal that their wooden houses were of relatively limited size (around 3 metres by 6 metres in floorspace), usually single-storey and, most intriguingly, able to be dismantled and carried away to a new site at the end of the lease.

We are helped in our reconstruction of the urban milieu by the revival of a genre of text known as the city description from the twelfth century onwards. For example, in his 'On the Marvels of the City of Milan', dating from 1288, Bonvesin della Riva, a friar, describes the physical appearance of the city, and whilst his account might be suspect on the grounds of civic pride, it conveys a sense of how populous Milan was at the end of the thirteenth century, claiming 12,500 houses as well as the public palaces. Reflecting the growing concern on the part of urban authorities for the health of the city, Bonvesin describes wide streets and alludes also to ten hospitals for the sick.

Living conditions in the majority of cities in Italy were crowded and squalid by modern standards, and documented disputes often broke out between neighbours over the inconsiderate disposal of human and animal waste. A Jewish merchant reported in the mid-eleventh century that it was impossible to walk the streets of Messina on Sicily because of the dirt. Only in the twelfth century, and more regularly in the thirteenth, do we begin to see attempts by civic authorities to regulate urban life with health as a motivation. We know that the Norman royal centre of Palermo had a municipal dung-heap. In the north, Milan saw regulations to place gaps between houses into which waste might be thrown; Perugia in Umbria provided a clean water supply and forbade women from washing themselves or their clothes in the civic fountains. In the south, Frederick II included in his codification of laws in 1231 several measures designed to limit disease from animal corpses and other waste.

How effective were such measures? Unfortunately, the science of paleopathology is still relatively young in Italy, and few skeletal samples have as yet emerged which can tell us much about the standard of living and health enjoyed by the Italians of the period. A recent necropolis excavated at the small town of Aversa, however, reveals high levels of infant mortality and an average age at death of between 30 and 40. Concomitant with a population whose main activity was agricultural, the researchers on the sample found much evidence of back complaints, arthritis, and fractures; surprisingly, scurvy affected several of the sample, signifying a lack of fresh fruit and vegetables, but there was a low incidence of dental disease, reflecting limited access to sugary substances (on diet and foodstuffs, however, see below).

Housing and sanitary conditions bring us closest to the everyday lives of individual inhabitants of both cities and the countryside in this period, but the public buildings of the period attest to the desire for display and prestige on the part of urban groups. Often, that desire translated into the importation of decorative or luxury fittings for, for example, churches and cathedrals. The bronze doors of Monreale cathedral in Sicily came from Pisa; those of Amalfi cathedral from Constantinople. The changing political scene in northern Italy also saw the rebuilding of whole cathedrals, and the construction of palaces, many of which still survive within later structures, for civic leaders.

The rural scene is much less clearly known. The inventory of Enardinus of Vicenza, drawn up in 1248, shows one of his heirs living in the *sedimen donicale* or main estate of the family in a rural setting. This consisted of a house with a tower (defence was just as necessary in the countryside) alongside a pigsty.

Personal possessions: the domestic life

One of the ironies of the medieval documentation in Italy is that the material life of women is recorded in more detail than that of men, through the medium of dowry lists drawn up on their marriage. A typical dowry in southern Italy might consist of the marital bed and bedding, clothes, and domestic items. Through such lists, and the rather more rare wills of women, we get a strong sense of the types of item that a moderately wealthy bride might take to her new husband, alongside a quantity of cash, and we can extrapolate from such documents up and down the social scale. Bedding consisted of mattresses and sheets, often of linen. Curtains and hangings might also be included, some quite elaborate with fringing and embroidered decoration. Domestic items might be carefully described if unusual, such as the spoon holder in the shape of a horse plus twelve bone spoons featuring in one dowry list. Other items of value included metal cauldrons and frying pans. Metal vessels appear quite frequently in wills, attesting to their relative value as possessions and their durability. A few pieces of metalware were an essential addition to more breakable pottery bowls (the inventory of Enardinus, however, includes 'two basins, one broken, the other complete', which suggests that even cracked pottery might still be carefully kept). Where there was no production of such goods, imports were needed, and Sardinia, for example, bought in quite basic pots and pans from northern Italy.

The bride's personal possessions included bone and ivory combs, a trousseau of clothes (rarely described, but illustrated in a unique eleventh-century document from Bari, showing the bride receiving the document itself), and jewellery. There have been isolated finds of pieces of jewellery, often in hoards, and southern examples, at least, demonstrate strong Byzantine influence in the disk brooches, crucifixes, and long, pendular earrings. The latter, as has been recently shown, became an item with rather less savoury connotations in northern Italy by the end of our period, as their use came to be associated with Jewish women and prostitutes, to the detriment of the former group.

Items in daily use are the hardest to find in documentary sources. Their very ubiquity may have precluded their inclusion in documents such as dowry lists or inventories, which were as much a public statement of the wealth of the bride's family as an accurate list of her belongings. Information about them has instead emerged as Italian archaeological excavations have increased in number and ambition. Excavations carried out in the city of Salerno, for example, revealed glazed pottery oil-lamps whose shape differs little from those of antiquity. Also found in Salerno, in the palace excavations, were glazed bowls of Sicilian manufacture, decorated in brown and green leaf patterns. Such wares would, presumably, only have been used in aristocratic households (the context of these particular finds certainly supports this), and several Sicilian items have been found in mainland excavations. Contemporary finds from elsewhere in the south reveal tableware of unglazed terracotta, with or without painted decoration. Pottery for everyday use, moreover, would be made locally in large quantities, and undecorated or red-banded ware seems to be the most common.

However, a revolution was about to take place, with imports of oriental pottery leading to the rediscovery of lost techniques of manufacture on the mainland. It seems that the Tyrrhenian coast looked to North Africa, Sicily, and southern Spain for its imports, whilst the Adriatic coast maintained strong links with Byzantium and bought from there. This resulted in a contrast between fine pottery found from the latter region, which tended to be monochrome, and the multicoloured ware preferred in the Islamic countries. Egyptian and Sicilian glazed ware was almost identical owing to regular trade between the two regions. The so-called Gela ware, decorated in green, yellow, and brown, was based on Sicilian models and highly glazed. Eventually, such Arabic designs and colours would find their way as *export* items from southern Italy to Byzantium and the Middle East, but both traditions found their way into Italian workshops. The colourful *protomaiolica* also found its way into the decoration of buildings, with round *bacini* being inserted into the fabric of buildings from Sorrento and Ravello in the south to Pisa further north by the twelfth century. Besides pottery bowls, vases, and lamps, archaeological investigations have also turned up considerable numbers of large amphorae, round-bottomed and wide-necked with handles, which were used in the transport of liquid or semi-solid foodstuffs. Such vessels were also used for the movement and storage of, for example, salted fish. By the beginning of the thirteenth century, the domestic tables of the wealthy might have been seeing increasing amounts of glassware alongside the more common pottery, bone, and wooden utensils. A Genoese charter of 1215 records a merchant of that city importing German glass, but does not state in what form it was arriving. Venice became a major centre of glass production: already by the tenth century some glassblowers had risen to the upper classes of the city. The city was also the first to exploit the discovery of eyeglasses and produce them commercially by the end of the thirteenth century.

Men's possessions are less systematically documented. As the use of documents penetrated deeply into Italian life after the twelfth century, however, we begin to see quite detailed inventories, such as that of the goods of the skinner, Armano, drawn up at Bonifacio on Corsica (then an outpost of Genoa) in 1239. In a lengthy document, his wife and daughter listed his estate including numerous lengths of various cloth, some made-up clothing, a variety of animal skins and furs, foodstuffs (see below), arms and armour, his tools (see below), and some metal implements, such as copper cauldrons, weighing-scales, axes, and horse tack. The cloth is of particular interest, since Armano clearly carried on other trades alongside his tanning. Indeed, the inventory includes a considerable list of debts and money held for commerce from other people. The colours of cloth were vermilion, green, purple, pink, black, yellow, and blue; and the types listed were linen, cotton, fustian (wool and cotton mixed, a product made in some quantities by the cities of the Po valley), and lace. Armano did not, apparently, deal in silk. However, the occurrence of women's clothing in the list suggests that he dealt in made-up goods as well as lengths of cloth. Several belts are also mentioned, each adorned with silver.

What is quite striking about this document is how few possessions listed can be described as personal to Armano himself. Apart from the suit of armour and swords, and maybe the belts and some of the small furniture such as chests and stools, the bulk of the inventory consists actually of trading commodities. This is understandable in the circumstances: such items and the records of outstanding business transactions held the key to his family's future, and his wife and daughter would therefore have been keen to see them minutely recorded.

The distinction between personal possessions and those which happened to be in the possession of the deceased at the time of his death is neatly expressed in the way the executors of a certain Zaccaria Roberti, merchant of Messina, wound up his estate in 1300. They returned several items, which Zaccaria had been holding (as pawns or investments or items to trade on) to Giacomo Zanterio of the same city. The list included high-value goods such as a small silver shield, candlesticks, silk purses embroidered with gold wire, a silk scabbard, as well as a quire of paper, a mattress, and other domestic items. Armano's inventory highlights the variety of cloth in circulation in Italy. The textile trade appears to have varied according to location. Sicily certainly produced raw cotton, but its manufacture into cloth took place in the north, and it actually imported finished cloth from there. The coastal city of Ancona, too, sold raw cotton to the workshops of central Italy, much of which had been imported from the Levant. The island also produced indigo, used for dyeing, although this and henna production seems to have gone into decline with the diminution of the Arab population of the island from the twelfth century onwards. From the north came woollen cloth, some home-produced, some imported from Flanders. Abulafia notes the change which occurred between the middle and end of the twelfth century, as more cloth was imported. Its price indicates that it was of the highest quality and superior to home-produced materials. Types varied and were often named after their colour and point of origin, such as 'green cloth of Ghent, brown cloth of Ypres, red cloth of Le Mans', and so on. The need for imports also reflects the fact that the Italian textile industry really exploded into life only in the late twelfth and early thirteenth centuries, with Milan and Piacenza major producers.

This expansion was reflected in changes in clothing habits: Roberto Lopez highlighted, for example, the rise of the shirt as an item of clothing. It was not an essential garment, but it added to the wearer's comfort, a major theme in the consumption patterns of the period. Indeed, the diversity of items in inventories often points to the rise of ownership of non-essential but desirable items. A case in point is the fork. First documented in Italy in the tenth century, when a Byzantine princess marrying into the Venetian ducal family was observed using this strange item to eat her food (a sign of the luxurious and dissolute nature of the Greeks, a slightly later observer noted!), forks occur with some regularity in inventories by the thirteenth century. That of Enardinus of Vicenza includes two iron forks (possibly larger versions designed for use in cooking) alongside a knife and a cleaver.

Tools and equipment

Among women's dowry and testamental lists, tools for spinning and weaving frequently make an appearance, testimony to the constant domestic labour of producing cloth and clothes both for family consumption and sale. Medieval women's work has been characterized as 'extended domestic labour', and spinning, in particular, could be carried out anywhere and easily set aside to continue later. Surviving material evidence is unusual, perhaps because such items were commonplace and thus subject to less care being taken of them. Highly durable stone loom-weights and spindle-whorls are the most common finds in archaeological exploration. Rather less common, it seems, are references to items that men might own as their tools of work. Even the inventory of Armano, mentioned above, is rather vague when it came to his tools. His wife and daughter simply state that they found '34 utensils' in a closet and 150 'instruments' (which might in fact refer to documents rather than tools).

Arms and armour might also be viewed as tools of a trade, particularly given the increasing importance of paid soldiers in the military campaigns of the period. Against the background of Norman conquest in southern Italy, and the campaigns of the German emperor, Frederick Barbarossa, in the north in the late twelfth century, the possession of arms was something of a necessity, and it appears that iron weaponry was exported from Genoa southwards to Sicily, including helmets, breastplates, and greaves. Pisa, too, was famous as a centre of production of iron goods, and its merchants are seen handling pieces of armour in their trading activities in Sicily. Venice handled iron, copper, and tin among its many trade commodities. Enardinus of Vicenza's inventory, which represents the property of a local, wealthy aristocrat, lists armour consisting of a breastplate, greaves, a helmet, a shield for use on horseback (he had also left the horse), another two large shields, two faceguards, and a wooden crossbow with five bolts. Further on in the list, his executors and co-heirs noted two swords, three lances, and two pairs of spurs.

At any given time there might be a need to store the raw materials of a trade either in a separate workshop or at home. We know that Sicily exported hides and rabbit skins, for example, in much the same way as it sent out raw cotton, and it is not unlikely that many of the skins mentioned in Armano's will were awaiting processing into finished goods.

Food and ephemera

Bonvesin of Milan, previously referred to, devotes a considerable part of his work to describing the bakeries, butchers, and fishmongers of that city, and goes on to recount the main crops grown in its *contado*, including grains, pulses, chestnuts, and soft fruits. He also draws attention to the provision of salt to the city. The latter, of course, was an essential element in preserving meat and fish (Messina in Sicily, for example, specialized in salted pork), and saltpans were valued property. The Venetian lagoons were a major source of salt, and other marshy coastal areas such as northern Apulia and southern Lazio also had saltpans. Meat, in particular, was a preserve of the rich, and it is doubtful whether peasants in northern or southern Italy would have had much opportunity to eat meat except, perhaps, on feast days. A much earlier record of the daily rations of the inmates of a Tuscan almshouse in 765 shows them receiving bread, wine, and a gruel of beans and millet soaked in oil or fat, and such a diet probably remained the standard fare of the poor.

At a more modest level, the inventory of Armano the skinner reveals him to have owned (probably for personal consumption) casks of grain, barrels of wine, packages of cheese, and a supply of pepper. The latter might sometimes be used in lieu of cash in business transactions, as is documented in twelfth-century Genoa, so perhaps it could be characterized as Armano's business 'float'.

It is worth remembering that foodstuffs themselves were the object of trade within Italy. Sicily, for example, exported wheat and meat to the north, and tunny-fishing was a major part of its economy. There was also a centre of cheese production at Syracuse, whose products were exported to Egypt (including some kosher cheese for the Jewish community there), and in Sardinia, which began to export pecorino cheese in this period. Indeed, dairy products were probably a central part of most diets, along with pulses and grains. The landed aristocracy, however, were also able to call upon the products of their estates to supply their needs. Enardinus of Vicenza's inventory includes reference to over forty separate small estates or pieces of land, most of which were held by tenants paying their rent in kind. Although there is clearly a formulaic element in the way in which these are listed, we can take at face value the information that the estates were expected to hand over a proportion of their grain, grape, and fruit production (casks of wine needing two carts to carry them and sacks of grain and flour are included in the inventory), plus a total of over 400 eggs, 15 pork shoulders, loaves, pullets, geese, and a capon. The inventory lists major food items already held by Enardinus, including sides of bacon, more pork shoulders, vinegar, mustard, and oil. Only the latter two seem not to have been readily available from his tenants. The eggs listed were to be delivered at Easter and on the feast day of St Felix; other leases often specify a date for delivery of meat, and we are also beginning to get some sense of the seasonal rhythm of the medieval diet in Italy through analysis of animal bones found in archaeological investigations. In addition, some cities had specialist trades in foodstuffs and other perishable commodities. San Gimignano, for instance, was renowned for its saffron, used as a dye, a drug ingredient, and a flavouring; Messina for its wine.

Luxury items

Luxury goods were sought after by both ecclesiastical and secular owners. The papal court, for example, was a major consumer of imported sugar, pepper, incense, and eastern cloth. This period sees some of the most decorative items surviving from the peninsula, including southern Italian ivory, worked into horns (oliphants), small boxes for writing instruments, and lockable chests, gold and silver work, and precious cloths such as Sicilian silk. The latter was manufactured on a relatively small scale in the town of Demona, which also made carpets. In the wealthiest circles, it is not hard to imagine that such items might have been prestigious status symbols, included in dowries or preserved for longer periods to hand on as family heirlooms.

The working of ivory seems largely to have been an innovation precipitated by the arrival of the Normans in southern Italy from the mid-eleventh century onwards; exceptional finds from earlier archaeological sites merely serve to underline the sharp rise in the number of items surviving from the later period. Some twenty oliphants (carved elephant tusks) are known, and were used as prestigious gifts to ecclesiastical houses more than for their musical quality. The leading centre for ivory production initially seems to have been Amalfi, which had the necessary trade links to procure the raw materials, but under the patronage of King Roger II from the mid-twelfth century, workshops were also created at Palermo. Little evidence survives of individuals specifically commissioning such works: a portable altar inscribed at the behest of, and presumably used by, Count Geoffrey of

Catanzaro appears to be the only definitive example. Highly decorated ivory boxes seem mainly to have had a secular use, before, in several cases, being donated to churches and having a second life as reliquaries. Several painted ivory boxes of Sicilian manufacture survive across Europe.

Silk manufacture, originally centred in the east Mediterranean, had arrived in southern Italy by the eleventh century, as even the bishop of Reggio di Calabria carefully listed his mulberry bushes for silkworms. Abulafia considers that the product was probably exchanged for foodstuffs for Calabrian monks. Apart from magnificent items such as the coronation robe of King Roger II, it is clear that members of the aristocracy also wore silk clothing as a sign of their social status: when, in 1984, the tomb of William of Hauteville in Salerno cathedral was opened, he was found to have been laid to rest in linen and silk clothes, some of which had survived. One of the main centres of silk manufacture was in fact Palermo, and one piece, dating from around 1140 and now in Vienna even has 'made in the royal workshops' woven into its edge. However, whether the Sicilian workshops produced for anything more than court consumption is open to question: there is little indication that the island's products were sold commercially, and the Tuscan city of Lucca may have dominated trade until the thirteenth century, when artisans moved with their skills and equipment to competing centres such as Bologna. Frederick II did try to encourage the expansion of silk production, using Jewish intermediaries, though it is not at all certain that these initiatives were a success. Lucchese silk remained superior, however, in its designs and technical quality. At the risk of exaggeration, Lopez even suggested that silk was in fact more important than wool in the Italian textile industry of the thirteenth century.

Another luxury item which might or might not indicate the literacy of its owner was the book. Italy has the reputation of having had a much higher per capita literacy rate among its laymen than other European countries in the early medieval period, and it is not difficult to find evidence in wills and inventories of book ownership. A list of goods carried by a Genoese merchant to Sicily in 1157 includes 'Saracen books', for which the island must still have provided a ready market. What is clear is the explosion of interest in the written document. Even these were undergoing change in the period under review, as parchment, still the primary material for written charters, was increasingly joined by paper: the cartulary of the Genoese notary Giovanni Scriba (1154–64) is written on paper which was imported from Alexandria in Egypt. Imported paper was joined by that made at Fabriano and, slightly after our period, Amalfi. Papyrus, too, was used, and the raw materials for this were grown in Sicily. Storage of documents and writing equipment was also thought of: the very wealthy Enardinus of Vicenza had owned two walnut letter-cases, presumably writing boxes. Women, too, are recorded as owners of such boxes. In neither case is this definitive proof of literacy: like book ownership, the items concerned were materially prestigious in themselves. Some of the ivory boxes which survive from the region may well have been used for a similar purpose.

Goldsmiths often became known by their trade in documents, with the surname Aurifex being handed on down families even if the trade did not. Besides jewellery, some of the finest examples of their work is to be found in jewelled and enamelled book-covers, mainly destined for ecclesiastical use. Workshops of this type operated in the Sicily of King Roger, making liberal use of precious stones and cloisonné enamel. Unique items such as the so-called crown of Constance of Aragon (d. 1220) also testify to the use of gold-plated silver, though unfortunately part of this decoration may be due to over-eager restorers. Records of items can sometimes come from unusual sources: the piracy which characterized the rivalry between the northern merchant cities resulted in 1194 in a list of items restored to the Genoese by the Pisans, including a silver vase and more gold.

Conclusions

In summary, therefore, Italy saw a growing diversity of consumer items in this period for those who could afford them. The products on sale reflected its continuing strong trade links with North Africa, Spain, and the Byzantine Empire, which were now joined by the Middle East after the First Crusade. The material culture of southern Italy may also have been affected by the demands of the incoming Normans as well. Chief among the changes visible are a switch to more glazed ware in pottery, taller and more sophisticated housing, an increased demand for spices and flavourings in food, and a more varied choice of cloth to wear and use as decoration in the home. Although archaeological evidence is still quite sparse, the sharp rise in written evidence in this period, particularly in the sphere of charters recording trading agreements, wills, and marital property exchanges, provides us with an often quite detailed picture of the material aspirations of the wealthier sections of Italian society. Those of the poor might have been limited simply to the struggle to survive; they come more into view in this period through the charitable efforts of both individuals and communes, which carefully recorded their beneficence for posterity.

Rural Italy

Duane Osheim

The Italian countryside in 1000 was covered thickly with forest and marsh. These uninhabited tracts in northern and central Italy were broken up by numerous small villages organized in a system of estates or manors, what the Italians call the *sistema curtense.* When these estates were first established in the eighth and ninth centuries, they consisted of some lands directly farmed by the landlord (demesne lands), other lands let by traditional long-term leases, as well as pasture and woodland used by all. These were not compact estates, but collections of pieces of land often spread among a number of villages. Villagers paid various rents in produce, in money, and even in labour. By 1000 very little of the land was directly farmed by the landlord. Peasants even held the demesne lands by traditional multigenerational or perpetual leases. Peasants tended to live in small villages or on isolated farmsteads.

The rural landscape: *castelli* and lords

After 1000, however, this landscape was transformed in many parts of Italy by *castelli.* These were not castles in the English sense of the word. For the most part, they were recently constructed rudimentary fortifications of small villages. In many cases a village was simply surrounded by a hedge or ditch. Palisades, if there were any, were simple wood structures. Since in most parts of Italy *castelli* are first mentioned in the late tenth or early eleventh centuries, it has been assumed that they were constructed as a response to the violence and disruption caused by Saracen and Hungarian raiders in the tenth century. Since the publication of Pierre Toubert's *The Structures of Medieval Latium*, however, the creation of these castelli has been a matter of great debate.[1] Toubert shows that in the neighbourhood of Rome castelli were not primarily constructed for defence of existing villages, but rather as a way to draw into a centralized area a population that otherwise would be scattered throughout a district. The impetus for this *incastellamento*, or the drawing of population into fortified villages, was the desire of landlords to effect a profound reorganization of country life. The primary goal was concentrating population to consolidate jurisdiction and control. Later, markets were established in and beside castelli and in many cases older churches were transferred to the neighbourhood of these new settlements. These new castelli, Toubert argued, became the economic and religious centres of the countryside. Claims of jurisdiction over the territory of the castello and its inhabitants often followed the first appearance of the fortification.

In a country as diverse as Italy, however, a general phenomenon like castle-building has more than a single explanation. Just to the south-east of Latium and Sabina, the area studied by Toubert, at San Vincenzo al Volturno, the appearance of castelli had a different economic and demographic significance. San Vincenzo was a recently refounded Benedictine monastery in a rich but underpopulated valley. In this case, it seems that the castelli, or fortified villages, were part of a programme of resettlement and economic development. Strategies of defence or control are much less evident. And far from being the product of a single organizer, contracts at San Vincenzo were often given to groups of men, up to forty in one case. In one contract a group of men promised 'they must build a castello in the neighbourhood (*in predictos fines*) and build houses with yards and kitchen gardens and live there with their families, their animals and their possessions'.[2] At San Vincenzo, at least, castelli were part of economic expansion. Further south, castelli were more clearly defensive. The most marked period of castle-building in the south followed the war

---

[1] Pierre Toubert, *Les Structures du Latium médiéval: le Latium méridional et la Sabine du IXe siècle à la fin du XIIe siècle*, 2 vols. (Rome, 1973).

[2] Quoted in Chris Wickham, 'The *terra* of San Vincenzo al Volturno in the 8th to 12th centuries: the historical framework', in Richard Hodges and John Mitchell (eds.), *San Vincenzo al Volturno: The Archaeology, Art and Territory of an Early Medieval Monastery* (Oxford, 1985), p. 239.

and unrest of the Norman expansion, especially in the twelfth century.[3] And the *castelli* of Norman Italy seem significantly different from the *castelli* of Latium. Norman invaders and their opponents in the twelfth century tended to build castles in a north European style. While they often did include a church and residence for a castellan and shelter for troops and even a market in the shadow of the walls, they seem to have had little or no impact on the settlement patterns of the countryside. New population centres were more likely to be *casali*, unfortified open settlements scattered throughout the countryside. Jurisdiction over these *casali* was most often in the hands of a local church or under the control of the sovereign. *Castelli* may reflect an attempt to control neighbourhoods militarily, but they had remarkably little impact on the southern countryside itself.[4]

It is perhaps easier to understand the impact on the rural landscape of *castelli* and newly fortified villages if we look at northern and central Italy. *Castelli* and fortified villages really seem to develop in several stages. It is clear that in the late tenth and early eleventh centuries *castelli* in northern Italy were primarily defensive in nature. Many were simply appended on to existing settlements and others, constructed in no discernible pattern, were highly temporary in nature. They might be mentioned in extant documentation once or twice and then disappear.[5] In Tuscany, perhaps 2,400 *castelli* and fortified centres are identified in the historical record, yet aerial surveys indicate that there may have been as many as 3,600 *castelli* at some point in the Middle Ages. Many of these *castelli* must have been constructed for defence and had little or no economic or social significance. In many cases these fortifications were uninhabited except

[3] Francesco Bosco, 'Incastellamento, territorio e popolamento dell'Italia centro-meridionale nella recente storiografia', *Bullettino della Deputazione abruzzese di Storia Patria*, 78 (1988), pp. 55–83.

[4] Bruno Figliuolo, 'Le fondazioni nuove in Italia meridionale in età normanna', in Rinaldo Comba and Aldo A. Settia (eds.), *I borghi nuovi, secoli XII–XIV* (Cuneo, 1993), pp. 100–13; Marco Tangheroni, 'I luoghi nuovi della Sardegna medievale', in *I borghi nuovi*. In the case of Sardinia, it was the appearance of towns in the thirteenth century and not villages that represented a profound change.

[5] On the debate over *castelli* see especially Ricardo Francovich *et al.*, 'Verso un atlante dei castelli della Toscana: primi risultati', in *Il Congresso nazionale di archeologia medievale* (Pisa, 1997), pp. 97–101; François Menant, *Campagnes lombardes du moyen age: l'économie et la société rurales dans la région de Bergame, de Crémone et de Brescia du Xe au XIIIe siècle* (Rome, 1993); Aldo A. Settia, *Castelli e villaggi nell'Italia padana: popolamento, potere, sicurezza fra IX e XIII secolo* (Naples, 1984).

in times of emergency. In other cases, peasants living in the neighbourhood might be required to maintain storage for their crops
within the walls. Even so, peasants generally preferred to live outside
the fortified area, perhaps even in temporary wooden or thatched
houses. One twelfth-century *castello* was described as a place where
'they store bread and wine and where they live with their wives in the
winter'.[6] Temporary refuges, especially if built at some distance from
local churches or manors, had little or no permanent effect on the
rural landscape.

A second stage of castle building, in the late eleventh and early
twelfth centuries, seems to have been significantly different. Later
castelli resembled the Norman castles of the south. They tended to be
better built and designed as a residence for a lord and for his retinue.
But unlike the southern castles, these *castelli*, often with a tower, castle
keep, and high walls, were symbolic of a changed countryside. *Castelli*
of the late twelfth and thirteenth centuries often represent legal and
political claims by rural lords. The locations of these *castelli* often
reflect this new political geography. In Tuscany *castelli* are almost
non-existent in the areas close to Lucca and Pisa. These are areas
where, as early as the first decades of the twelfth century, towns took
control of the surrounding countryside. In other parts of Italy, on the
edge of the Apennines and in the Po valley, *castelli* and claims to
lordship were much more common in the twelfth and thirteenth
centuries than they had been previously.

Yet even the claims of rural lords did not transform the rural
landscape itself. While it is true that lords did claim rights to labour
services, hunting and fishing rights on otherwise public lands, as well
as rights to hold court, they did not significantly alter population
patterns. Their *castelli* were meant to be private, the earliest intim-
ations of what would become the villas and hunting lodges of the
Renaissance elites. The most significant transformation of the countryside was associated with the construction of new or refounded
towns, the Villanuovas, Borgo Nuovos, and Castelfrancos found
throughout Italy. Like the older *castelli*, there is no single explanation
for these new foundations. They were constructed to promote economic expansion and to protect roads or borderlands. The distinction between *castelli* and *borghi nuovi*, or new settlements, may seem

---

[6] Settia, 'Castelli e villaggi', p. 441.

a bit artificial, but the *borghi nuovi* did tend to be larger, to be founded by towns or bishops and to follow a much clearer geographical pattern than the casual appearance of the *castelli*.[7] Towns, bishops, and nobles promoted new settlements for a number of reasons. For some, new settlements were part of an economic reorganization of the countryside. More often, however, new settlements were strategic, protecting a road or establishing a claim along a border.

Perhaps the most famous example of a new settlement for economic reasons was Verona's foundation of Villafranca in the 1180s as part of a movement to settle a large area on the right bank of the Adige just below the city. Each settler was to have 22 *campi* (about 6.5 hectares or 14 acres) of tillable land, another *campo* for a house and kitchen garden plus access to a large common area of wood and meadow. This was a rehearsal for an even more ambitious undertaking in the draining and clearance of lands and the creation of the settlement of Palù. These settlements were necessary to produce much needed food for Verona's growing population. Perugia, in central Italy, sponsored similar projects in the area of Lake Trasimeno, again in order to grow grain for its urban population.[8]

By far the greatest number of *borghi nuovi*, however, were founded for strategic purposes. In the second half of the twelfth century, strategic new settlements were common in Lombardy and Piedmont and they became important in Tuscany during the thirteenth century. They were primarily used by bishops and communes to protect their territories. One of the earliest examples would be the Milanese foundation of Galliate Nuovo in 1092 with the intention of drawing population away from Galliate, a settlement under the jurisdiction of the neighbouring bishop of Novara.[9] Other strategic settlements were built in Piedmont and Liguria, along the Via Francigena, the most important medieval highway leading south to Rome. There are

---

[7] Id., 'Le pedine e la scacchiera: iniziative di popolamento nel secolo XII', in Comba and Settia (eds.), *I borghi nuovi*, pp. 63–81.

[8] Andrea Castagnetti, 'Primi aspetti di politica annonaria nell'Italia comunale. La bonifica della "Palus Comunis Verone" (1194–1199)', *Studi medievali*, ser. 3, 15 (1974), pp. 363–481, which describes the foundation of Villafranca as well as the later work at Palù; on settlements at Perugia, Paolo Pirilli, 'Borghi e terre nuovi dell'Italia centrale', in Comba and Settia (eds.), *I borghi nuovi*, p. 86.

[9] Settia, 'Le pedine e la scacchiera', pp. 63–81, esp. p. 69 on Galiate.

countless examples along the foothills of the Alps from Piedmont to the Veneto of new settlements meant to draw population from one jurisdiction to another, or to fortify a strategic centre. The picturesque town of Biella with its suburb of Piazzo on a hill overlooking the city is the result of a failed resettlement. The bishop of Vercelli tried unsuccessfully to move the population from the valley to the mountaintop in 1160. The upper village was never popular and most of the population remained in the valley.

Similar military and strategic interests led to the creation of new settlements in Tuscany in the second half of the thirteenth century. Lucca built Castelfranco di Sotto and Santa Croce Valdarno in a desperate and eventually unsuccessful attempt to reduce Pisan and then Florentine influence in the lower Arno valley. They were more successful when they built Pietrasanta and Camaiore in the coastal region of Versiglia in the 1260s. The Sienese and especially the Florentines quickly followed the Lucchese example. The Florentines founded five new towns in the first half of the fourteenth century. Florentine new towns demonstrate the planning and strategic thought at the heart of the undertaking. All five were in the Apennines to the north and east of the city along a critical communication route to Bologna and the Romagna, in an area dominated by rebellious nobles. All of these fortified new towns had similar characteristics. The most successful new towns were founded on newly cleared or common lands, areas where it was most simple to acquire sufficient property. They had a regular rectangular shape that focused on a public piazza at the centre of the town.[10]

The Tuscan and probably most of the other new settlements were part of an administrative transformation of the countryside. Initially, the Danish historian Johann Plesner suggested that there had been a transport revolution with new roads running through newly reclaimed lands. More recently Thomas Szabó has argued for a more profound revolution.[11] In the years after 1000 roads and bridges were

---

[10] David Friedman, *Florentine New Towns: Urban Design in the Late Middle Ages* (New York and Cambridge, Mass., 1988); and Riccardo Francovich, Erica Boldrini, and Daniele De Luca, 'Archeologia delle terre nuove in Toscana: il caso di San Giovanni Valdarno', in Comba and Settia (eds.), *I borghi nuovi*, pp. 155–94.

[11] Johann Plesner, *Una rivoluzione stradale del Dugento* (Florence, 1980; first printed Aarhus, 1938); Thomas Szabó, *Comuni e politica stradale in Toscana e in Italia nel medioevo* (Bologna, 1992), especially pp. 257–69 on Plesner's work.

often built and maintained by ecclesiastical institutions or even private lords. From as early as the third decade of the thirteenth century and especially after 1250, Tuscan communes reorganized the administration of the countryside requiring rural parishes and communities to maintain roads and bridges in their neighbourhoods and even dig wells at important stopping points on the main roads in the countryside. Residents of local villages could be required to clear drainage ditches, fill potholes in the roads, and cover highways with gravel. By 1300, the rural settlement pattern had been profoundly transformed. Lands had been cleared and drained. But more importantly, in central and northern Italy, communes had taken a lead in the reorganization of the countryside. Castles and new *borghi nuovi* had been constructed at critical points throughout the north and centre of Italy, and they were tied together by a network of locally maintained bridges and roads.

Parallel developments in southern Italy

There were similar initiatives as far south as Sicily, where under royal and ecclesiastical patronage areas such as the slopes of Etna were settled and exploited for their resources; what is noticeable there is the greater role of the central government and of the feudal baronage. The so-called Lombard settlers, north Italians who came in considerable numbers to Sicily, were apparently attracted south by generous tax exemption privileges, typical of many a frontier society. The great fear of the Sicilian and south Italian rulers was that land would lie empty and that revenue from it would therefore collapse. In Sicily, years of conflict between Christians and Muslims left large open tracts which were made still larger when the rebellious Muslim population was carried off to Apulia. This resettlement of the Sicilian Muslims at Lucera was partly motivated by the wish of Emperor Frederick II to ensure that the fertile soils of the Capitanata would be intensively cultivated, and he provided the Muslim peasantry there with oxen and with tools. Capitanata as a whole became an important source of grain on the international markets. We see the evolution of the *masserie*, large granges which concentrated on production for the market, beginning as several patches of land under one owner but becoming increasingly integrated into substantial continuous estates. This was part of a wider process whereby the kings of Sicily and southern Italy sought to extract maximum benefit from the lively export trade in wheat and barley, offering privileges to Genoese, Florentine, Venetian, and Catalan merchants who sought to feed the hungry cities of northern Italy and of the lands of the crown of Aragon with imported grain (Sardinia too became the target of Italian and Catalan grain shippers, and is discussed in a separate chapter). The effect of these initiatives was to encourage grain cultivation at the expense of other products which had traditionally been produced in Sicily in particular, such as cotton and dyestuffs. The monarchy also gave its support, from the time of the Norman king William II onwards, to the regulation of transhumance in Apulia, and the rising numbers of sheep which moved back and forth from hill to plain foreshadowed the evolution in the fifteenth century of the tightly controlled *Dogana delle Pecore*, which was to become a major source of revenue to the Neapolitan kings. Around 1300 attempts to increase wool production as the basis for a woollen cloth industry in Naples met with only limited success, however. Under Frederick II in particular, encouragement was given to silk cultivation, in which the south Italian Jews were closely involved.

The rural communes

By the end of the Middle Ages urban control of the countryside depended on a network of administrators located in rural communes. Viewed from Italy's thriving cities, rural communes often seemed little more than administrative arms of the urban communes. The reality was much more complex. It was once thought that the rural associations that formed communes reached back into Late Antique and Roman times. It seems more likely that they were formed much later, perhaps the late eleventh century at the earliest.[12] In many cases our first hints of rural communes occur in documents

---

[12] Chris Wickham, *Community and Clientele in Twelfth-Century Tuscany: The Origins of the Rural Commune in the Plain of Lucca* (Oxford, 1998; Italian edn. Rome, 1995), pp. 1–7 for a discussion of earlier theories of rural communal origins.

where the *vicini*, that is residents, of a local parish, make an agreement over dues or tithes with a bishop or local lord. Rural communes were often quite informal associations. Urban officials frequently slipped easily between describing individuals as residents of a parish or members of a commune. Since much of the business of the rural commune revolved around the parish, notaries often would indiscriminately describe neighbourhood representatives as *operari* of the parish (officials responsible for the fabric of the local church) or consuls of the commune.

Urban critics complained that rural communes were made up of 'a multitude of thieves, highwaymen and escaped serfs'.[13] In fact, the population that made up the rural communes in the twelfth century was varied. Public documents often distinguished between knights and people, or between those who could afford a horse and could serve in a militia and those who were simple *rustici*, that is peasants.[14] Throughout the twelfth century rural communes continued to include an elite of notaries, artisans, and landowners who tended to dominate public life. In the thirteenth century, this rural elite was less in evidence, especially in the small communities close to Italy's dominant cities. The disappearance of the wealthiest group from the rural communes happened for a variety of reasons. First of all, ambitious individuals were drawn by the economic opportunities available in towns. In parts of Lombardy, especially in Milan, the movement was evident by the twelfth century. In the late twelfth and thirteenth centuries, however, the movement may owe as much to governmental policy as it did to economic opportunity. In the aftermath of the political struggles between the emperor Frederick Barbarossa and the urban communes, rural communities found themselves increasingly subject to a host of exactions and controls by the urban communes. It was this urban influence as much as the economic opportunities of the city that changed the social and political landscape in the countryside.

In Lombardy, the history of the *fodrum*, an extraordinary tax on imperial vassals, is indicative of what happened to rural communes.[15]

---

[13] Settia, 'Le pedine e la scacchiera', p. 72; he is specifically describing Alessandria and Crema, two of the *borghi nuovi* founded in the twelfth century.

[14] On the important issue of rural communes, see, especially, Wickham, *Community and Clientele*, esp. p. 233 where he sums up his observations; and Menant, *Campagnes lombardes*, pp. 489–559.

[15] On the *fodrum*, see the discussion in Menant, *Campagnes lombardes*, pp. 463–877.

The *fodrum* was a tax paid in money rather than in kind that was levied in those years that the emperor was in Italy. Thus it was an irregular tax paid by only a portion of the Italian population. First mentioned in the eleventh century, it was changed and expanded over the first half of the twelfth century. The *fodrum* was transformed and extended in three ways. First, it evolved from a tax collected from imperial vassals and their dependants to a tax on all the residents of a subject commune. This occurred as the term *fodrum* came to be used to describe almost any tax paid in money instead of kind. Even a feudal aid paid on the marriage of a lord's daughter was once referred to as a *fodrum*. From that point it was easy for the deputy collectors authorized to collect the imperial tax to extend the *fodrum* to all the residents of a village or commune. As deputy collectors, officials of Santa Giulia of Brescia did just that, claiming *fodrum* not only from their own dependants, but all the residents of villages in which the dependants lived. Frederick Barbarossa's campaigns against the Lombard towns also changed the *fodrum*. Rather than being imposed once a generation, Frederick's frequent presence in Lombardy in the 1160s and 1170s meant that the *fodrum* was regularly claimed by his officials. Finally, when Frederick conceded imperial rights to the Lombard communes and some rural lords, the *fodrum* became a communal tax collected from rural communities. The effect on rural communes could be dramatic. While some lords and towns only exacted the *fodrum* in special circumstances, others demanded payments on an annual basis. Further, the *fodrum* began as a relatively light tax traditionally fixed at 6–8 pence per head. Yet many communes raised the rate to perhaps ten times the traditional rate. Eventually urban communes assessed each rural commune at a sum to be divided among residents according to their ability to pay. And finally, in the thirteenth century, urban communes began to talk of a *taglia* or direct tax rather than an imperial *fodrum*.[16]

By the end of the thirteenth century, urban governments were claiming a host of direct and indirect taxes from rural communes. In Siena, by the end of the century most of the indirect taxes were unified in a single *gabelle* of the *contado* collected annually from all the rural communes in the Sienese state. In normal years, this *gabelle*

---

[16] On taxation of the countryside the best work is William M. Bowsky, *The Finance of the Commune of Siena, 1287–1355* (Oxford, 1970), see esp. pp. 225–55.

probably represented about 10 to 15 per cent of the city's budget. In addition to this *gabelle*, however, rural communes could also be expected to pay a *dazio*, or direct tax based on estimated wealth, offer special forced loans to the commune, and pay the costs of communal officials sent out to the rural communes. And this was in addition to military and labour services that rural communes could be expected to contribute to urban government. It is difficult to know how heavily burdened rural communities were by these taxes and dues. In Tuscany and Lombardy there are some complaints and occasionally communes may have refused to co-operate. But the little village of Almanno near Brescia may have been typical. Hard pressed by a host of small dues and taxes, the commune found its dues rising to the point that it had to sell off its communal grazing lands in order to settle its debts.[17] And throughout late medieval central and northern Italy, common lands, grazing lands, woodlands, and marsh were most likely to survive in the hills and mountainous regions at a distance from the urban communes, areas less easily dominated and controlled than the suburban villages.

Finally, urban communal desires to protect their own economies had a negative impact on the surrounding countryside. Urban governments enforced export bans (*divieti*) by which villagers were forbidden to export their grains, livestock, or even wood products outside the boundaries of the city-state. They were most often required to sell grain in communal grain markets where the urban commune could ensure that the prices paid by urban consumers remained low. In times of dearth, urban officials even carried out inquests to establish how much grain villagers did have and could be expected to supply to the urban market. The net effect was an ever widening class of poor farmers, so poor that they were merely noted as paupers in village tax registers. Given the burdens placed on the rural communes, it is not surprising that those who could leave the countryside did so. Immigration of countrymen of all economic levels was a key to the population growth of Italy's vibrant towns. There is evidence that urban communes eventually recognized the dangers to villages and did what they could to prop up marginal communes. Bologna's dramatic redemption of 1257, freeing nearly 6,000 serfs, was a desperate and ultimately unsuccessful attempt to

[17] Menant, *Campagnes lombardes*, p. 546.

prop up rural communes. These newly freed serfs were free to move where they wished within the Bolognese countryside so long as within three months they were enrolled as taxpayers in one of the hard-pressed rural communes.[18] At other times, communes attempted to force immigrants who had left rural communes to return, or at least obliged them to continue to pay the taxes and dues they had paid in their villages. The problem was so great that tax collectors had to face what were called broken communes, villages so reduced in size they could no longer pay the expected taxes. Bolognese officials discussed the issue of the villages frankly. Describing the villages in the lands of the bishop of Bologna officials complained 'no one but paupers remain there and they do not pay taxes nor do they carry out the public works required by the city of Bologna'. The city council of Siena debated similar problems.[19]

The pressures on the rural communes could be enormous. Urban governments carefully inserted in their statutes a variety of requirements for rural communities. Rural communes often had the right to deal with minor civil or criminal issues, but the overlords quickly intervened in more serious matters. It was not uncommon in the thirteenth century for towns and signorial lords to seize the houses and possessions of peasants in an effort to get them to pay rents or obey statutes. Near Milan, the abbot of Sant'Ambrogio regularly seized houses belonging to his tenants, promising to return them once overdue rents and taxes were paid.[20] Nunzios from the city often arrived with demands that consuls of rural communes impound properties or turn them over to urban claimants. And there were stiff penalties if the rural commune failed to act within the required deadline. Rural communal officials were increasingly viewed as little more than administrative representatives of the urban government. The power of the urban communes was overwhelming, yet in some cases they chose to moderate their demands. Some communes reduced or forgave taxes or dues from especially hard pressed rural areas. This most often happened along borders, regions most subject to border

---

[18] Antonio Ivan Pini, 'Un aspetto dei rapporti fra città e territorio nel medioevo: la politica demografica "ad elastico" di Bologna fra il XII e il XIV secolo', in *Studi in memoria di Federigo Melis*, i (Naples, 1978), esp. pp. 376–89 on Bologna's demographic interests and their impact on rural life.

[19] Pini, 'Rapporti fra città e territorio', p. 382; Bowsky, *Finance*, pp. 237, 250–5.

[20] Rosario Romeo, *Il comune rurale di Origgio nel secolo XIII* (Milan, 1992), pp. 53–4.

warfare, and where it was easiest for peasants to slip away into another jurisdiction. Yet urban landlords and communes did moderate their demands at other times as well. To understand when and why, it is necessary to look more closely at the functioning of the rural communes themselves.

When viewed from the city, the rural commune was the administrative arm of the central government. The perspective of the village was significantly different. In the twelfth century and in those villages at some distance from the nearest urban commune, villages contained a mix of people, including those whom local documents often identified as knights and who were distinguished from the common people. These men tended to dominate public life. They regularly controlled the administration of local churches and chapels. They often served as administrators to religious and secular landlords with interests in the district. They often contracted for highly profitable tax farms in areas distant from the urban centre.[21] Rural communes closer to vibrant urban centres like Milan, Lucca, or Perugia had a very different make-up. By the end of the twelfth century, these elites had largely been drawn into the city and urban influence was clear at all levels of the rural communities.[22] None the less even in areas where the old rural elites had become urbanized landlords, the rural communities retained a sense of community and of communal interests. The local church was a key to the formation and the continuation of this sense of community identity. As we noted previously, communes tended to emerge at the end of the eleventh century and the beginning of the twelfth century. In most cases the boundaries of the rural communes were identical with the parish boundaries of the local church. On the plain of Lucca, for example, it has been argued that nearly every church listed in a papal tax of the early fourteenth century had become a rural commune by the end of the twelfth.[23]

Villagers tended to gather in the precincts of a local church and identify themselves and their properties by their association with the church. Participation in the affairs of the local church quickly became a matter of right. *Operari* of a church or chapel often negotiated with

---

[21] Duane J. Osheim, *An Italian Lordship: The Bishopric of Lucca in the Late Middle Ages* (Berkeley, 1977), pp. 40–1; similarly at Origgio, near Milan, Romeo, *Origgio*, pp. 32–3.

[22] Wickham, *Community and Clientele*, pp. 172–6, for his summary observations; Romeo, *Origgio*, p. 4, makes a similar point.

[23] Wickham, *Community and Clientele*, p. 68.

the bishop or parish clergy or elites who might claim patronage over a church. In some cases villagers wanted to ensure that certain religious feasts were observed. In others, they successfully claimed the right to participate in the selection of parish clergy. Villagers could act forcefully if they felt aggrieved. They took their complaints to the bishop; they even locked out clerics who they felt were unacceptable. Parishioners were especially interested in maintaining the cycle of feasts, particularly of local patrons. This included participation in *luminaria*, or candlelight processions, blessing of holy water for the baptismal font, and charitable donations for the local poor. These are all part of traditional medieval piety, but in the villages they could take on a particularly communal feeling.[24] In villages in the lower Arno valley, for example, each family was expected to bring water for the baptismal font at the beginning of Holy Week.

Rites surrounding death and burial show most clearly the connection between church, commune, and community. By the twelfth century parish boundaries clearly noted who belonged and who did not. In one infamous case near Lucca, the body of a stranger who died along a contested boundary was stolen, buried, and then reburied in a long fight to enforce parish, and communal, rights. For the rector of the local church, boundaries were about preserving burial dues and fees for memorial services. For the community it was much more. Rural communities, much like religious brotherhoods, looked out for their members' needs, and at no time more than at death. In some rural communities, residents, male and female, were expected to attend the sick and remain with the dead until burial. The stable rural communes offered more than just religious consolation. In many cases the residents leased land from each other, borrowed implements, stored crops, and co-operated to harvest and transport food-stuffs and lumber to local and regional markets. In the late thirteenth century it was not uncommon for peasants near Lucca to be making numerous rent payments. Most often these were for typical leases of land, but others clearly reflect loans and investments by one villager to another. In the rural commune of Santa Margarita, some 15 per

---

[24] The following section is based on Duane J. Osheim, 'The Country Parish at Late Medieval Lucca', in Paula Findlen, Michelle Fontaine, and Duane J. Osheim (eds.), *Beyond Florence: The Contours of Medieval and Early Modern Italy* (Stanford, Calif., 2003), esp. pp. 66–71.

cent of the farmers were both making and collecting payments for such small loans. The effect was that, so long as the system was not disrupted by political upheavals or economic decline, villages were tightly knitted together in a web of dependence. In healthy rural communes, tenants often put up a common front against outsiders whose claims were thought to be unjust. During the fourteenth century there were numerous complaints from merchants and speculators at Lucca who had to deal with dangerously independent rural residents.[25] Residents of the commune of Origgio, near Milan, burned 135 trees belonging to the monastery of Sant'Ambrogio when they felt that their just claims were being ignored.[26]

Communal equality and solidarity were easily destroyed. War, epidemic, and population movements in the fourteenth century destroyed much of the cohesion on the plain of Lucca. In fact many of the shattered small communes were consolidated and separated from their local churches. In the second half of the fourteenth century, communal solidarity was less widespread than it had been previously.[27] Communal feeling was also threatened by the steady impoverishment of residents with little or no land. They were the residents most dependent on the village's common lands. Waste lands, or lands held communally, were an essential part of community structure in the Middle Ages. In the eleventh century, especially in the Po valley, villagers preferred to live along water courses. There they could hunt, fish, and raise swine in addition to cultivating grains in the small fields in the region. Landlords, like the great Benedictine abbey of San Benedetto Polirone, often required tenants to provide fish from common waters as well as grain from specific fields. In other parts of Italy as well, common woodlands were an essential part of the village economy.[28] By the thirteenth century there had been significant changes. Common lands were largely replaced by grain fields in the countryside close to the cities. Even where lands were still held in

[25] Duane J. Osheim, 'Countrymen and the Law in Late Medieval Tuscany', *Speculum*, 64 (1989), pp. 317–38.

[26] Romeo, *Origgio*, pp. 65–7.

[27] Franca Leverotti, *Popolazione, famiglie, insediamento: le Sei Miglia lucchesi nel XIV e XV secolo* (Pisa, 1992), pp. 190–7; and Osheim, 'Countrymen' pp. 335–8.

[28] Vito Fumagalli, 'Il paesaggio si trasforma: colonizzazione e bonifica durante il medioevo. L'esempio emiliano', in Bruno Andreolli (ed.), *Le campagne italiane prima e dopo il Mille* (Bologna, 1985), pp. 98–105.

common, they were often leased and tilled. Further from the cities, villagers who were emigrating often sold their rights to common fields to merchant speculators. Poor immigrants often arrived in these villages and discovered they had no right to put animals on the common or to gather wood or nuts. The net effect was that, by the fourteenth century, the disappearance of the common lands exacerbated the distinctions between rich and poor in the rural communes. Lacking common resources, poor peasants were increasingly dependent on urban landlords for farmland and the small consumption loans that were essential to the rural poor. The structure of the village was an essential variable in the structure of the rural economy.

The rural economy

The profound changes that transformed the Italian rural economy in the later Middle Ages are often credited to the impact of urban growth and the obvious influence of urban landlords. By the late thirteenth century most urban merchants and even many artisans also owned land in the countryside. In the eyes of Philip Jones, for example, the consolidation of estates, the introduction of commercial crops, and short-term leases were all the work of urban speculators.[29] Italian cities played a role, but this was not simply due to the material and organizational skills of the urban merchant. We can perhaps better understand the influence of the city if we discuss the roles of landlords and the changes in crops, and finally discuss the crisis in the rural economy at the end of the Middle Ages.

When we look at how agricultural lands were organized, it is clear that the influence of urban speculators was more muted than is commonly assumed.[30] And regional differences may be more important than general trends. In northern Italy, much of the land was organized in large estates founded by major Benedictine or Cistercian religious houses. The grange founded by the abbey of Staffarda in

[29] Philip Jones, *The Italian City-State: From Commune to Signoria* (Oxford, 1997), pp. 285–7.
[30] Elisa Occhipinti, *Il contado milanese nel secolo XIII: l'amministrazione della proprietà fondiaria del Monastero Maggiore* (Bologna, 1982), pp. 182–5; Osheim, *An Italian Lordship*, pp. 107–13.

Piedmont is an interesting example. After its initial creation in 1138, the monks worked to consolidate a series of compact estates farmed by a combination of religious brothers and wage labourers. For perhaps a century after the initial foundation of the house, the monks bought, sold, and traded lands to create compact estates. Much of the land, both fallow ploughland and meadow, was used as winter grazing for flocks of sheep that spent the summer along the coast or in the Alps.[31]

The construction of the grange of Valera, a possession of the great Cistercian house of Chiaravalle near Milan, shows how religious houses transformed rural life.[32] After an initial acquisition of land in Valera in the mid-twelfth century, the monks received donations, bought, and eventually traded tracts of land until they had created a vast estate that in the late Middle Ages probably measured over 750 hectares (or about 1,650 acres). Much of the land at Valera was recently cleared and drained. The rest was a mix of pasture and woodland. Some of the lands were worked by day labourers and lay brothers of the monastery, but for the most part lay brothers merely managed the monastery's mills, dairies, and flocks. The monks tended to lease these lands to peasants on short-term oral leases claiming in return one-third of the produce from the lands. The monks preferred oral contracts because they could be voided quickly if necessary; and the monks could and did change the terms when necessary.

The monks of Chiaravalle must have been efficient managers because their estates continued to expand in the thirteenth century. When the monks did end their direct supervision of Valera, it was for political rather than economic reasons. In 1255–6, in response to destruction brought on by the communal army of Pavia, the monks abandoned direct supervision of the grange and reorganized their lands in a series of group leases. Tenants were offered compact farmsteads on fifteen-year leases and for a rent of one-third of their crops which they agreed to carry either to a nearby grange or to the more distant monastery in the suburbs of Milan.

---

[31] Francesco Panero, 'Le grange e la gestione del patrimonio fondiario dell'abbazia di Staffarda (secoli XII–XIV)', in Rinaldo Comba and Francesco Panero (eds.), *Aziende agrarie nel medioevo: forme della conduzione fondiaria nell'Italia nord-occidentale, secoli 9–15* (Cuneo, 2000), pp. 156–65.

[32] Luisa Chiappa Mauri, 'La costruzione del paesaggio agrario padano: la grangia di Valera', *Studi Storici*, 26 (1985), pp. 263–313.

Group leases, which often included jurisdictional claims by the landlords, could be found in other parts of Italy. The best known and most dramatic were probably the leases used by the abbey of San Benedetto Polirone near Mantua. The powers of ecclesiastical land-lords were and remained extensive. On the lands of San Benedetto, tenants were not allowed to appeal to communal courts or sell lands to outsiders. Women even needed the permission of the abbot to marry outside the village.[33] Even in cases where religious houses even-tually leased out their granges, the organization does not seem to have changed very dramatically. In Mantua, peasant complaints about the monks of San Benedetto continued into the sixteenth cen-tury. Further to the south, especially in Tuscany, extensive granges were uncommon by the thirteenth century. In central Italy even churchmen were more likely to lease lands to tenants on traditional perpetual or multigenerational leases. The well-documented estates of the cathedral canons of San Martino in Lucca were almost entirely leased to individuals by the late twelfth century. Ecclesiastical estates in the Florentine countryside were directly farmed for a longer time, but in the thirteenth century they too were divided and leased to individuals.[34]

Although direct farming was unusual in north-central Italy, mon-asteries, canonries, and bishoprics in Tuscany also concentrated their holdings through gift, exchange, or purchase. Further, ecclesiastical landlords tended to make small consumption loans or purchase rent increases when their tenants needed funds to buy animals, seed, or food. One peasant near Lucca explained to his landlord that he needed the money, 'for the glory of God and the marriage of my daughter Agnese'.[35] It was through such simple loans that a landlord could expand influence, defuse village crises, and eventually extend ownership over lands.

In the thirteenth and fourteenth centuries, both ecclesiastical and lay landlords increasingly described their lands as compact, unified

[33] Rosolino Bellodi, *Il monastero di San Benedetto in Polirone nella storia e nell'arte* (San Benedetto Po, 1974; repr. from Mantua, 1905), pp. 43–7.

[34] On estates in Tuscany see generally, Philip Jones, 'An Italian Estate, 900–1200', *Economic History Review*, 2nd ser., 7 (1955), pp. 18–32; id., 'From Manor to Mezzadria: A Tuscan Case-Study in the Medieval Origins of Modern Agrarian Soceity', in Nicolai Rubinstein (ed.), *Florentine Studies: Politics and Society in Renaissance Florence* (London, 1968), pp. 193–241.

[35] Osheim, *An Italian Lordship*, p. 103.

farms complete with house, threshing floor, and stalls for animals as well as all the lands necessary for an individual farmer. If a single landlord could control all the land a particular peasant held, and if he was the only sure source of small loans and emergency aid, tenants had little leverage when negotiating over leases. In late thirteenth- and fourteenth-century Italy the position of peasant farmers became increasingly perilous. Peasants had often lived at the margin, depending on what they could hunt or gather on common lands and on the little they could earn as wage labourers to supplement what they harvested in their fields. As ecclesiastical and lay landlords concentrated their lands in compact estates, they laid claim to most and eventually all of the common lands. As one peasant in Piedmont complained about the Cistercians when they began constructing a new grange, 'they will cut down the trees and the hunting grounds for pigs, wild boar and deer will be lost'.[36] The loss of rights to common lands was exacerbated in many parts of Italy by the declining size of peasant holdings. Because of population pressures, peasants tended to divide their lands among all their children, or at least those who did not emigrate to the cities. In parts of the Romagna, peasant holdings at the end of the thirteenth century might have been only one-third of their size in the previous century.[37]

Difficult economic conditions for peasants created opportunities for merchant speculators. Hard-pressed countrymen often were forced to sell anticipated harvests to urban merchants extending even further the cycle of debt in which they were caught. Other landlords and speculators dominated villages simply because they were the only people with any money to spare. Although they did it more efficiently and ruthlessly, urban speculators were following a strategy of reorganization begun by ecclesiastical landlords a century before.[38] It was not the urban landlord who transformed late medieval Italian

[36] Paolo Grillo, 'La Mansio Aymondini: creazione e gestione di una grangia cistercense nel saluzzese fra XII e XIV secolo', in Comba and Panero (eds.), *Aziende agrarie*, p. 173.
[37] Vito Fumagalli, 'L'evoluzione dell'economia agraria e dei patti colonici dall'alto al basso medioevo', in Andreolli (ed.), *Le campagne italiane*, p. 30; Menant, *Campagnes lombardes*, p. 311.
[38] Charles de la Roncière, *Un changeur florentin du trecento: Lippo di Fede del Sega (1285 env.–1363 env.)* (Paris, 1973); Sante Polica, 'An attempted "Reconversion" of wealth in XVth century Lucca: the lands of Michele di Giovanni Guinigi', *Journal of European Economic History*, 9 (1980), pp. 655–707.

rural life. It was rather the urban market. Rental contracts make clear the overwhelming interest of landlords in rents paid in wheat or other bread grains. But they obscure the nature of the Italian farm, and how a farmer's activities were affected by urban markets.

Distance from urban markets seems to have been a key variable. In the twelfth century and even later in areas at some distance from population centres, peasants raised a variety of crops and animals. The major innovation was the planting of chestnut groves, especially in the hills and lower areas of the mountains. Chestnuts remained an important source of food for peasants throughout the Middle Ages. They were eaten dried, boiled, or ground up into polenta. By the thirteenth century, there were varieties prized for the sweet taste of their dried fruit. In addition to wood for building and the construction of tools, chestnuts provided kindling and charcoal for household and foundries. Rental contracts in many parts of central and northern Italy often required regular plantings of chestnut trees to ensure food as well as wood. Grain crops and hardwoods may have been of primary interest to landlords, but the chestnut was essential for the peasantry.[39]

Countrymen preferred diversity as a way to ensure that the household always had enough. In addition to wood, nuts, fish, and small game from common lands, peasants liked to mix crops in their fields. They tended to mix fruit trees and vines, often even using trees instead of pergolas to support new vines. These were often planted along the edge of a field, or sometimes in wide rows leaving space between in which grains, legumes, and garden crops could be planted. Even grain fields often were planted in a mix of wheat and less prized grains, ensuring that whatever the conditions there would be a crop. None the less, throughout the late Middle Ages, landlords tended to convert more and more of their rents to wheat, the grain most prized in urban markets. Even in areas where barley or rye were more productive, landlords wanted wheat. The *martilogio* of the bishopric of Lucca from the mid-fourteenth century underlines the predominance

---

[39] Pietro Piussi and Odile Redon, 'Storia agraria e storia di selvicoltura', in Alfio Cortonesi and Massimo Montanari (eds.), *Medievistica italiana e storia agraria: risultati e prospettive di una stagione storiografica: Atti del Convegno di Montalcino, 12–14 Dicembre 1997* (Bologna, 2001), pp. 197–9. Renzo Zagnoni, 'La coltivazione del castagno nella montagna fra Bologna e Pistoia nei secoli XI–XIII', in Giuliano Pinto (ed.), *Villaggi, boschi e campi dell'Appennino* (Pistoia, 1997), pp. 41–57.

of wheat, especially on episcopal lands close to the city.[40] Demand for wheat was always strong and it remained a profitable commodity for merchants and speculators.

Wine and oil should have been equally important, but because of transport costs neither product was as profitable as we might have expected. Olives were cultivated throughout Italy, even in areas were olive trees were relatively unproductive. Churches required oil for liturgical purposes and to light the church's countless lamps. Even olive branches were prized since it was believed that burning a blessed olive branch could prevent hail.[41] But because of the length of time necessary to bring olive trees into production, the difficulty of transporting large quantities of oil, and the ready availability of animal fats for cooking, plots of olive trees in most parts of Italy tended to be small, perhaps ten or so trees, and located near churches. The largest groves were found in Liguria and north-west Tuscany, then as now famed for its oil.

There was no substitute for wine. It has been estimated that in fifteenth-century Bologna the average individual consumed 200 litres of wine annually. Consumption in fourteenth-century Lucca may, if anything, have been even greater. The wine was generally young, of a modest alcohol level, and easily spoiled. Again, most specialized vineyards were found in the immediate suburbs of Italy's towns. Thirteenth-century Bologna, for example, probably produced 98 per cent of the wine consumed there. Vineyards, even producing high quality wines, were not necessarily profitable if they were at some distance from a sure market. The Romagnol wines of Imola were highly prized, but only so long as they could be transported by barge. When political changes closed river access to Venetian and Lombard markets, production withered.[42]

---

[40] Pietro Guidi and Eugenio Pellegrinetti (eds.), *Inventari del vescovato, della cattedrale e di altre chiese di Lucca*, Studi e Testi, 34 (Rome, 1921), no. XIV.

[41] Antonio Ivan Pini, *Vite e vino nel medioevo* (Bologna, 1989), p. 41 n. 37.

[42] Antonio Ivan Pini, 'Il medioevo nel bicchiere', *Quaderni Medievali*, 29 (1990), pp. 26–8.

Conclusion

By the fourteenth century rural Italy had been profoundly transformed. Vast tracts had been cleared and drained. Villages and fortified towns had been strategically placed to tie towns and countryside together into strong administrative units. But perhaps most importantly, urban markets and commercial crops had changed the nature of farming. The growing demand for grain, meat, and garden crops as well as wood for construction and for kindling, led ecclesiastical institutions, merchant speculators, and small landowners alike to clear vast tracts of land. This had a serious impact on rural villagers who had depended on common lands and woods and marshes for game, nuts, and other wild plants to supplement their grain-based diets. The net effect was a further impoverishment of the poorest members of the rural communities.

Clearance also had an impact on the rural environment. By the late thirteenth century in many parts of central and northern Italy, urban governments were concerned about deforestation. Many required new planting of trees, or promoted leaving tree trunks *azucati*, that is as a large stump from which quick growing suckers could later be harvested. By the end of the Middle Ages, draining marshes, clearing wastes to create new grain fields, and clear-cutting hillsides to provide timber and kindling profoundly changed the rural landscape. Flooding was a greater danger in parts of Lombardy, Romagna, and Tuscany than it had been previously.[43] By the end of the Middle Ages, the Italian countryside was tied closely to the urban world. But this integration exacted a high price from countrymen and the rural environment alike.

[43] On environmental changes, see Fumagalli, 'Il paesaggio si trasforma', pp. 108–9.

8

The family

Steven Epstein

During the period 1100–1350 'Italy' remained largely a geographical expression, but the peninsula and the islands of Sicily and Sardinia form a cohesive yet also diverse unit of study. 'The family' did not exist; instead, there were millions of individual families for which the sources are few and difficult to interpret. Some historians have preferred to discuss households, those living under one roof and not necessarily kin. Households are easier to define (and tax) than families, but both social categories can serve to illuminate the changes in Italian domestic history during the central Middle Ages. There is no particular logic to this period from the vantage point of social history. Only at the end, with the devastating outbreak of bubonic plague in 1347 in the south of Italy, do we have a conclusion to one particular story: the dramatic rise of population in medieval Italy and its sudden collapse. Italian families existed long before 1100, but it is possible to set a starting-point around that time because the sources become much more abundant in the twelfth century.

It is useful to begin with some parameters for the search for the distinctive features of Italian families during the period from 1100 to 1350. The rich variety of historical experience in the peninsula and islands must be kept in mind. In the Mezzogiorno, Muslim and Byzantine rule no longer existed, but Islamic and Greek Orthodox teachings on the family remained important in Sicily and Calabria respectively for most of this period. The North–South issue in Italian social history remains the most salient, but other strong divisions also affected family history. Northern Italy was in the process of becoming one of the most urbanized areas of Europe, but even there the contrasts between city and rural life had a profound impact on family life. Throughout the peninsula and the islands the legacy of ancient

Rome endured, particularly in its rich family law. By 1100 much of this law was irrelevant, or superseded in some places by later sets of rules like the important Lombard laws. Yet even later codes of law continued to respect what had become the common law of the region, a vulgarized but still vibrant legal tradition in Latin (and in Greek in parts of the south). Finally, most social historians have come to accept, with some reservations, that there was a durable concept called 'Mediterranean honour' and that Italy remained one of the places where it was most strong. Honour, and its companion shame, were always deeply embedded in family values and particularly in the ways that male members of a family treated 'their' women. This code of honour was not confined to the families of noble warriors, but was spread throughout society. This theme reminds us that class also shaped family life, but that a sense of honour was common to all Italian peoples. Honour is a finite resource, like many others in the often harsh Italian patriarchal environment. Struggles over honour in the family, as well as in the relations among families, help to illuminate the fates of the men, women, and children who remain the real subjects here.

General themes

It is necessary to begin with those features of family life that were common to communities across Europe. These features, that tie Italian experience to wider social realities, need to be kept in mind in any reading of the distinctive aspects of Italian families. Muslim families in Italy virtually disappeared over the course of this period, and Jewish ones, with their own traditions, clung on to a precarious position, mainly in the Mezzogiorno. First, the teachings of the Roman Catholic Church on the family, and its rules embodied in canon law, were the same for every believer across Europe. Italians, in the persons of important popes such as Innocent III (Lotario de' Segni from Rome) and Innocent IV (Sinibaldo Fieschi of Genoa) and theologians such as St Thomas Aquinas (from Aquino in the Mezzogiorno) had major roles in defining these rules, so Italian experiences and practices remained a vital part of the general teachings of the Church. The Church taught, among other things, that consent made a marriage, that divorce was wrong and monogamy the rule, that incest was a sin, and that marriage was prohibited among close kin. The question of consent raised the problem of the age at which people were deemed capable of becoming engaged as well as forming a family. The Lateran Council of 1215 changed the prohibited degrees of kinship from seven to four, in practice making it a little easier to marry distant cousins. But exogamy remained the general rule, and this ran up against endogamy—family desires to buttress kin ties and conserve wealth by fostering marriages among blood relatives.

Marriage was, however, receiving recognition as a sacrament, and even though marriages were not yet regularly performed in churches, the Church retained a powerful grip on the rules of marriage. The first clear evidence for the giving of a ring at marriage ceremonies comes from thirteenth-century Italy. Another sacrament, baptism, conferred membership in the family of believers. Godparenthood created a spiritual family that the Church intended to supplement the ties of blood. Bonds to godmothers, godfathers, and godchildren remained important in Italian culture. In Florence with its common baptistery, baptism records (black beans for boys and white ones for girls) provided in the early fourteenth century, according to the chronicler Giovanni Villani, the first demographic evidence on births (between 5,500 and 6,000 baptisms a year) and sex ratios in any European city. Villani's finding that slightly more males than females were baptized has raised questions about the missing girls, and explanations have run from prenatal deaths to infanticide. Finally, the Holy Family itself, Mary, Joseph, and the infant Jesus, remained a complex and interesting model for family life across Europe. Yet there is no doubt that this family remained an especially powerful image in Italy. Francis of Assisi was after all the first to assemble the Christmas crèche, an image with the strongest possible lessons for family life. The people of Loreto, near Ancona, believed that the Virgin's own house in Nazareth had been miraculously transported in 1294 to the non-Muslim environment of their own city. The Church defined the moral aspects of family life, and those definitions had a strong Italian context.

A second general theme concerns the age of husband and wife at first marriage, and the broader differences between the so-called Mediterranean and European models of marriage. In Italy the Mediterranean pattern reveals itself in the relatively young age of women at first marriage; according to the saints' lives of the period, St Umiliana of Florence married at 16, and St Clare of Pisa married at 12. What little evidence survives from the twelfth century suggests that women's age at first marriage was falling, with a floor set at the canonical age of 12. Less information exists about the ages of men, but the few hints we have suggest that non-aristocratic men seldom married before the age of 20, and were often years older. The developing form of the Italian urban family over the course of the thirteenth and early fourteenth centuries seems to fit the pattern of a growing gap between the ages of men and women. This marital strategy was of course one way to control overall marital fertility, since many of these young wives were destined for long periods of widowhood. (The European marriage model affected fertility by delaying marriage for both partners.) Another complicating factor concerning women's age at marriage was the dowry, which loomed large in Italian family life. Even the poorest women required a dowry to attract a spouse, and it became a relatively common charity for the rich to leave money to dower poor women. A consequence of this marriage market and dowry practice was to push down the age of first marriage for young women, because the dowry varied by age, and it became increasingly costly to marry off older women. This system also pushed many women into lifelong celibacy, inside or outside a convent or brothel.

A final general theme concerns the family as an economic unit. Family size and opportunities for its members naturally depended on wealth. In turn, families with few or no children forced spouses to plan for old age without the support of the next generation. Children were, in Italy as elsewhere, an investment that could guarantee the survival of both noble lineages and family workshops. Notices of legal adoptions became increasingly widespread in medieval Italy as some families raised, 'for the love of God', children whose parents were unwilling or unable to support them. Differences between rich, middle, and poor households became increasingly important. Both in the *contado* and in the growing cities, the households were also units of production. Much of agriculture and artisanal manufacture remained based on family farms and workshops. The extended family, including kin as well as journeymen and women, apprentices, hired labourers, and occasional slaves, was a moral as well as economic unit.

These broad influences on the Italian family prepare the way for a closer look at particular themes in the period from 1100 to 1350. The aims here are to show changes over time and to give some sense of regional variations. The traditional teaching on the family held that its purposes were to bring legitimate children into the world, to provide companionship for husband and wife, and to help the partners avoid vice. These three goals provide an additional framework for investigating the Italian family.

Wives, husbands, and children

One purpose of the family was to produce legitimate children who inherited the family's wealth, enabling the family to continue to exist over time even as its specific members crossed over to the next world. Inevitably, the concept of the family itself defined some children as illegitimate, and in practice these offspring had a poor chance of fully sharing in the family's wealth. The last will and testament captures this generational picture of family life as the testator divided his or her wealth among the heirs, almost always the children, when they survived. A will is a portrait of family life existing in one moment of time as the testator contemplated death and his or her desire to reach beyond the grave and continue to affect family life.

A large, unique number of wills survive from Genoa for the period 1150 to 1250 and provide a detailed glimpse of noble, *Popolo*, and even rather poor families. Statistics based on this small sample are perilous, but the information, used cautiously, provides a glimpse of the realities of family life not always apparent in the legal sources. The main issue in a will was how to divide up an estate. Genoese wills reveal 1.87 children per family for the entire sample, and 2.5 children per couple with children. At Palermo from 1298 to 1309 there were 1.9 children living at the time of a married person's will. These figures suggest that many couples were childless, and that families were small, especially since the wills provide evidence for high levels of infant and child mortality. In the countryside there may have been more children with better chances of survival, but the evidence is very thin on rural families. One-third of Genoese families had only one child. This narrow pool of potential heirs demonstrates that the medieval Italian family, in household form those living under one roof, resembled the typical nuclear family. These wills also suggest that grandparents were relatively rare, especially grandfathers, so the households were almost always two generational. Large and increasing numbers of domestic servants (and in cities like Genoa or Palermo slaves) populated the households of the wealthy, and although these people were not potential heirs, they often received legacies and were part of the emotional life of the family.

In Palermo 17 per cent of the testators before 1350 were not married, and this figure reminds us that not everyone attempted or perhaps wanted to establish a conventional nuclear family. These single people, often young, almost always named a surviving parent as the main heir. The Genoese wills indicate that testators, male and female alike, usually divided their estates evenly between sons and daughters. Married daughters might have received their portion upon marriage, but the collective choices, not dictated by law or religion, suggest a social consensus that the children should share alike, regardless of gender. Given the small size of most Genoese families, and the substantial number that included only one or more daughters, it should not be surprising that even in a patrilineal society blood ties, even to women, still trumped patriarchy when it came to inheriting family wealth. The testators were also scrupulous about remembering their deceased children by endowing masses for them or in a few cases securing the rights of grandchildren. Wills are often dry documents, but the Genoese wills provide much evidence of strong, emotional attachments within the family, in this world and the next. Wealthy families, like the Doria, were already establishing family tombs and monuments that are further testimony to family solidarity and a strong sense of lineage.

Wills from Genoa and other cities also show that male testators were concerned about the remarriage of their wives, who were often younger and probably longer lived. On Sardinia both men and women married late, with both low birth and high death rates. In late medieval Palermo nearly 40 per cent of the women making wills were widows. The men seemed to have hoped that their widows would remain 'good wives without husbands', and they often included many financial incentives for their wives to avoid remarriage and stay with the deceased's children. Remarriage was not illegal, but it was frowned upon because of the complications it could cause for the family's wealth. A man's fear seems to have been that his own children would be slighted if his wife went on to have another family. A man's kin were naturally concerned that the family's wealth might easily be diverted to these 'strangers'. The story of 'La Cenerentola' (in English 'Cinderella') was old and deeply embedded in Italian culture, and while in this case the fate of the stepdaughter was a happy one, it was not always this way. In addition to literally bribing his wife to remain unmarried, a man could protect his children by appointing guardians among his own kin to administer their property (along with his wife) and in general to look after their interests. For both parents, the issues surrounding the guardians were important, for there were also many tales about faithless protectors who robbed their charges. Testators saw siblings, godparents, or even better older brothers if they existed, as ideal guardians or in legal terms tutors. The wills, wherever they survive, reveal the familial aspirations to protect and nurture the next generation, and to conserve family wealth. The deserving poor, the proverbial widows and orphans, also received charitable bequests administered by the Church. The concern for those whose families had somehow failed them reveals deep-seated fears about the possible fragility of family life. Companionship in marriage did not require medieval Italian husbands and wives to be the same age; rather, it remained the antidote to the loneliness of the widowed, and the plight of the neglected orphan.

The career of St Francis, hardly a typical adolescent, nevertheless serves as a reminder that possessing or inheriting wealth was not the only issue in family life. Renouncing riches was a path few chose. To live the life of a saint also meant the renunciation of ordinary family life. In these centuries Italian regions produced increasing numbers of saints who came from the ranks of ordinary city and country folk. Yet even the lives of the Italian saints are filled with examples of concern for children, from Angela of Foligno's embracing of the infant Jesus to St Catherine of Siena's care for her own numerous siblings and then her extended family of followers. The combined weight of the evidence from wills, hagiography, and other sources has proved beyond doubt that medieval Italians made high levels of emotional as well as economic investment in their children. High levels of childhood mortality (in some unhealthy places such as Sardinia as high as 50 per cent before the age of 10) may have produced much experience of grief, but it did not come close to extinguishing love for children. Childhood may not have lasted long, in terms of idleness, in a society that put so many boys and girls to work as apprentices or on the farm in their early teens. Yet even here, the terms of apprenticeship contracts, which obliged the master to exercise quasi-parental care over his or her apprentices, again testify to high levels of concern about how children were treated. No doubt harsh parents and employers existed, and at times the family, the workshop, or the farm was a place of sorrow as well as a refuge for children. But childhood remained a distinct and valued stage of human life in medieval Italian society filling the space between the speechless time of infancy and the assumption of responsibilities during adolescence.

The role of government

Stronger urban governments in the north, and royal legislation for the Norman, then Hohenstaufen, and then Angevin and Aragonese kingdoms in the Mezzogiorno, were able and eager to legislate on family matters. Seldom did family law enrich the coffers of states; rather, the intention here was in some instances to affect the property aspects of marriage, and in others to impose morality. For example, governments, both monarchic and communal, regulated, and even taxed, prostitution, but did not make it illegal. Avoiding even worse vices was the ostensible reason for this general leniency, but such laws also reflected the pervasive double standard so durable in Italian culture. Such rule-making reveals the aspirations of those, invariably men, with the power to make the rules.

An early example occurred in the commune of Genoa, where in 1143 the consuls ruled that women were no longer entitled to one-third of their late husbands' estate, and that their marriage gifts should no longer exceed £100. The famous *tercia*, whose loss prompted an illustration in the Genoese official chronicle showing women in mourning over it, was an old tradition. Its abolition meant that the husband's heirs, presumably his children, would receive a larger share of his goods. Older Lombard law had guaranteed wives a quarter of their husband's estate, and Milanese law in 1216 referred to this as the 'hated quarter', an obvious target for abolition. It is possible to interpret these changes as early signs that the males who made the rules were consciously trying to keep family wealth in their own patrilineages. What is new is the use of a relatively recent institution, the commune, to regulate a detail of family life. The other part of this new rule concerns the marriage gift, or counter-dowry, the smaller donation that the husband made to his wife in return for the larger dowry. Again, the men making the rules did not limit the dowry they received, but the amount of wealth that would be the personal property, if not under their direct control, of their wives. Enforcing these provisions depended on written, public records of marriage settlements, and the notarial records are replete with such contracts. Marriage was becoming a civil institution as well as a sacrament, and this development left governments free to impose regulations in the name of the common, male good.

The dowry, a property matter, was the most obvious point at which the makers of local laws could shape the realities of family life. Florentine statutes set the marriage gift at £100 in 1253, and in this period and beyond never adjusted the figure, even as dowries spiralled upward. The statutes of Pistoia in 1296 set the minimum age of marriage for girls at 12, another sign that the dowry itself was affecting the age of marriage for women. Here, too, a commune was legislating on a matter determined in canon law, but not to the satisfaction of the Pistoiese. As Italian families became increasingly patrilineal, the dowry became the daughter's major and in some cases only share of family wealth. Her family retained an interest in this wealth, especially if the marriage were childless. In turn, it became common for women to help pay for their own daughter's dowry from these funds.

In the kingdom of Sicily rulers revealed self-interest by legislating on family life as it affected marriage between nobles and the inheritance of fiefs. The great collection of southern law, the Constitutions of Melfi promulgated by Frederick II in 1231, demanded that marriages, especially for nobles, be public, and that the king's vassals obtain his licence to marry. The services due to the crown from vassals holding fiefs gave it a legitimate interest in the marriage strategies of the nobility. Frederick III (1296–1337), Aragonese king of Sicily, had a strong desire to foster moral reform among his subjects. His General Ordinances (of about 1310) imposed very detailed rules for all marriage ceremonies, with the intention of regulating the bride's dress, the celebrations, even the number of guests. The same laws required modesty in clothing for all women. Frederick's purpose seems to have been to reduce ostentatious display and expense in order to foster modesty and presumably reduce family rivalries. To use the law in this sophisticated way showed that the monarch had the power to intrude into formerly private family matters. Frederick III prohibited women from mourning in public, allowed them to wear distinctive black dress only for their husbands, and imposed serious fines to enforce his edicts. A time of crisis and high levels of mortality may have motivated the king to restrict traditional behaviour, but here too women bore the brunt of the law's rigour. Even a well-intentioned paternalist like Frederick III must have noted that he denied women the right to mourn their own children in public. The power to dictate or prohibit behaviour was not limited to monarchs, and urban authorities in the north also issued sumptuary legislation on the same moralistic grounds.

Finally, another legally recognized entity begins to emerge in the records after 1000 and to become even more important in later centuries. The *consorteria* was a descent group of males who continued to hold property and rights in common, usually derived from some common ancestor through inheritance. The tension here was between the importance of the nuclear family and the powerful pull of male lineage and of property too complex or valuable to divide. The *consorteria* of the Corbolani family in Lucca in 1287 actually had a formal set of rules and even family officials. In Genoa a parallel institution, called the *albergo*, appeared in the late thirteenth century; it was basically a noble clan. These broad kinship groups, based on agnatic ties, acted as factions and played an important part in various Genoese governments and show the tensions between narrow and wider concepts of kinship. Clans active in government and feuds demonstrate that they developed a strong political role passing down power and grievances from one generation to the next.

Names

One of the most important developments over these centuries was the rise of an obvious but momentous way to distinguish families. They began to be given names. Family names were still relatively rare in 1100 and many noble lineages were known by the first name of a common ancestor or a toponym, a name derived from a place they owned, or where they lived. But even at this early date in cities such as Venice some family names like Giustiniani, Contarini, and Gradenigo had already emerged and, as the *longhi* (old names), they would continue to dominate the city for centuries. By 1350 the habit of having a family name was more universal but remained uncommon in many rural areas, and especially in the interior of Sicily and Sardinia. Naming a thing, as St Thomas Aquinas observed, conferred a power over it, and the idea that a family needed naming suggests that its members were becoming more aware of its meaning and identity.

The earliest family names derived from a wide array of associations, but a common type of surname in Italy was the patronym, derived from the father's name—for example 'Piero di Giovanni'. This type of identification could gradually lead to a family called 'di Giovanni'. Toponyms, occupations, and nicknames all lent themselves as possible surnames—everywhere the squinters became the Guercio family. For the great *consorterie*, like the Colonna and Orsini of Rome or the Fieschi and Doria of Genoa, a surname gradually spread to different nuclear families that still felt a strong bond to the common lineage. Matronyms were extremely rare, another sign of the growing importance of the male line after 1100. Especially in the urban environment with its increasing reliance on the written word, surnames became more necessary for the middle and upper classes. The *Popolo minuto*, in the city and the countryside, with less official business to conduct, were the last to adopt surnames, and many around 1350 remained without them.

One change in Christian or first names deserves mention here, and that is the increasing reliance in this period on the names of prominent saints for children. As older Lombard and other forms of first names disappeared, Italian first names for men were derived from a smaller pool of familiar names, with the new 'Francesco' adding to the list. David Herlihy dated this contraction to the years between 1280 and 1320. Two trends would reinforce this pattern over time. First, some Italians had the habit of alternating names in the male line, with a boy sharing the name of his, usually paternal, grandfather. This conservatism in naming would over time produce a greater similarity of names. Secondly, the growing tradition of naming some children for a saint's day, with an eye towards attracting a spiritual patron for the child, would also diminish the pool of names. But some local saints, like Giovanni Battista in Florence or Gennaro in

Naples, produced far more names than the number of children actually born on their feast days. First names for women followed the same pattern, but this pool of names remained for some reason richer and more various. Yet common names for women, like Maria, Maddalena, Lucia, and Caterina, shared by slaves as well as free women, were also intended to teach lessons about proper, subservient behaviour as women were expected to emulate the behaviour of their namesake. Parents none the less exercised more imagination when it came to naming daughters, and perhaps it was the mothers who decided to give their daughters a bit more individuality. After all, the daughters would mostly lose their own family name upon marriage. The most likely explanation for these changes in the naming of children is that lay piety was becoming deeper over these centuries as parents sought spiritual protection for their children by associating them with powerful heavenly patrons and good role models such as Giorgio, Michele, Giovanni, Maria, and all the rest of the angelic host.

Stories of family life

The period before 1350 lacks the diaries and personal letters that permit the social historian to illuminate in detail the experiences of individual families. The childhood of saints tends to fall into predictable patterns. Folk tales lack specifics of date and context, and become vague and timeless. Yet a few witnesses to family life open up some families in the early Trecento for closer inspection. Dante Alighieri (1265–1321) is probably the best known and most intensely studied Italian in this period. His wife and children pale into anonymity compared to the immortality he conferred on Beatrice, the object of his extramarital, lifelong infatuation. Dante certainly serves as a reminder that 'relationships', both emotional and physical, extended beyond the traditional norms of family life. Yet Dante's *Commedia* is a rich source on Florentine family life, especially in Hell, where the damned have often sinned against family yet remain intensely interested in the fates of their surviving kin. One detail merits notice here. At the very bottom of Hell, in Canto 32, Dante reserved a special place for those who were treacherous to their kin. Betraying one's family was a horrifying crime; and no doubt Dante was faithfully mirroring here the sentiments of his Italian contemporaries. This part of Dante's Hell, named after Cain, prompted him to recall the worst betrayers, those who murdered their relatives. As in the case of the Alberti brothers who ended up killing one another over a castle, property often caused the worst intra-family disputes. Frozen in shame for eternity, these violators of family bonds provoked in Dante the rare comment that he shuddered when he remembered their fate. Dante passed quickly to those betraying their country and God, but it is notable that the family ranks with these ties.

Giovanni Boccaccio (1313–75) wrote just at the end of this period, between 1348 and 1352, his *Decameron*, with its hundred stories intended to divert his readers from the calamity of the plague. Three small points help to conclude this survey of the Italian family from 1100 to 1350. Boccaccio too experienced youthful infatuation, in his case with the mysterious Fiammetta (hardly a saint's name) at the court of Naples. Boccaccio spent his life in minor Church orders, never married, and (himself an illegitimate child) fathered at least five children of his own, an indication that many people may have lived outside the conventions of regular family life. Yet his Florentine relatives looked out for Boccaccio and got him a job as a bank clerk when he was 14. The *Decameron* is a collection of stories whose main theme is relationship, familial or sexual. The tales are not a collective sociology of the Italian family, but they are good evidence for at least some norms of behaviour. Boccaccio gave a special place, in the last tale, to the story of Griselda. This long and complex story of how a peasant girl attracts a noble and ultimately cruel and suspicious husband, was already in Boccaccio's time an old and well-known story. Boccaccio gave it a sharp focus and fleshed out the basic story with many details, inventing the name 'Griselda' and making the husband Gualtieri, marchese of Saluzzo in the north-west corner of Italy. Griselda became the archetype for the patient, suffering wife, subject to the tests and deceits of a strange husband. Gualtieri even pretended to have a papal dispensation to divorce his wife and marry another. Griselda endured slights and even the cruel pretence that her children were murdered. Eventually the marchese tired of putting Griselda's endless patience to the test, and he restored her children and his wife's place in society. Boccaccio intended to suggest that a peasant could have a finer character and be a better spouse than a noble. Griselda's patience, easy to scorn, was also a strategy for survival in a world where patriarchy could turn suddenly vicious and the law and religion were slight obstacles to it. The family could be a prison as well as a safe refuge in a harsh world filled with war and now plague.

Language and culture

Alberto Varvaro

Language in Italy *c.*1000

The first signs of the appearance of a vernacular Italian are the well-known *Riddle of Verona* and some graffiti in the Catacombs of Comodilla in Rome, both around AD 800. After these, the vernacular was documented at Capua and Teano, today in the province of Caserta, in AD 960–3. These fragments only underline the overall lack of textual evidence, which is not sufficient to give even a vague idea of the linguistic situation over the entire peninsula around the year 1000. Accordingly, it is possible to infer that awareness of the difference between Latin and the vernacular was not particularly fierce at the time.

As with other cultural aspects, the linguistic situation on the peninsula underlined an overall lack of political unity. There were two main opposing trends. The coastal areas, more in the south than the north, maintained a Mediterranean orientation that went back to antiquity. Links with Constantinople, which continued to possess provinces in Italy until the Norman conquest, had reinforced the use of Greek, which for many centuries had been spoken along the southern Italian coast, particularly in the Salento area, Calabria, and eastern Sicily. Also influential was immigration from the east, particularly by Christians fleeing Muslim conquests. The Muslims themselves had occupied Sicily from the ninth century, and had then proceeded further up the peninsula, establishing long-lasting settlements. Entire parts of Sicily were Arabic-speaking, and the use of Arabic words spread north, particularly along trade routes.

The situation to the north and inland was rather different. The kingdom of Italy looked towards the Holy Roman Empire and thus towards Europe beyond the Alps. The Longobard language was extinct or just about extinct in its last stronghold, Benevento, but there were isolated examples of immigrants who continued to speak their own languages, such as the Bulgars.[1] Along the southern reaches of the Apennine mountains, in Basilicata, there were settlements where Greek was spoken, and others that used an archaic romance dialect, traces of which still exist today. South of the Tiber river, there had formed a linguistic type that might be labelled 'Sabine', characterized by the loss of the -*mb*- and -*nd*- sounds (for example, *gamma* for 'gamba' and *monno* for 'mondo') that subsequently spread to all of southern Italy. Various texts were produced in this area, particularly in the Benedictine monasteries between Farfa and Monte Cassino.

The territory on the Adriatic side, from the Marches down to the Gulf of Taranto, had its own linguistic character, more open to influence from the north. In the Po valley the most important and populous centres were on the low plains, from Pavia and Milan to Treviso and Padua. The most linguistically conservative areas, which for example kept the final 's' of Latin, were to be found in the high Alpine valleys and towards Friuli, which would preserve Ladin and Rhaeto-Romance ('Romansch'). The Apennine valleys were more easily penetrated, and innovations such as the lenition, or softening, of voiceless intervocalic consonants (ACU > *ago*) spread into central Italy either along the Via Francigena towards Lucca or to the east along the ancient Via Flaminia towards Umbria.

Tuscan at this stage had neither an autonomous profile nor the prestige that it was to acquire three centuries later, but during this period traders from Pisa started arriving in Corsica and Sardinia and their linguistic influence began to modify the very conservative character of the local spoken language. It is worth remembering that Sard is not a dialect of Italian but an autonomous variant within the neo-Latin languages, with its own vocalic system (the only Romance language to merge the Latin pairs of short and long vowels), taking the

---

[1] Presumably still using Turkic rather than Slavic.

article from *ipse* and conservating the Latin final 's' (*sas domos* for *le case*, 'the houses'), and so on.

There is no proof that the inhabitants of the peninsula thought they all spoke the same language; if anything quite the reverse. Even if in the present it is difficult to decide exactly what 'Italy' means, the absence of the adjective 'Italian' cannot escape our notice. The first conscious affirmation of unity among spoken languages on the peninsula would have to wait for the definition by Dante of the 'lingua del sì'.

Linguistic change up to 1300

There was much change between 1000 and 1300. Above all Arabic fell into almost complete disuse. This was not an immediate consequence of the Norman invasions, since Count Roger I (1031–1101) and his successors had no particular linguistic policies, but the effect of the Norman presence was to revive the Romance elements in Sicilian speech. It was the civil wars of around 1200, the rebellion against Frederick II (1198–1250), and the Arabs' subsequent expulsion which effectively meant Arabic was only used on the island by the Jewish communities, until their own expulsion in 1492.[2] In general, the Crusades resulted in a changed relationship with the Muslim world which effectively closed the road to lexical borrowing from Arabic. The use of Greek also went into an irreversible decline, although small pockets of Greek usage have survived in Calabria and the Salentino up to the present.[3]

The disappearance of Arabic and the decline of Greek coincided with heavy immigration from the rest of the peninsula, particularly from Tuscany and the north, towards southern Italy and Sicily. The newcomers, who were referred to collectively as 'Lombards',

[2] The Saracen colony in Lucera, in the Capitanata district, was dispersed in 1300 and left no linguistic legacy, although Franco-Provençal settlers brought around this time into the same region have preserved their own dialects over many centuries. Arabic remained in use on the islands of Pantelleria, Malta, and Gozo, which were part of the Sicilian kingdom. On Pantelleria Arabic had been replaced by Sicilian by the sixteenth century and Malta developed its own language, still in use today, which is effectively a relic of medieval Sicilian Arabic.

[3] In Sicily, Greek was used in Messina until about 1500.

dispersed in large numbers over a wide area, although in some localities their population density created linguistically distinct islands,
some of which have survived into the present. These areas are to be
found in Basilicata between Potenza and Tito down to Rivello and
Trecchina, and also in Sicily, from San Fratello and Novara di Sicilia
to Piazza Armerina and Aidone. The migration process is not well
documented, but the linguistic characteristics of these colonies indicate the provenance of the migrants from southern Piedmont and
western Liguria.

The complete Romanization of language in Sicily was not due to
the demographic increase of those who spoke Romance languages
before the conquest, but rather their mingling with immigrants,
whether from the Italian peninsula or France, and also with speakers
of Greek whose language had changed. The result was a language that
contained various linguistic features. The area's characteristic vocalic
system, which has only five phonemes (*a, e, i, o, u*), where the Latin
short and long (i) and the long (e) give rise to the same *i* sound and
the Latin short and long (u) and the long (o) give rise to the same *u*
sound (so that the word *nivi* has the same vowel sounds as *vivu* and
cruci sounds like *muru*), seem to be the result of close contact with
the vocalic system of varieties of Greek. The same system is also
found in southern Calabria and the Salento area. At the time of
Frederick II (1198–1250) a poetic language based on Sicilian was established, even though the emperor's court only spent a short time on
the island (Frederick had passed his youth there, however). After the
kingdom had passed to Charles I of Anjou and even more so after
the revolt of the Sicilian Vespers (1282), Naples became the centre
of the kingdom: the language of Sicily lost its importance, particularly as the island passed into the Catalan political orbit. In effect
Naples would crush many of the linguistic features of other parts of
the kingdom, but this phenomenon was only evident after about two
centuries. Meanwhile the southern linguistic varieties were defined as
'Longobard' (as opposed to Lombard), or as 'Apulian', an indication
of the prevalence of Apennine and Pugliese influence.

It should be noted that Rome did not have a particular linguistic
influence at the time. Its language type was still very southern, and
would remain so until at least the second half of the fifteenth century,
when Tuscan influence helped to create the modern Roman dialect.
Tuscany assumed an increasingly important linguistic role from

around 1200. Initially this was a polycentric phenomenon, with linguistic varieties in Lucca, Pisa, Pistoia, Florence, Siena, and Arezzo. Later, Florence became increasingly dominant. Usually this is explained through the great prestige of Florentine fourteenth-century literature, but the process is in fact older and less monocausal. In the 1200s Tuscany witnessed an extraordinary economic, political, and cultural development, with a concomitant diffusion of writings. The flow of linguistic features from the north was halted, and the Tuscan language began to radiate northwards itself, particularly towards Bologna and the Veneto. By 1300 the written language of the Emilian city was different from that of Florence only because it was less idiomatic.

It has been mentioned already that the spoken languages of the Po valley are termed Lombard. This denomination includes the great variety of distinct linguistic types extending from Piedmontese to Veneto and Romagnolo (the city of Venice for the time being remained a case apart). A dense network of intersecting linguistic boundaries covering the entire plain is now well documented, although no single linguistic type dominated. These differences were maintained by the fragmentation of political power, competing economic interests, and cultural differences.

The periphery of the Italian linguistic area included the Alps and the Alpine foothills: Occitan and Franco-Provençal to the west, Rhaeto-Romance, Ladin, and Friulian to the north and east. Also peripheral are Istrian in Istria and Dalmatian in Veglia and isolated places along the coast to Ragusa (now Dubrovnik). In Corsica by this time the dialects retained few remnants of antiquity, by sharp contrast with Sardinia, except for the northern areas around Sassari.

Cultural centres, schools, and libraries

Throughout the period from 1000 to 1300 the language of Italian high culture remained Latin, though in some cases Greek and Arabic were used. Latin was the language of the Roman Church,[4] but the Church

---

[4] In the south, however, the use of Greek persisted in churches subject to Roman authority.

Reform Movement, the most important cultural phenomenon of the period, had Italy as its point of reference. Italy was not, however, the Reform Movement's driving force: apart from personalities like Peter Damian, it is in France—first at Cluny and then at Clairvaux—that we need to search. Later still, the Church was governed from Rome, but its intellectual centre was Paris—it was not mere chance that prompted Thomas Aquinas to move from southern Italy to France.

Thomas Aquinas brings us to the question of universities. In Italy, universities were established in Bologna (by the end of the twelfth century), Padua (1222), and Naples (1224). They excelled in the field of law, particularly Roman law, and turned out administrators for government and the Church. Canon law, on the other hand, had its capital in Paris. The medical school at Salerno was famous, having been founded before 1000 and flourishing in the eleventh century under Constantine the African; yet the school remained outside the true university structure, giving instruction in practical skills. The schools of the mendicant orders in the 1200s are particularly interesting, but here again primacy goes to Paris. We know little about grammar schools, which were certainly more common. There is nothing to suggest that levels of literacy were higher than elsewhere, though there were enormous differences from one part of the peninsula to another. Merchants had to be able to write, and it is no surprise that the largest number of texts in the vernacular emanated from Tuscany, where economic activity was most intense. They included accounts, business appointment books, lists of creditors and debtors, payments, taxes, and the like.

Less striking is the literary production of the period in Latin, which is not comparable to the volume of work produced in France and the Rhine valley. Formerly, the slow development of Italian literature relative to German and French was justified by reference to the fact that educated Italians retained solid ties to Latin, which they felt to be their mother tongue, but this does not seem to be the case. The areas which witnessed the greatest growth in the production of literature in Latin in the twelfth and thirteenth centuries were substantially the same as those where literature in the vernacular also flourished. Until 1300 Italy was peripheral for both types.[5]

---

[5] There are of course some exceptions: certain works in Latin written in Italy were very successful. More than 1,000 manuscript copies of Jacopo da Varazze's *Legenda*

This suggests that both characteristics were related to analogous external conditions: the potential reading public, the schools, and libraries. The golden age of Italian libraries had been earlier in the Middle Ages, the period of Monte Cassino, Verona, Bobbio, and Vercelli, but during the period under consideration dust covered their treasures thickly and it would only be removed in the second half of the fourteenth century by indignant humanists. Between 1000 and 1300 the great monastic centres seem to have been in decline, and noble families did not have sufficient continuity to acquire books and establish cultural traditions. We do know that at least Frederick II was interested in books, but it is not possible to say how many he had or whether they were organized into a stable and permanent library.[6] Even the papal collections were begun after the period under consideration.

We have already mentioned the idea that primary education was reasonably widespread (though mainly in urban areas), and this was obviously connected with the needs of the Church and the legal profession. The beginnings of commerce and finance had also provided reasons for the young to learn how to read, write, and do arithmetic, but only in Tuscany and certain restricted areas.[7] In effect merchants had already been writing frequently since the early 1200s, but this does not mean that literacy was common outside the Church and the legal profession. Notaries in particular were often writers as well. Giacomo da Lentini was a notary, and between the thirteenth and fourteenth centuries notaries in Bologna used to fill the blanks in their registers with transcriptions of poetry. The Italian clergy, on

aurea still exist, but much of its success was owed to the Church and in particular the Dominican Order. The success of the *Historia destructionis Troiae* by the Messinese Guido delle Colonne, which became the standard account of the Trojan Wars in all of Europe right up to Chaucer and Shakespeare, was completely secular in character.

[6] We do, on the other hand, know that he carried with him valuable codices such as the illuminated *De arte venandi*, which the Parmans took by force when they besieged his camp at Vittoria.

[7] The most significant literary product of mercantile culture at the end of the thirteenth century was Marco Polo's *Milione*, dictated by the author to Rustichello da Pisa while in prison in Genoa, and subsequently written down in French. Produced in innumerable versions and adaptations, the work would remain one of the most important texts of the later Middle Ages. Another work in French by an Italian author which was successful in the thirteenth century was an encyclopaedia by Brunetto Latini, Dante's teacher. It was entitled *Tresor*, and was translated in both Italy and Spain.

the other hand, with the exception of the texts produced at Monte Cassino, played a less important role in the development of literature than their French brethren, possibly because the Italian clergy seemed to be more administrative than intellectual. Notable exceptions were provided by the likes of St Francis of Assisi, who recognized the importance of poetry and was the author of the *Laudes creaturarum* (1224–6). Also noteworthy was the production of religious poetry known as *laudi* ('lodi' or 'praises'), which reached their highest point with the *Stabat mater* of Jacopone di Todi. The secular clergy remained at the periphery of literary production, as did the aristocracy, which elsewhere provided essential patronage.

The first documents in the vernacular and para-literary traditions

The number of documents written in the vernacular and dating prior to about 1211, details of which were collected some years ago by Livio Petrucci, amounted to no more than about twenty for the entire Italian peninsula (excluding Sardinia; Sicily counted none). Also interesting is their geographical distribution. Apart from the *Riddle of Verona* and the *Glossary of Monza*, which in a strict sense do not count as vernacular, from the north there is only an inscription from Casale Monferrato (dating from before 1106), the Venetian *Recordacione* of P. Corner (*c.*1150–75), the *Declaration of Paxia* (Savona, 1182–93), the *Ritmo bellunese* (Belluno-Feltre, *c.*1200, but extant only in much later copies), the *Subalpine Sermons* (*c.*1200), and the *Ricordi Veronesi* (*c.*1205). Of these, only the Sermons present a text of any length, and it is still a matter of debate whether they are in Gallo-Romance or Italian. Writings from the south are even rarer. After the *Placiti campani* of 960–3 there was nothing until the *Ritmo cassinese*, the three verses of the Cassinese *Pianto di Maria*, and the inventory of S. Maria at Fondi, all from about 1200, and all from northern Campania.[8] At the northern limit of the southern linguistic area we find two brief Roman texts: the already mentioned graffito of

---

[8] Fondi and Monte Cassino were within the kingdom. Only with the establishment of the province of Latina (1926) were these areas transferred to Lazio.

Comodilla and the inscription of San Clemente (*c.*1100). On the other side of the peninsula there is the *memoratorio* of Monte Capraro (1171) in Molise.

Tuscany and the central areas were much richer. There are the *Postilla amiatina* of 1087, the naval accounts of Pisa of about 1100, the testimonies of Travale (1158), the *Decime* of Arlotto (1160–80), the inscription on the tomb of Giratto at Pisa (1174–80), the *Ritmo laurenziano* (between 1188 and 1207), the *Declaratoria pistoiese* (from the middle of the twelfth century), the Pistoiese annotation dated between 1187 and 1208, the rents and notes of Coltibuono (*c.*1200), and finally the Florentine banking accounts of 1211. From the area of Umbria and the Marches we have the Umbrian confessional formula (before 1080), and the charters of Osimo (1151), Fabriano (1186), and Piceno (1193).

Sardinia represents a case apart. During the same period the island produced at least fifteen legal documents, from the *privilegio logudorese* of 1080–5 to the charter of Cagliari of 1200–12. There are seven texts from Logudoro, which represent the most conservative linguistic type, four from Arborea, three from Cagliari, and one from Gallura. Although the linguistic features vary from region to region, the textual typology is similar among all the texts, to the extent that they are all juridical documents using highly official language.[9]

It should be noted that there is nothing from the better part of the Mezzogiorno, including Sicily, nor from most of the Po valley, including Milan, Bologna, Verona, Padua, and Venice. Typologically the majority of these texts, which are usually brief, are linked to a practical function, generally connected with the law or religion. Very few of them are even slightly literary. Consider the scant lines of the *Ritmo bellunese*, which celebrate the victory of the militias of the communes of Belluno and Feltre over the commune of Treviso in a local skirmish:

> De Castel d'Ard avi li nostri bona part
> I lo getà tutto intro lo flumo d'Ard.
> E sex cavaler de Tarvis li plui fer
> Con sé dusé li nostre cavaler.

---

[9] Because of the high proportion of juridical texts, mainly registers of ecclesiastical property, the editing of ancient Sardinian texts has often been undertaken by historians of law, more interested in their legal substance than the linguistic aspects.

From Castel d'Ardo came our better part, and they threw it all into the River
Ardo. Six horsemen from most proud Treviso took our horsemen with
them.

Whether or not it is complete, this very humble text, in epic decasyl-
lables with caesura after the fourth syllable, refers to the sorts of events
which are likely to have inspired numerous other poetic works. The
celebration of occasions in small warlike communities must certainly
have been recorded in poetry, both for the purposes of spreading the
word and for boasting about victories. From the 1200s we have three
texts that refer to such situations: the *Serventese* of the Lambertazzi
and Geremei (1280) and the *Serventese romagnolo* of almost the same
date, as well as the older *Ritmo lucchese*. Communal pride, which was
to be so important in Dante's *Commedia*, permeates much of this
literary production, the greater part of which was lost. Similar
attention to founding myths is preserved in municipal chronicles. In
the cities of the Po valley, this production is in Latin prose, whereas in
Tuscany the vernacular was used relatively early on. The myth of the
origins of Florence in Fiesole was known not just to the educated, but
to the whole commune.

Minstrels played an important role in the celebration of local
feasts, but little record of their performances has been preserved. It is
to a jester, perhaps from Volterra, that we owe the *Ritmo laurenziano*
('Salva lo vescovo senato lo meglior k'unqua sia nato . . .'), in which
the bishop of Jesi is celebrated because he had given a horse to the
poet. Religious minstrels were responsible for the *Ritmo cassinese*,
which compares the contemplative to the active life.

Minstrels, as well as the lower clergy, also put on dramatic works
that were precursors of modern theatre. The fragment of the *Pianto
cassinese di Maria* belongs to this category, as do certain texts by
Jacopone. The inscription of San Clemente contains the depiction of
a dramatic work. This shows the miracle in which the saint's persecutors are forced to drag a heavy marble column rather than the saint's
body; the persecutors utter phrases in the vernacular ('Fàlite dereto
colo palo, Carvoncelle', etc.), while the saint uses solemn Latin
('Duritiam cordis vestris saxa traere meruistis'). Drama as an aspect
of literature was of less importance, but it had its place, especially the
elementary form of the *contrasto*, a poetic 'dialogue' that had no need
of scenery and where the same actor played both parts. There are

three examples of such works from the thirteenth century: the *Contrasto di Cielo d'Alcamo* (mentioned by Dante as an example of rustic Sicilian), the *Song of Castra*, and the dialogue 'O Zerbitana retica'.

The establishment of literary traditions

The communal poem and the dramatic dialogue are two examples of the slow emergence of literary traditions. Already these examples pose the problem of whether they are autochthonous or not. The decasyllabic *Ritmo bellunese* seems to have some of the characteristics of French epic poetry, a form that spread quite early in northern Italy and gave rise to a hybrid linguistic form, Franco-Italian. Among other works, there is a version of the *Song of Roland* in this hybrid language. The *contrasto* also has characteristics that come from outside Italy: among the oldest Italians texts we should include stanzas by the Occitan troubadour Raimbaut de Vaqueiras. These amount to two stanzas (which can only be judged as generically Italian) of the plurilingual 'Eras quan vey verdeyar' and half of the *contrasto* 'Domna, tant vos ai preiada', considered Genoese. These texts, both from the end of the twelfth century, provide examples of the diffusion in Italy of troubadour poetry, as well as their presence in the peninsula and their attention to the local spoken language.

Traditionally the relationship between the Italian language and Occitan poetry has been considered in linear terms: troubadours arrive in Italy and perform their own compositions, then certain Italians adopt Occitan and imitate its forms and motifs. In a third phase some Italian poets adopt their own language, continuing to imitate Occitan models. By about 1200 there were already numerous Occitan poets visiting Italian courts, particularly in the north. The troubadour Peire Vidal participated in the social and literary life of the peninsula, as did Uc de Saint Circ, who became the biographer of his teachers and colleagues. There were already northern Italian poets who had adopted Occitan for their own poetry for some decades. The most famous figure of the 1200s would be Sordello da Goito. Rather later, around 1230, Frederick II would promote the poetic production of his court, usually referred to as the Sicilian poetic school. A few years ago there was an important discovery: a *canzone*, datable to around 1200, transcribed in Ravenna, in a language that was not local but appeared to be a mixture of southern forms that had passed though a more northern filter. It begins 'Quando eu stava in le tu' cathene'. Besides this there was a partial copy of another, rather different, composition. A short time earlier there had been a discovery in relation to Sicilian poets. In the Zentralbibliothek of Zurich a poem by Giacomino Pugliese, written around 1234–6, had been found. This copy must have been made near Lake Constance, where it seems to have arrived via Aquileia.

These two discoveries led to a rethinking of old assumptions. 'Quando eu stava' without doubt shows familiarity with Occitan models, but it lacks the imprint of the themes of Occitan poetry, which are, on the other hand, more evident in the smaller fragment. The two poems indicate that in Italy at the end of the 1100s compositions displayed form and content that was influenced by the Provençal model but was also relatively autonomous. Even more interesting is the language, which is far from representing a local model, and thus indicates the existence of a supra-local practice, which also applied in more southern areas. By rereading other, anonymous compositions, apparently of a later date, it may be possible to discover further fragments of this prehistory of the Italian language.

Nearly all Sicilian poetry has come down to us in Tuscan guise through the collections produced there in the thirteenth and fourteenth centuries. There exist only a few stanzas in the original language, but these were copied in the sixteenth century and their origin is therefore open to doubt. The language of the Zurich poem, which dates back to the emperor Frederick II, shows no Tuscan influences and is written in a Sicilian enriched by supra-local influences.[10] Overall, this text, along with the one from Ravenna, seems to indicate the existence of a poetic and literary non-dialect language that predated Frederick.

The relationship with Provençal poetry thus becomes more dialectic, and there is another sign of this. Occitan poetry brought courtly manners to Italy and with them the formula of courtly love, or 'fin'amore'. This formula appears in the work of Sicilian poets,

---

[10] Even in this case the copy is probably of other copies, and it certainly cannot be considered original.

notably John of Brienne and above all Rinaldo d'Aquino. But elements of this formula had already appeared much earlier in personal names. In Genoa as early as 1191 and then in 1201 there were people called *Finis Amoris* and *Jacomus Finis Amoris*, and later, in 1232, in Pistoia there was a Dominam *Finamorem*. These people would not have been children when their names were registered in archival documents, and their adopted names indicate the popularity of the formulas of courtly poetry long before they were harnessed by the pens of John of Brienne or Rinaldo d'Aquino.

The fact that today the background is much more complex detracts nothing from the importance of Frederick II. At his coronation in 1220 there were troubadours, Provençal poets, and German *Minnesänger*, but there is no record of performances by Italians. It is undoubtedly to his credit to be the first lord, as far as we know, consciously to assume the role not just of protector but promoter of vernacular poetry, encouraging the members of his court, and participating himself, in the writing of poetry. The emperor's intervention needs to be seen in the light of his overall aim to increase the prestige of his court, partly through these manifestations of refinement. The model was certainly Occitan, but it was not a passive imitation. The emperor was not keen on political content, so important in the poems of many troubadours, beginning with Bertran de Born; even moral themes are transposed to the plane of theory rather than relating to real people or classes. Alongside moral themes the theme of love was important, but even here there was a certain autonomy with respect to the Occitan model. This autonomy was even more marked at the level of form: it was the Sicilians, and above all Giacomo da Lentini, who invented the sonnet. This was unknown to the Provençal tradition, but would remain the canonic form of short poetry in Italy and the rest of Europe.

Even beyond the initiative of Frederick II and the not inconsiderable achievements of other poets, particularly Giacomo da Lentini, the Sicilian poetic school has further historic significance, of which Dante himself was fully aware. Even before the fall of the Hohenstaufen dynasty at Benevento (1266) there were traces of its influence in Tuscany, a region strongly linked to King Manfred. Thus we have a group of poets described as Siculo-Tuscan. Afterwards there was constant innovation, from Guittone d'Arezzo to the Bolognese Guido Guinizelli and from Guido Calvalcanti to Dante.

Dante's 'Dolce Stil Nuovo' characterizes this last group of poets as a school, a community, despite differences of personality, style, and poetry. The tradition of Italian lyrical poetry, in its two principal forms of the *canzone* and the sonnet, took on its definitive shape among this group. Later, with Petrarch, it would become a model of perfection that would continue for centuries, even beyond Italy. Thus the Sicilians created a tradition of lyric poetry. Having mentioned Guinizelli, it might be added that other poets writing in Bologna tended to imitate Tuscan poetic circles, and in the same city prose writers composed books on more learned subjects than in Tuscany. With Boncompagno da Signa and Guido Faba, vernacular texts began to be produced in the universities, and formed the basis for lectures to an educated public, which was constantly expanding in size.

Less lasting were other poetic traditions. The Po valley area witnessed a flowering of didactic poetry in the 1200s, often but not always religious, sometimes anonymous (as in the case of the so-called 'Anonimo Genovese') but sometimes by authors such as Girardo Patecchio di Cremona, Ugucione da Lodi, Giacomino da Verona, and the Milanese Bonvesin da la Riva. These names are already enough to indicate that vernacular poetry originated in many places, but none of them succeeded in establishing stable models or continuity. More fortunate was another genre of poetry, the so-called 'comic-realistic' begun by the Florentine Rustico Filippo, continued by the Sienese Cecco Angiolieri, and then developed by Folgore da San Gimignano. There are echoes of this genre in Dante's *Inferno*.

The foregoing schematic indications are sufficient to demonstrate that by about 1200 Italy, with its many linguistic variations, was home to rich and differentiated poetic traditions, which went from the poetry of courtly love to religious, moral, and comic-realistic work, and to occasional poetry with political overtones. Dramatic poetry is likely to have existed, but there is little documentation. Epic poetry was noticeably lacking. Italian prose was probably not particularly original but covers a broad range, from the novel to science. We also see the beginnings of the most successful genre of pre-modern Italy, the *novella*.[11] Behind this maturing literature stood Latin culture.

---

[11] The *Novellino* is often considered to have appeared at the end of the 1200s, but the earliest manuscripts are later than 1320.

The sum of these Italian and European traditions was the extra-ordinary appearance of Dante Alighieri. One the one hand, Dante participated in the 'Dolce Stil Nuovo', but his interests were much broader. His lyric production is seen in the *Vita Nuova*, whose complex structure foreshadows Petrarch's *Canzoniere*. But Dante was interested in conscious linguistic selection and the style of literature (the *De vulgari eloquentia*), in culture as a whole (the encyclopaedic, if incomplete *Convivio*), and in the theory and practice of politics (*De Monarchia*). These are interests that went beyond the theoretical. His passionate participation in Florentine political life, the price of which was a long period of exile, is proof of his commitment to high ideals. It was on the basis of this life and culture that the ambitious structure of the *Commedia* was based. This was an extraordinary project for a poem that embraced all of human experience, from the terrestrial to the eternal. It was both a summing up of, and a point of departure from, medieval culture in all its aspects, yet it was always linked to the personal experience of the author, his beloved Florence, and the places of his exile.

PART III

THE OTHER FACES OF ITALY

The Italian other: Greeks, Muslims, and Jews

David Abulafia

The history of medieval Italy is often written as the history of an evolving *Italianità*, 'Italianness'. It is true, as Alberto Varvaro has indicated in this volume, that it is in this period that a group of interrelated forms of romance came into existence which came, by the fifteenth century, to be dominated in many areas by Tuscanized Italian. Yet this preoccupation with Italianness obscures several realities. The south, substantially ignored by so many historians of Italy, standing at the point where Latin, Greek, and Arabic cultures and polities met one another, was exposed to influences from many directions. It was also, before the fifteenth century, the main centre of Italian Judaism which, even though it accounted for only perhaps 5 per cent of the population of southern Italy and Sicily, also bears witness to important cultural exchanges between the Greek, Arab, and Latin worlds, and which had a vibrant history of its own. It is necessary to take the Jews, Greeks, and Muslims out of their historiographical ghetto and to show what role these groups played in the economic, cultural, and political life of Italy in the central Middle Ages.

The first point is that the presence of the Greeks was not simply related to the long-standing political interests of the Byzantine emperors in southern Italy and Sicily. In the eleventh century, Latin bishops and their flocks were often as enthusiastic about their

allegiance to Constantinople as were Greeks; and Greeks were sometimes willing to countenance submission to non-Byzantine rulers, if
these were willing to protect their communities. In other words,
Greekness and submission to Byzantium were not the same thing.
This became even more obvious once, in the ninth century, the island
of Sicily fell under Muslim rule, despite intermittent but often energetic Byzantine attempts to regain a foothold at least in the east of
Sicily; the Muslim conquest left large numbers of Greeks, perhaps
40 per cent of the island population, under Islamic rule. Other
indistinct boundaries between Christians and Muslims emerged: the
Maltese, though Christian by the early thirteenth century, did not lose
their Siculo-Arabic language, which persists to this day; and the
Sicilian Jews remained attached to the use of Arabic in daily speech
until 1400 or later.

This sense that southern Italy and Sicily were less (or even less)
homogeneous in ethnic identity, language, and religious affiliation
than the north is accentuated by the presence in the south of very
diverse ethnic pockets: Slavs fleeing wars in the Balkans, Armenians
dumped in southern Italy by Byzantine emperors who used population transfers as a solution to political tensions in their eastern lands,
Berbers who reached Sicily in the wake of the Muslim conquest, not
to mention the Lombards (whose Germanic language long persisted
at Benevento), the Normans, few but potent, and a vast influx of
settlers from northern Italy, Provence, and adjacent areas, who filled
gaps left by departing or displaced Muslims and others; and some of
those Sicilian Muslims were themselves transported to the plains of
Apulia, where they lived in relative isolation until 1300. In other
words, the picture, from the tenth century to the fourteenth century,
is one of constant flux. More problematic is the question whether
these population movements had a substantial genetic effect; in other
words, whether the invasions and settlements were superficial in
character, leaving a fairly stable native population whose genes can be
traced back to pre-medieval times. The tendency of modern genetic
research is to insist that, throughout the Italian peninsula, genetic
stability has prevailed. But genes are only part of the question. The
cultural, linguistic, and religious identity of the population under-
went significant changes, nowhere more than in southern Italy and
Sicily.

The Greeks

The Greeks in Italy were not simply the descendants of the inhabitants of ancient Magna Graecia, of the Greek colonies that had been
established in southern Italy and Sicily since the seventh century BC.
Greek settlement occurred in subsequent centuries too, but there was
an essential continuity from late antiquity. The major areas of concentration of Greek population, in the ninth century, were Sicily,
Calabria, and the towns that ran down the Adriatic coast, though here
the distribution of Greeks was variable, with significant Latin populations in such major centres as Bari, and also rural Greek populations
who continued to construct their churches in the traditional Orthodox
style. Of these Greeks only tiny communities have survived into the
twenty-first century. However, what was distinctive about the Greek
culture of tenth- and eleventh-century southern Italy was the vitality
of religious life. Particularly important is the role of St Nilus of
Rossano (Rossano remained a Greek bishopric right up to the fifteenth
century, and is well documented since most of the Greek manuscripts
survived and are now in the Vatican Library). Nilus is a figure of
contradiction, drawn to the eremitical life, but also aware of the need
to spread his spiritual message, so that he was the founder of monastic communities in Calabria and the south, while his northernmost
community, at Grottaferrata, stands at the gates of Rome, and still
conducts a Greek liturgy.

This serves as a reminder that the Roman Church itself, up to
the tenth century, was subject to powerful Greek influences. Some
were mediated through political contacts: Theophano, the mother of
the German emperor Otto III, was a Byzantine princess, and did not
let anyone forget the fact. But there were also other contacts: the
last Greek to occupy the papal throne was the Calabrian Zacharias
(d. 752), and the Greek community in Rome had an important base at
the church of Santa Maria in Cosmedin ('in schola graeca'), favoured
by Pope Hadrian I in the late eighth century. By the eleventh century,
however, deteriorating relations between the Roman pontiffs and the
patriarchs of Constantinople, which were entangled with the political
rivalries of Normans, Byzantines, Germans, and Lombards in southern Italy, saw the Roman Church distancing itself ever further from

Greek influences and practices: the Latin Church sought to promote clerical celibacy, while the Greek Church accepted married priests; the Latin Church used unleavened wafers in the Mass, but the Greeks denounced this as a 'Jewish' practice, shared by the Latins with the even more despised Armenians; above all, the Greek Church was not prepared to accept papal claims to authority over the text of the Creed and the exact terms used to describe the nature of the Trinity. The issue here was, perhaps, the semantic richness of Greek which could not be reproduced in Latin without long periphrases, but simply adding further words to the Creed was, the Greeks insisted, unacceptable without the consent of all the five patriarchs of Rome, Constantinople, Antioch, Alexandria, and Jerusalem meeting in a Council. Constantinople did not deny that special honour and even precedence attached to the Church of Rome, but there was no room in Byzantine thinking for the idea of papal plenitude of power, all the more so when it was the emperor, rather than the patriarch, who was presented in Byzantium as Christ's vicar on earth.

These disagreements, which were already foreshadowed during the so-called Photian Schism of the ninth century, became especially bitter in 1054 when Cardinal Humbert slammed a bull of excommunication directed at the Byzantine emperor and the patriarch of Constantinople on the High Altar of Hagia Sophia in Constantinople. This itself has to be seen as part of the concerted effort by the papacy in the late eleventh century to assert its authority throughout Christendom, the so-called Reform Movement that reached its peak under Gregory VII (d. 1085); other divergent liturgies in Spain, Milan, and northern Europe were increasingly brought into line with Roman usage. In Sardinia, where an isolated Greek Church survived until the eleventh century, the Latin ecclesiastical conquest was particularly thorough; churches built on the Greek cross plan gave way to Romanesque structures built for the Pisan and Provençal monasteries that gained estates and power on the island.

What the papacy sought in the south of Italy was not the suppression of the Greek rite, for after all Greek was one of the canonical languages. Rather, the aim was to create what would later be termed a Uniate Church, a Greek Church that recognized papal authority. Indeed, the presence of Greeks under papal authority only served to emphasize the universality of that authority, at a time when the Greeks disputed papal claims to leadership. Although at a local level

Greek churches survived, ecclesiastical leadership in the Norman south passed into Latin hands. Given the fragile loyalty of the south Italian Greeks towards Constantinople, and given the lack of interference in the internal affairs of Greek parishes, this system worked well enough, though in the long term the numbers following the Greek rite fell away.

Still in the realms of high politics, we can observe how the Byzantines sought to make their control of southern Italy real at the end of the tenth and beginning of the eleventh centuries, and how this left a lasting legacy in the urban layout of south-eastern Italy. The construction of a line of fortress towns, including Lucera, in the region subsequently known as Capitanata, was accompanied by attempts by both Constantinople and Rome to endow the new cathedrals of these towns with generous privileges, all part of a campaign to win over hearts, souls, and bodies. However, the settlements seem to have been more Latin than Greek in ethnic and religious character. Still, the name Capitanata is a reminder of the political changes taking place in this zone: the name derives from the title Katapano (Κατάπάνω) accorded to the military and civil governor of the province known as Langobardia, the land of the Lombards. Byzantium sought to shore up its defences in this region because of a simple strategic rule: the empire was like an onion, and it was wise to create as many outer layers of defence as possible, to protect the centre. With the loss of Sicily, provinces in Calabria and Langobardia acted as a bulwark against Muslim raids (bearing in mind the fact that in the late ninth century Bari was for some years in Arab hands), and protected the Balkans against Arab incursions.

However, this policy did little to protect Calabria, and the history of the Greek communities there, which has been studied in detail by André Guillou, shows that there occurred regular cycles of devastation followed by recovery.[1] The end of the tenth century was certainly a time when the political temperature was high in Calabria; the fever was only exacerbated by the intervention of the German emperor Otto II, who met defeat at Arab hands at Cotrone (982). What the Byzantine rulers wanted least of all was that the saviours of southern Italy should not be themselves but the Latins. Limited

---

[1] A. Guillou, *Studies on Byzantine Italy* (London, 1970); A. Guillou, *Culture et société en Italie Byzantine (VIe–XIe siècle)* (London, 1978).

Muslim settlement occurred in Calabria, but until the Norman conquest this remained a Greek province of the Byzantine world. There are signs that government recovered and that economic recovery was made possible by the extension of mulberry cultivation in Calabria: Guillou argued that phenomenal amounts of silk were produced in early eleventh-century Calabria, and, even if his mathematics prove rather optimistic, it is clear that vineyards were being extended, towns were being revived, and the region was experiencing economic recovery when the Normans arrived in the 1060s. Roger I used Calabria as his base for the conquest of Sicily, and the link between Sicily and Calabria remained an intimate one throughout the Norman period, expressed not merely in the vibrant trade between Messina, in Sicily, and the Calabrian coast, but also in the use at the Norman court of Calabrian officialdom: the Maleinos family, Calabrian aristocrats, served the Norman government in Sicily, enabling the administration in Palermo to produce Greek documents and to imitate Byzantine protocol. For in Sicily itself memories of Byzantine administrative practices had long withered away.

Muslim-ruled Sicily presents to view another aspect of the Greek presence in Italy: the Greeks appear here as *dhimmis*, protected peoples under Islam, between the mid-ninth and the mid-eleventh centuries. Concentrated more in the east of the island, the Greeks maintained several successful monastic foundations, for example at Maniace, and were as deeply rooted in the rural communities as in the cities. It is clear that the Norman conquest brought a rapid improvement in status: freedom from the poll tax or *jizya* imposed by the Muslims; more opportunities to work in government; benefactions from the Norman rulers (the Normans only gradually shifted their attention to Latin foundations, and even under Roger II Greek monasteries were receiving generous donations from the Hautevilles). Moreover, the Greek civil servants in the Norman administration endowed Greek churches; thus George of Antioch, King Roger II's admiral, founded the church of Santa Maria dell'Ammiraglio (later known as the 'Martorana') in Palermo, with its magnificent Byzantine mosaics.

The 'ordinary' Greeks of the countryside are more of a mystery. Evidence from charters suggests that they were actually able to recruit new members in the twelfth century, as the Muslim population went into decline through emigration, slaughter, and conversion; but the conversion was more often to Greek than to Latin Christianity, according to Jeremy Johns. It is not difficult to see why this should be so. The Greek *papas* or local priest was a more familiar figure to Muslim peasants than the grand ecclesiastics who fluttered around the royal court. Thus we see personal names like Ali giving way to names such as John. Most likely (bearing in mind studies of conversion in early medieval Spain) this was not so much a conversion as a gradual process of osmosis by which allegiances shifted from the mosque to the church as the obvious focus of social life and moral authority in the community. In the longer term, the arrival of the Normans did lead to decline in the numbers speaking Greek and worshipping in the Greek fashion: by the fourteenth century eastern Sicily had a Latin majority. We can thus characterize the Norman conquest as good for the Greeks in the short term, bad for them in the long term.

The cultural life of Norman Sicily was heavily influenced by Greek models: the kings imitated Byzantine ideas of rulership, and they adopted Byzantine methods of administration (such as the use of purple parchment for particularly grand decrees). King Roger II signed his name in Greek and very few of his Sicilian charters were in Latin (even a privilege to the Genoese in 1116 was written in Greek). However, it is likely that the immediate model for the day-to-day Byzantine methods of government on which they drew was the provincial government of Byzantine Calabria, which Roger I had conquered, rather than Constantinople itself. Constantinople was, however, a powerful influence in the arts and letters, as will be seen. In the late twelfth century, the administrator Eugenius, who wrote Greek poetry, was also practised in the production of Latin texts, as he had to be by now, in a trilingual administration in which Latin rather than Greek had become the prime language of government. The finest examples of twelfth-century Byzantine mosaic workmanship to have survived are those from Palermo, Cefalù, and Monreale, and Greek craftsmen were brought to the island to create the magnificent mosaics in the royal palace at Palermo. Equally, the work of translation, fostered by courtiers such as the Latin Henry Aristippus, was made possible as a result of the acquisition of the texts of Plato, Ptolemy, and so on from Constantinople, rather than as a result of discoveries of texts in local libraries: there simply was not a local tradition of Greek scholarship upon which to draw. The high culture of Norman Sicily was impregnated with Byzantine influences; it was now (rather than when the island was under Byzantine or Arab rule) that Greek culture really flourished in Sicily, for it was a Greek court culture dependent on active royal patronage.

In the north of Italy the Greek presence was very limited. There were historic ties between Constantinople and Venice, expressed mainly in trade but also, between 1082 and 1176, in a notional Venetian dependence on the Byzantine emperor; and, as in Sicily, the Venetians capitalized on their links to Constantinople to hire superb mosaicists in the twelfth and thirteenth centuries in order to adorn the Doge's chapel, better known as the Church of St Mark. Burgundio of Pisa translated John Damascene's Greek classic *De orthodoxa fide* in the mid-twelfth century, evidence that contact between Constantinople and Pisa bore fruit in intellectual as well as commercial contacts. But Latins sought to establish themselves in Greek lands (for trade) rather than Greeks in Latin lands. Further south, exceptionally, Ancona recognized Byzantine suzerainty in the years around 1173, but the Greek presence was minute.[2]

The Muslims

The Muslim presence in Italy had a rather different character. The best way to explain this is to compare Sicily with Spain. The Arab-Berber invasion of Spain took place in 711, followed by a very slow but steady Islamization, so that more than half of Muslim-ruled Spain was Muslim by religion before the end of the tenth century. Sicily, on the other hand, was only invaded in 827 and the Islamization of the island had reached a point by the 1060s, when the Normans invaded, at which (at a reasonable estimate) about 60 per cent of the population was Muslim. Another contrast is in the cultural field. Just as Byzantine Sicily had been something of a backwater compared even to southern Italy, Muslim-ruled Sicily lacked the magnificence that was to characterize the period of Norman rule. Indeed, the paradox is the same as with Byzantine culture: the real efflorescence of Muslim

---

[2] Boncompagno da Signa, *The History of the Siege of Ancona*, ed. and trans. A. F. Stone, Archivio del Litorale Adriatico, vi (Venice, 2002).

culture in Sicily occurred when the island had passed into Christian hands, and it owed much to foreign models, particularly Fatimid Egypt and the palace culture of Ifriqiya (modern Tunisia).

Indeed, early eleventh-century Sicily lived in the shadow of Tunisia. It supplied towns such as al-Mahdiyyah with grain, and cotton from Sicily was also crucial in the development of the urban industries of Ifriqiya, as has been revealed in the Cairo Genizah letters, written by Jewish merchants based in Fustat (Old Cairo) and mainly preserved in Cambridge. Palermo became a major port, servicing both the trade of the Islamic world, and supplying exotic goods to a few western entrepreneurs, in particular the merchants of Amalfi, who issued their own gold coins in imitation of the gold *tarí* or quarter-dinars of Sicily, which were manufactured out of the gold that was brought from Tunisia in payment for Sicilian products. Islamic Sicily also saw, in the same way as Islamic Spain, the introduction of specialized crops which had originated further to the east, but which were in heavy demand in the Islamic Mediterranean: indigo, henna, sugar. Following the Norman conquest these products lost their significance, so that wheat emerged as the prime export of Sicily. In the thirteenth century, Emperor Frederick II tried to reinvigorate the production of these specialized commodities, bringing skilled Jewish workers from the Maghrib.

These promising economic developments within Sicily were vitiated by internal political rivalries which in the end opened the door to the Norman invaders. Under the rule of the Kalbites Sicily fell within the sphere of influence of the Shi'ite Fatimid caliphate, whose origins lay in early tenth-century Ifriqiya; but by the eleventh century, when the Fatimid power base was in Egypt, Fatimid control over Sicilian affairs was weaker than ever. By the mid-eleventh century the island was divided between three main emirates, and ibn ath-Thimnah of Catania appealed in 1060 for the aid of Norman cavalry against his foes, after which they stayed and took over. However, in conquering Sicily the Normans had to work out a relationship with the native Muslims, even though they posed as liberators of the Christian population of Sicily and Malta, and secured papal approval. By the time of the fall of Palermo in 1072 the technique they adopted had become standardized: in return for surrender and acceptance of Christian rule, the Muslims were guaranteed the right to practise their religion, though their major mosques were confiscated (as in

Palermo) and all Muslims, along with Jews, were to pay a poll tax, the
gesia, whose name indicates that it was simply a continuation of the
jizyah tax paid by Christians and Jews in pre-Norman times. The aim
was continuity and stability; and this was also expressed through the
adoption of Muslim administrative practices, though many of the key
administrators were Greeks or at any rate converted Muslims.[3]

The most difficult question concerns the social standing of the
Muslims in the countryside following the Norman conquest. Did
conquest make them freer or less free? The question can be
rephrased: did conquest actually lead to a loss of local autonomy? If
we accept that the Normans adapted the Muslim system by which the
dhimmi or protected Jew or Christian paid taxes but retained a high
degree of self-government (making the Muslims into the new
dhimmis), then the issue becomes that of how deeply Norman government penetrated into the localities. The government in Palermo
sought peace within the island and a chance to maximize its revenues
from taxation and from the sale of wheat and cotton. In the west and
south-east of Sicily large areas retained considerable internal autonomy. Yet gradually the pressure on rural and urban Muslims increased.
The *History of the Tyrants of Sicily* attributed to Hugo Falcandus
indicates that the Lombard settlers based in Piazza Armerina
launched raids on Muslim villages in the 1160s, and sought to create
more room for themselves in the east of the island; they were actively
exploiting political unrest within the kingdom:

They made unprovoked attacks on nearby places, and massacred both those
who lived alongside the Christians in various towns as well as those who
owned their own estates, forming distinct communities. They made no distinction of sex or age. The number of those of that community who died is
not easy to reckon, and the few who experienced a better fate (either by
escaping by secret flight or by assuming the guise of Christians), fled to less
dangerous Muslim towns in the southern part of Sicily. To the present day
they hate the Lombard race so much that they have not only refused to live in
that part of Sicily again, but even avoid going there at all.[4]

[3] A fuller discussion of the relationship between Fatimid, Byzantine, and Norman
administrative systems is provided by Hiroshi Takayama in his chapter on 'Law and
monarchy in the south' in this volume.

[4] Cited from *History of the Tyrants of Sicily by 'Hugo Falcandus'*, ed. and trans.
G. A. Loud and T. Wiedemann (Manchester, 1998), pp. 121–2, with minor alterations.

To what extent this reflected a deep rivalry between Christians and Muslims, and to what extent it was simply the result of a breakdown of order which was exploited by the Lombard agitators, it is hard to say. Further internal movements meant that by the end of the century the concentration of Muslims in the west of the island had become pronounced. It was in this area that the crown granted the abbey (later archbishopric) of Monreale vast estates, effectively granting the abbey oversight over the remaining rural Muslim communities.

The Muslims were, in fact, being forced into a tight corner and numbers were continuing to decline quite steeply. The Granadan traveller ibn Jubayr visited Sicily in 1184–5, penetrating as far as the royal palace in Palermo: there he found Muslim men and women in royal service, but he also insisted that many were afraid to avow their Islamic faith publicly, while suggesting that the king turned a blind eye to their devotions. He also described a meeting with ibn Hammud, leader of the Muslim community in Sicily, which conveys similar ambivalence: ibn Hammud was allowed access to the court (when not in disgrace), but he also was subject to vexation, culminating in the seizure of much of his wealth.[5] Ibn Jubayr tells of parents sending their daughters to Islamic lands to marry for fear they will be forced to turn Christian; and, as has been seen, charter evidence suggests that many Muslims were converting. The text cited from Falcandus hints at the existence of crypto-Muslims who pretended to be Christians; in any case, conversion, emigration, and sheer slaughter brought Muslim numbers down and down, so that at the time Frederick II deported the last Muslims there may only have been 20–40,000 left in Sicily.

In the arts, the Muslims of twelfth-century Sicily did play a notable role, even if the preponderant influences came from Ifriqiya and Egypt. At a demotic level, we have the expansion of production of tin-glazed pottery. Finely crafted ivory caskets, of which one of the most spectacular examples is the reliquary of St Petroc preserved in Bodmin, Cornwall, betray the influence of Fatimid artists. The largest series of medieval Muslim figurative paintings in the Mediterranean adorns the wooden ceiling of the Palatine Chapel in Palermo, again betraying very strong Egyptian influence. The silk workshops of Sicily, whose personnel appears to have been male and female, Muslim and

---

[5] *The Travels of ibn Jubayr*, trans. R. J. C. Broadhurst (London, 1952).

Greco-Jewish, produced magnificent robes which still exist in Vienna as part of the coronation vestments of the Holy Roman Emperors, having earlier served the Norman and Hohenstaufen rulers. More striking still is the design of the surviving palaces: the Zisa in Palermo, with its Arabic-style fountain and stucco work; or the Cuba, also in Palermo, another pleasure palace in the North African style. These styles coexisted with Byzantine and western ones; whether the aim was to symbolize the meeting of religions in Sicily or (more likely) it was simply a question of buying the biggest and the best irrespective of artistic coherence has been much debated. A similar question applies to a tombstone of 1148 in Greek, Latin, Arabic, and Judaeo-Arabic: often seen as a symbol of the easy coexistence of Greeks, Latins, Muslims, and Jews in Sicily, it is more likely that it was a loud proclamation of the wish to convert Jews and Muslims. One means by which the royal court hoped to achieve this was the introduction of a Christian liturgy in Arabic. The Palatine Chapel appears to have hosted Christian services in Greek, Latin, and Arabic, and a gospel book in Arabic from Norman Sicily is preserved in the British Library.

Yet it has been seen that the longer-term prospects for the Sicilian Muslims were poor. In the 1190s the Muslims rose up against the government; power at the centre had collapsed, and the papacy began to worry at the resurgence of Islam on the island. But in fact the rebellion, which smouldered for several decades, was concentrated mainly in the west around Jato (the rebels even minted their own coins). One of the first tasks of Frederick II on his return to the island in 1221 after years in Germany was the merciless suppression of the revolt, and his solution to Saracen restiveness was a traditional Mediterranean one: mass deportation to Lucera in Capitanata, where he was looking for skilled manpower to till fertile fields. Islam and Arabic culture in Sicily were thereafter confined to numerous slaves, occasional merchants who settled for a while, and the inhabitants of peripheral islands: Malta was largely Christianized by the 1240s but remained Arabic-speaking, while Pantelleria was in effect a neutralized condominium shared by Sicily and Tunisia, and again Arabic-speaking. Frederick's many admirers, who see in him a paragon of inter-faith understanding and tolerance, tend to stress not these drastic events but his insistence that his Christian subjects must not vex Jews and Muslims, because they are too greatly persecuted at present (thus, not so much disapproval of persecution as disapproval of violent persecution). Again, Frederick's many admirers point to the presence of Muslim scholars at court, but these were much more noticeable under Norman rule, and the translators who worked for Frederick and later for Manfred and Charles I of Anjou were predominantly Jews or converts from Judaism with a knowledge of Arabic.

The creation of Lucera Saracenorum (Lucera of the Saracens), was a remarkable feat. The pre-existing Christian population was scattered to the winds, though it is possible the bishop tried at first to hold on; and yet in the early days of settlement Frederick did insist that it was his intention to convert the Muslims, isolating them from the rest of Islam and allowing Dominican preachers into the city. Conversions were few; the main value of Lucera to Frederick and his successors was as a source of wheat and of skilled military manpower: the emperor's Muslim bodyguard even accompanied him on crusade. The invasion of southern Italy by Charles I of Anjou in 1266 was advertised in part as a crusade against the Lucera Muslims; but even Charles, faced with stiff resistance, showed grudging admiration, and the community was permitted to survive. Franco-Provençal settlers brought down to Capitanata to till the fertile soil around Lucera in place of the Muslims were in the end given outlying villages rather than the city itself, which contained a massive and heavily fortified royal palace; among the items excavators found there were fragments of Chinese celadon ware which graced the tables of Hohenstaufen or Angevin kings. The Saracens of Lucera sent representatives to the king's parliaments in Naples; the leading families, such as that of Abdolasisius (Abd al-Aziz) were honoured by a succession of kings, and eminent Saracens were actually knighted. It was only in 1300 that Charles II of Anjou, short of money and high in religious fervour, decided to arrest the Lucerans and to sell the entire population as slaves: they were already the *servi camere regie*, 'servants of the royal chamber', and in a sense possessed by the king, but it was probably his civil lawyers who argued that this meant they were actually his slaves and that he could sell them to whomever he might choose. They moved from the ambiguous status of the king's *servi* to that of *sclavi*, slaves, subject to many owners. After this disaster small knots of Muslims did survive in the region, as poor, scattered cultivators. The last vestige of Islam in the region is the funeral stone of the military captain Jachia (Yahya) Albosasso, reported by Norman Douglas, which carried the Muslim date equivalent to 5 April 1345.[6] 'It breathes a spirit of noble resignation', Douglas wrote, though it has also been suggested that it arrived in Lucera in more modern times from the Middle East. At any rate, there certainly were scattered Muslim traders and slaves in southern Italy and, particularly, Sicily, even including settled artisans in fifteenth-century Palermo; but they did not form a community. Palermo, as a significant slave market, saw many sales of Muslim slaves, already well documented in the first notarial registers from the city, at the end of the thirteenth century. It was also in the guise of slaves that Muslims occasionally appeared in such northern cities as Genoa; Islam discouraged Muslim merchants from trading in infidel lands, and even the embassies that arranged treaties between the Italian mercantile republics and the north African states tended to be Christian embassies sent to Muslim lands, and very rarely the reverse. The sight of free Muslims was therefore a great rarity in northern Italy. Sardinia, for its part, had experienced Muslim raids in the early eleventh century, but it was never occupied by Muslim armies in a meaningful sense. Ironically, merchants and invaders sometimes treated the native Sards as if they were infidels, selling them into slavery, but that is evidence of greed and prejudice rather than of the survival of Islam in Sardinia.

The Jews

The Lucera Muslims were implanted outsiders; but the Jews of southern Italy and Sicily were, if anything, one of the more stable elements in the shifting population of southern Italy. This fact helped protect the Jews: they were not, as in northern Europe, outsiders who had been pushed to the margins of society, forced into unpopular occupations such as moneylending; they were another distinctive group among the many in medieval southern Italy. When significant numbers of Jews first settled in southern Italy it is impossible to say. More revealing than scraps of evidence from ancient Pompeii or Puteoli-Pozzuoli is the sense, among the Jews of the tenth and eleventh

[6] N. Douglas, *Old Calabria* (2nd edn., Harmondsworth, 1962), p. 19.

centuries, that their history had begun in the days of Titus, who had supposedly settled several thousand Jewish captives in Taranto, Otranto, and nearby. In other words, there developed by about 1000 an awareness of the depth of Jewish roots in the heel of Italy. The city of Venosa still preserves many Hebrew inscriptions, indicating that there was a lively community of Jews in the sixth to ninth centuries, often speaking Greek. Jewish communities sprang up around the new centres of commerce that emerged in southern Italy in the early Middle Ages: at Salerno, Amalfi, and so on, and a Jew of Salerno was, according to legend, involved in founding the famous medical school of Salerno. The Jewish settlements in the heel of Italy were substantial. Here one of the major centres of Jewish scholarship was Oria, but the reputation for learning of the Apulian Jews was summarized in the saying: 'From Bari shall go forth the Law, and the word of the Lord from Otranto.' At the end of the tenth century, the physician, astronomer, and Hebrew scholar Shabbetai Donnolo appears to have had good relations with the monk St Nilus of Rossano.

More is known about the Jewish communities of Islamic Sicily: this is the result of the survival for a thousand years in Old Cairo of a synagogue storeroom containing many thousands of business letters and personal documents. Their speciality was the luxury trade: among notable imports handled by Sicilian Jews were dyestuffs such as brazilwood and lapis lazuli; silk was both imported and exported. These were commodities which were traded along the very extended trade routes that carried Jews to Yemen, even India. One important feature of the trade of the Sicilian Jews in the Islamic and early Norman period is the fluidity of the community itself; Spanish and Egyptian Jews would come to settle in Palermo, buying houses, marrying, and making business deals. However, the coming of the Normans gradually and indirectly undermined these Jewish merchants: Christian hegemony over the Mediterranean and victories against Islam in Sicily and the Holy Land brought Genoa, Pisa, and Venice mastery over the spice trade and over the trade routes past Sicily.

However, the Normans had no difficulty in accepting that the Jews were part of the fabric of local society. Normans and Jews even converged: one of the more colourful figures was the son of a Norman knight, Obadiah the Proselyte, who brought with him, and adapted to Hebrew use, the church music with which he was familiar. The archbishop of Bari, Andreas, also apparently became a Jew, but fled to Constantinople and Egypt out of harm's way.[7] A further indication of the relatively untroubled state of the Jewish community comes from the reign of the first Norman king of Sicily and southern Italy, Roger II. In 1153 a Jew exchanged some land with an abbess in order to acquire a plot for a prayer room between the main synagogue of Naples and a nearby church. A dozen or so years later the Spanish Jew Benjamin of Tudela visited southern Italy, and recorded the existence of flourishing communities in Salerno, Capua, and Benevento, in all of which their numbers supposedly ran into hundreds, in the case of Naples into thousands.[8] He also provides rich evidence for the flourishing state of the Jewish community of Palermo, which was mainly concentrated in one area close to the present-day Martorana church and close to a water course (vital for clothworkers). For the Jewish population in southern Italy and Sicily consisted primarily of artisans. The preparation, especially dyeing, of cloth, including silk, dominated their economic life. Within the towns, Jews often sought a monopoly over the slaughtering of animals and they cultivated vines, two activities which ensured supplies of kosher products for Jewish consumption. The Jews were not particularly deeply involved in moneylending. Thomas Aquinas emphasized the difference between the Jews of his Neapolitan homeland and the Jews of northern Europe, often forced into this occupation.

It has been seen that direct contact between the royal court and Muslim scholars was limited in the era of Frederick II. The Jews, with their knowledge of Arabic, served as intermediaries between Islamic and Christian culture. Frederick looked for a wise Jew and was put in touch with the Castilian scholar Judah ben Solomon ha-Cohen, the star pupil of the influential Toledo rabbi Meir Abulafia; after some correspondence, the Jew and the emperor met, and evidently Frederick enjoyed his contact with such a lively philosophical mind. The translators appear to have been organized by Michael Scot, Frederick's astrologer, and were drawn from a common background: they were mostly members of the ibn Tibbon family, Provençal Jews of Spanish

---

[7] There is a large literature on Obadiah. See for the context J. Prawer, 'The autobiography of Obadyah the Norman', in I. Twersky (ed.), *Studies in Medieval Jewish History and Literature* (Cambridge, Mass., 1979), pp. 110–34.

[8] *The Itinerary of Benjamin of Tudela*, ed. M. N. Adler (London, 1907), pp. 7–9.

origin, or their close associates. Jacob Anatoli, brother-in-law of Moses ibn Tibbon, translated Ptolemy's Almagest and works by Averroes; but to imagine him frequenting the imperial court on easy terms is to stretch the evidence too far. The Jewish scholars who worked for Frederick were thus products of Spanish and southern French Hebrew learning; they were not torch-bearers of the Jewish scholarship of the Regno, though Faraj of Girgenti (Agrigento), who worked for King Charles I, was a Sicilian.

In fact, the Sicilian Jews were still living in the shadow of Islamic culture in the centuries after the Christian conquest of Sicily. The Spanish kabbalist Abraham Abulafia, writing at the end of the thirteenth century, observed:

Note that the Jews who live among the Ishmaelites speak Arabic like them; those who live among the Greeks speak Greek; those who inhabit Italy speak Italian, the Germans [Ashkenazim] speak German, the inhabitants of Turkish lands speak Turkish, and so on. But the great wonder is what happens among the Jews in all Sicily, who not only speak the local language or Greek, as do all those who dwell there with them, but have preserved the Arabic tongue which they had learned in former times, when the Ishmaelites were dwelling there.

Thus many of the Jews of Erice in western Sicily around 1300 had Arabic names, and we have already encountered Faraj of Girgenti. The Jews of Sicily were 'Arabs by language, Jews by religion', to cite Henri Bresc, though others would stress the gradual erosion of this distinctive identity, which disappeared in Sicily just as it had already vanished in most of Spain.[9] In scholarly attainment, the Sicilian Jews could not match the Sephardim of Spain, however. By contrast, as will be seen, the Jews of areas such as the Marches used the local romance vernacular.

Frederick II's reign marks the beginning of a process of transition. In many respects his attitude to the Jews was highly traditional, and he actively defended the Jews of his German kingdom against vehement detractors. The removal of the Muslim population from Sicily had effects on the Jews as well, since it left them as the sole non-Christian element in the island's population. The influence of the papacy on his legislation can be seen in his decrees issued at Messina

[9] H. Bresc, *Arabi per lingua, Ebrei per religione: l'evoluzione dell'ebraismo siciliano in ambiente latino dal XII al XV secolo* (Messina, 2001; also French edn., Paris, 2001).

in the spring of 1221. Jews were classed alongside prostitutes as a group of outcasts who threatened to contaminate those Christians with whom they had contact: each group must be made visible in its costume (male Jews must sport beards); and where appropriate they must be physically segregated from the mass of Christians. In further legislation of 1231, also to be seen as a statement of principle, Frederick warns against persecuting Jews and Muslims, who must have the same right to initiate legal proceedings as anyone else, and who are at the moment too severely persecuted. By 1237, importing terminology he had applied in Germany, Jews were defined as *servi camere* 'servants of the [royal] chamber'; this term indicated that they were ultimately the possessions of the ruler, but that he would also protect them and actually expected them to be well treated by non-Jews for the service they did to the king. It is worth adding that this terminology was immediately applied to the Muslims of Sicily and then to those of Lucera as well.

The great demographic contrast between medieval and early modern Italian Jewry was that in the former period the great majority of Jews lived in the south, whereas after the mid-sixteenth century it was the south that was empty of Jews, who now gathered in the towns of the north and centre. Rome, however, poised between north and south, had a continuous history of Jewish settlement, and the claim is often made that 'the Jewish community of Rome is probably the oldest in the world, with a continuous history from classical times down to the present day'.[10] This continuity is not in doubt. The distinctive liturgy of the Jews of Rome (which is still in use) was of enormous influence in the wider history of European Jewry, laying the foundations of the German or Ashkenazi rite, which eventually took on an identity of its own. Benjamin of Tudela's travel narrative testifies to the strength of the Jewish community in Rome. There, indeed, the Jewish community acquired additional and unwanted attention when the papacy was contested between two candidates, one of whom Anacletus, pope from 1130 to 1139, was a member of the Pierleoni family, a family of Jewish descent. The famous monk St Bernard vigorously denounced the idea that a 'Jew' could sit on the throne of St Peter, an odd statement because Anacletus was at most the grandson of practising Jews, not to mention the fact that Bernard

---

[10] To cite the Israeli *Encyclopaedia Judaica*, vol. xiv, p. 239, s.v. 'Rome'.

appeared to have forgotten St Peter's Jewish birth. According to Benjamin of Tudela, another financier, Jehiel ben Anav, acted as bookkeeper to Pope Alexander III in the twelfth century, when there were probably 200 Jewish families in the city, among whom the Anav family claimed particular antiquity and prestige. Another member of the same family, Benjamin ben Abraham Anav, was very active in the writing of Hebrew religious poetry, some of which is still recited in the Tempio Maggiore or Great Synagogue in Rome, notably on the Day of Atonement:

Bemiqdash El ve-heikhalav, ha-yonah shir terev, u-vat le-saper mahalalav . . .

In the Divine sanctuary and in its halls the dove [Israel] immerses itself in psalmody, beginning from the morning onwards to enumerate God's marvels and celebrate his glory with sweet melody.[11]

The Jewish community of Rome lived in the area around the Tiber island that remains to this day the main focus of Jewish life in Rome: a Jewish quarter, but not, until the sixteenth century, a Jewish ghetto. Relations with the pope existed on two levels: as lord of the city, the pope might claim vexatious special taxes from the Jews, as Boniface VIII did in 1295; as head of the Catholic Church, the pope presided over occasions such as the Fourth Lateran Council of 1215, which legislated generally concerning the Jews, demanding, for instance, the wearing of Jewish badges, initially to little apparent effect. In 1257 Jewish badges were enforced, though such regulations tended to be imposed solely in order to secure a pay-off from the Jews in return for suspending the order; a decade later the Jewish cemetery was desecrated. Despite such very unpleasant incidents, the overall picture is not radically different from that in southern Italy: the community was accepted as part of the fabric of Roman society, and the Jews often found protectors among those who ruled the city, whether in the occasional benevolent pope or local leaders such as Cola di Rienzo in the middle of the fourteenth century. Perhaps one indication of the generally peaceful relationship between the Jews and other Romans is the career of the spirited poet Immanuel Romano; he mocked Guelfs and Ghibellines in Italian and left a Hebrew account of his journey to Heaven which has sometimes been cited as evidence

---

[11] D. Disegni (ed.), *Preghiere del giorno di Espiazione secondo il Rito Italiano* (Rome and Turin, 5726/1966), pp. 128, 132, and esp. 260.

that he was close to Dante, not that Dante's comments about Jews were always complimentary.

Further north, Pisa and Lucca had Jewish communities, and had been lively centres of Jewish culture since the tenth and eleventh centuries, when a number of important liturgical texts, later adopted in the German liturgy, were written by the rabbis of Lucca such as Meshullam ben Kalonymos. The other major centres of trade, Genoa and Venice, were home to very few Jews and sometimes explicitly discouraged Jewish settlement; the idea that the wealthy merchant of twelfth-century Genoa, Solomon of Salerno, was a Jew is no longer taken seriously. Jewish settlement in northern Italy only became significant in the fourteenth century, with the foundation of loan banks staffed by German and other Jewish immigrants. However, an early sign of the Jewish presence in the Marches or nearby is the Judaeo-Italian elegy of the early thirteenth century, a romance text written for the fast on the ninth of Av, the day in the Jewish calendar when the destruction of the First and Second Temples is commemorated:

> La ienti de Siòn plange e lutta . . .
> The people of Zion weeps and mourns . . .
> La notti e la die sta plorando
> Li soi grandezi remembrando,
> E mo pe lo mundu vao gattivandu
> Night and day it sheds tears,
> Remembering their greatness,
> And now throughout the world lives in subjection . . .[12]

On the other hand, scholars of both Italian and Jewish history have decisively rebutted the recent claim that a Jew of Ancona called Jacob left a travel diary describing his voyage to China at the end of the thirteenth century; such long-distance contacts, barely conceivable in the age of the Cairo Genizah, were now unthinkable.

Political strife in Italy in the thirteenth century had a severe impact on the Jews. The conquest of southern Italy by the Angevin dynasty in 1266 signalled the coming of a new, anti-Talmudic approach to Judaism, which had developed particularly in the circle of King Louis IX of France, whose brother Charles now became king of Sicily and southern Italy. Under Charles I, the convert Manuforte was permitted

---

[12] R. Sampson, *Early Romance Texts: An Anthology* (Cambridge, 1980), pp. 181–3.

to organize a preaching campaign in the hope of converting Jews. Spasmodic acts of this sort were transformed into a veritable campaign against the Jews under his son Charles II: it was the image of the Jew as a literally bloodsucking murderer, guilty of human sacrifice, that appears to have motivated the persecutions of the 1290s. Jews were given the choice of expulsion or conversion, and one bitterly anti-Jewish source boasts that 8,000 converted. Communities of converts, *neofiti*, emerged, notably around Trani in Apulia, which was evidently the focal point of the persecutions. Charles II's motivation must be sought in the attempt of the Angevin kings to articulate a view of themselves as Christian monarchs, ruling Christian subjects; as has been seen, the persecution also extended to Muslims, most of whom were rounded up and sold as slaves in 1300. The Christian identity of the kingdom offered a platform for a policy of centralization and the assertion of royal authority, after twenty years of chaos and civil war.

These wars saw the island of Sicily break away from the mainland and reconstitute itself as a separate kingdom; but there too the Jews found themselves in the firing line. The reformist ruler of Sicily Frederick III, a Catalan, was inspired by Church legislation as well as by Spanish examples to decree the evacuation of the Jews of Palermo from the Cassaro region of Palermo and their concentration in a new walled Jewish quarter or *giudecca*; Jews were also not to eat and drink with Christians, nor to possess Christian slaves or servants. This type of physical separation needs to be seen as a form of 'internal expulsion', and similar measures were taken a little earlier in such places as Majorca. Such policies stopped short of the expulsions of Jews so freely practised in northern Europe; they gave the crown the opportunity to continue to draw income from its Jews, rather than simply seizing their goods once and for all, as often happened with expulsions. The wish to keep the Jews may also have been influenced by hopes that they could still be converted into useful Christian citizens; missionaries such as the prolific Ramon Llull, from Majorca, continued to target the Jews of Sicily and southern Italy, though Llull at least seems to have converted not a soul. On the other hand, the Catalan–Aragonese invasion of Sardinia gave impetus to the growth of a small but economically successful Jewish community, largely of Catalan origin, on that island.

Yet at this time what was happening on the ground was far less sinister for the Jews than the thinking at the royal courts of Naples and Sicily might indicate. At Erice in western Sicily Jews and Christians lived side by side around the same courtyards on good terms, and the Jews even made intensive use of a Christian notary.[13] Campaigns against Jews seem to have been directed from above, and it was only in the late fourteenth and fifteenth centuries that popular anti-Judaism became a powerful force which some rulers resisted and others supported. This decline in relations may be linked to the late spread of moneylending activities among the Jews of the Italian south during the fifteenth century.

Conclusion

The intention here has been to show that the history of Italy is not the same as the history of Catholics speaking a variety of romance dialects. The Jews and the Greeks were very ancient inhabitants of Italy; the Muslims included many native Sicilians who had converted to Islam and whose descendants would eventually convert back to Christianity. There are indeed many Italies, and some of them do not look (in the traditional historiography) very Italian; but they are decidedly Italian all the same, in the sense that these communities existed for long periods on the soil of the peninsula and its islands, contributing significantly to economic, cultural, and sometimes political life within those lands.

---

[13] The most recent edition is that of A. Sparti, *Il registro del notaio Giovanni Maiorana*, 2 vols. (Palermo, 1982); for a discussion, see D. Abulafia, 'Una comunità ebraica della Sicilia occidentale: Erice 1298–1304', *Archivio storico per la Sicilia orientale*, 80 (1984), pp. 157–90; repr. in D. Abulafia, *Commerce and Conquest in the Mediterranean, 1100–1500* (Aldershot, 1993); Hebrew version with English summary in *Zion: A Quarterly for Research in Jewish History*, 51 (1986), pp. 295–317.

11

Sardinia and Italy

Marco Tangheroni

In Dante's famous *De vulgari eloquentia*, a treatise on literary language written around 1305, the author describes Sardinia as 'associated' with Italy, rather than part of it, and he describes the Sardinian language as a laboured and mechanical imitation of Latin, 'as if of monkeys'. This reflects an idea, common in authors both before and after Dante, such as Raimbaut de Vaiqueiras or Fazio degli Uberti, that Sard was a barbarous and incomprehensible language. Linguists now consider Sard a language in its own right, due to its particular characteristics, evident in documents written in the vernacular as early as the last decades of the eleventh century. In the *Commedia*, the poem that brought Dante universal fame, certain passages convey the idea of Sardinia as a strange and remote island, plagued by malaria: in the Barbagia area (the mountainous internal region of Sardinia), women would walk about with their breasts shamelessly uncovered. Such ideas are commonplaces, but were widely held. In a chronicle of the twelfth century one reads that Sardinia was inhabited by 'rude, rustic, savage, obstinate, effeminate, and monstrous men'. And in the thirteenth century the archbishop of Pisa, Federigo Visconti, asked himself 'how will we go to that land of horror and solitude . . . which one visits only when pressed by necessity?'

Nevertheless, other events and characters in Dante's *Commedia* underline the many historic links between Sardinia and the Italian peninsula (in Sardo the *terramana*, or 'great land'). The significant historiographical work on medieval Sardinia of recent decades confirms these links, despite periods of isolation (which in any case were never absolute), and indicates growing relationships of interdependence with Italian history, in particular with Genoa and Pisa (but not only these places: it is enough to remember the importance of links

with the papacy and the empire). The notion of a relation of interdependence revises what some historians have portrayed exclusively
as dependence on Sardinia's part.

The emperor Justinian had maintained Sardinia administratively
and politically as part of Africa. Subject to attacks by the Longobards,
it continued to form part of the Eastern Roman Empire, and even
repeated Muslim raids, while contributing to the downfall of the
ancient cities and desertion of coastal centres, had not diverted the
island from a distinctive political and juridical development, increasingly detached from Byzantium. At the beginning of the eleventh
century, Sardinia was divided into four kingdoms, known as *giudicati*,
or judicatures: Torres in the north-west, Gallura in the north-east,
Arborea in the centre-west, and Cagliari in the south. Compared with
the rest of Europe these states were characterized by the strong per-
sistence of public law. In private law local customs had developed,
such as marriage *a sa sardisca*, based on the communion of goods
between spouses, rather than a dowry. The literary, cultural, and
ecclesiastical traditions of the island were largely of Greek origin.

In this period Mujahid of Denia, the ruler of the Balearic Islands,
tried to take control of Sardinia, with the aim of establishing a maritime Islamic state that would have been capable of controlling the
entire western Mediterranean. The city-states of Genoa and Pisa,
encouraged by the pope, intervened to defend Sardinia, defeating
Mujahid in two successive campaigns (1015–16). This was the beginning of the Christian reconquest of the Mediterranean, as explained
in another chapter of this book. For Sardinia it was the beginning of
domination by the two maritime city-states, which were soon to enter
into open competition with each other. At the same time, the pope
became concerned with the problem of how to bring the Sardinian
Church back into the Latin fold and effect ecclesiastical reforms.

The papacy and Sardinia: political and ecclesiastical intervention

Pope Gregory VII, who had wanted to consecrate the new archbishops of Cagliari and Torres personally from the first months of his

pontificate, wrote a stern letter to the four judge-kings of the island. After reprimanding them for allowing 'the Christian religion to reach a point of maximum decadence', he recalled them to their duty to behave 'as the legitimate offspring of your mother the Roman Church'. The pope also criticized the behaviour of their predecessors, accusing them of negligence in relation to Sardinia and its Church. In successive letters, beginning in 1080, in response to reports from one of his legates, the pope revealed significant dissatisfaction with the conduct of the judges, in particular the ruler of Cagliari. Yet the pope did not have pretensions to political control over the island: the issue close to Gregory VII's heart was the 'latinization' of the island's Church, and the spread of reform, both to suppress Greek influence and rites (such as the bishops' habit of not shaving, and the relationship between metropolitan and suffragan bishops), and to control the judges' tendencies to intervene in the nomination of bishops and prelates. Nevertheless, Gregory VII did not hesitate to enlist the judges to spread reform against the resistance of the clerics themselves.

Already under the pontificate of Alexander II, there had been a subdivision of the island into three ecclesiastical provinces, and probably also the creation of a large number of suffragan dioceses. And in previous years, beginning with the pontificate of Gregory VII, the island had witnessed the establishment of monastic communities originating from the mainland, often at the request of the judges themselves. For example, in 1063 Barisone of Torres had asked the abbot of Monte Cassino to establish a monastery in his judicature. After an initial nucleus of twelve monks was captured by pirates, the first settlements of monks from Monte Cassino were established, thanks to donations of churches and property by Barisone.

For his part, Gregory VII favoured the establishment of monks from St Victor of Marseilles (known as the Victorines) in the judicature of Cagliari, as well as the donation of a church to the cathedral church of Pisa by the judge of Torres. The motivation for this donation, described in a document drafted in the presence of, and with 'the counsel' of, the pontifical legate, is interesting: the donation was made after it was ascertained that there was 'an absence of religiosity and ecclesiastical instruction' and the spread of 'nefarious sins due to the negligence of the clergy', who lived in a very similar way to lay people. The judge expressed the hope that the bishop and the canons of Pisa would be able to reform this deplorable state of affairs. The hope was also shared by Gregory VII, since at that time the diocese of Pisa was still loyal to the pope and engaged in ecclesiastical reform. Urban II continued the same line, entrusting the pontifical legation of Sardinia in perpetuity to Daimberto (who was promoted to the rank of archbishop) and his successors. A general synod ratified the island's adhesion to a programme of reform.

During the twelfth century monastic institutions gradually spread throughout Sardinia. Besides the monks of Monte Cassino and of St Victor (who, as well as their vast latifundia, also controlled the rich salt marshes of Cagliari), Benedictines from Camaldoli and Vallombrosa also settled, as well as Cistercians. In general the monks' patrimonial lands, donated by the judges and various noble families, were very extensive and also included numerous serfs. Disagreements between bishops and monasteries were not unknown. For example, in 1118 the archbishop of Cagliari wrote to the pope to protest at the lack of respect shown by the Victorine monks of San Saturno: 'I am ashamed, and blush in having to recount the ruin, suffering, and restrictions suffered by the once powerful and respected Church of Cagliari.' It was only in the thirteenth century that the great monastic properties went into crisis. Later, when Franciscans and Dominicans arrived, they tended to settle in the cities.

Above all it was the Pisan archbishops, several of whom made personal visits, who repeatedly intervened in the ecclesiastical affairs of the island. In 1138, Innocent II added the two dioceses of Gallura to the perpetual legation in Sardinia conferred on the Pisan archdiocese. In 1176, the primacy of the archbishops of Pisa was extended to all Sardinian dioceses. But beginning with the pontificate of Innocent III (1198–1216), partly due to the Ghibelline tendencies emerging in Pisa, the popes began to intervene frequently to make sure that privileges conceded to Pisa did not impinge on the rights of the Holy See. These interventions became more decisive after the conflict with the emperor Frederick I, and the idea that Sardinia formed part of the patrimony of the Roman Church began to gain strength.

A Sardinian council held at Santa Giusta in 1226 to activate decrees made at the Fourth Lateran Council, presided over by a papal legate, denounced the intrigues of lay clergy and clergy from Pisa, allegedly aiming to 'impose the dominion of Pisa over Sardinia, which in fact belongs to the Roman Church'. The council established the principle that the nomination of Pisan bishops and canons in Sardinia would only be possible with the specific approval of the pope himself. It was without such permission that in 1263 the Pisan archbishop Federico Visconti made a pastoral visit to Sardinia. Deprived of legatine powers derived from Rome, he appealed to 'patriarchal' rights of 'primacy' over the entire island.

As Turtas has written, this was a total reversal of the line followed from Gregory VII to Alexander III. This was a result not only of changed relations between Pisa and the papacy, but also of the popes' desire to assert their temporal rights over Sardinia, inherent in the supposed Donation of Constantine. They also wanted to put an end to the increasing tendency of the noble houses of Pisa to appropriate the various judicatures of the island. The end result would be the feudal gift of the 'Kingdom of Sardinia and Corsica' by Boniface VIII to James II of Aragon. This took place in the general context of an agreement aiming to make peace in the Mediterranean and to resolve the question of the kingdom of Sicily thrown up by the revolt of the Vespers in 1282. After James II had given concrete meaning to Boniface's gift with a large military expedition, a few Pisan monasteries lived on, though not for more than a few decades. After that, the Sardinian episcopacy was increasingly under the influence of Catalonia.

The political penetration of Pisa and Genoa in the eleventh and twelfth centuries

It is preferable—in our view—to speak of Pisans and Genoese, rather than Pisa and Genoa. It is true that the two cities, after alternating phases of anti-Muslim collaboration and the early conflicts of the eleventh century, appear to have been locked into an almost permanent war against each other for the entire twelfth century, during which control over Sardinia and Corsica was one of the central issues. Nevertheless, it is important to underline the variety of Pisan and Genoese forces holding an interest in Sardinia. It is misleading to talk of 'dominators' and 'dominated', as if these words represented monolithic groups. Among them were a variety of interests: the great

Ligurian and Tuscan noble families, religious orders, great merchants, lesser merchants and artisans, and even barely known individuals. These interests gathered together in various ways, sometimes with converging objectives, at other times with opposing ones. Furthermore, at least in the eleventh and twelfth centuries, the four insular kingdoms were capable of their own political initiatives, taking advantage of the possibility of aligning here with Genoa, there with Pisa—a dangerous political strategy that in the end would drag them towards dissolution.

To chronicle the minutiae of a political situation that was in constant flux would be outside the scope of this chapter, but a few examples will serve to illustrate the general trends. When the judge of Torres, Costantino, died in 1127, the powerful Athen family tried to appropriate the throne, taking advantage of the minority of the heir, Gonario, but certain rich Pisan merchants came to his aid. Taken to Pisa, where he was educated, he was then able to take the throne with Pisan military aid, before ending his life as a monk at Citeaux. More significant still is the case of the judge Barisone of Arborea, who conceived a very ambitious political plan in the middle of the twelfth century. After marrying a noble Catalan woman, he tried to organize a Pisan–Catalan alliance for a new expedition against the Balearic Islands. But Pisa, which had established favourable commercial agreements with the Muslim world, was not interested in new military undertakings. Barisone then shifted his attention to Genoa, with whose political and financial support he was crowned 'king of Sardinia' by the emperor Frederick I Barbarossa, at Pavia in 1164. However, far from bringing about political unity on the island, Barisone found himself in grave financial difficulties due to his inability to repay loans taken from Genoese financiers. He was forced to remain in Genoa, virtually a prisoner of his own debts. Less than a year later, on the other hand, Barbarossa allied himself with Pisa, promising the city every power and jurisdiction over Sardinia, with 'all that is in Sardinia and all that will be there in the future'. This act provoked an immediate reaction from the pope, who considered the island part of the dominions of the Holy See.

In later years Pietro of Cagliari forged an alliance with Genoa, allowing free commerce between the city and his judicature, from which he expelled the Pisans. A Genoese consul came to the island and Pietro swore faith to the commune of Genoa and its archbishop.

At the same time the Genoese increased their influence within the judicature of Torres, particularly after the conquest of the fortress of Bonifacio in southern Corsica. By about 1180 it seemed that the Ligurian republic was outstripping Pisa in terms of influence in Sardinia. But the Pisans were not slow to respond, and in doing so they opened a new phase: that of judges from the mainland of Italy.

Judicial dynasties and mainland lords

Beginning in 1187, supported by Pisa, of which he had become a citizen, the marquis Guglielmo di Massa, a member of the noble house of the Obertenghi, went to Sardinia with an army and entered the political struggles among the judicatures. He ascended the throne of Cagliari and attacked Arborea and Torres. The example was soon imitated by another very politically powerful Pisan family, the Visconti (not to be confused with the Visconti of Milan), supported in their activities on the island by noble and mercantile families from Pisa.

In 1207 Lamberto Visconti married the heir of the judge of Gallura, Elena. He began to contest the initiatives of the great Genoese families, the Doria, the Spinola, and the Malaspina, all intent on carving out baronies within the judicature of Torres. Lamberto's son Ubaldo married Adelasia, the daughter of the judge Mariano. When Ubaldo died, Adelasia married Enzo, the illegitimate son of the emperor Frederick II. The marriage, which was opposed by the pope, the clergy, and many of the important families of the judicature, was approved by the Genoese.

In the judicature of Cagliari, the Visconti and the commune of Pisa took advantage of the weakness of the judge Benedetta de Massa in order to construct a new fortified city on the hill above the Gulf of Cagliari, Castel di Castro, a few kilometres from the judicial capital, Santa Igia. The Catalans called the new city Castell de Caller, whence the name Cagliari. Conflicts between Pisan families, such as the clash between the Visconti and the Gherardesca, also played themselves out in Sardinia: a war broke out between the two families, the former now supported by the pope, and the latter by the city of Pisa. In the judicature of Arborea, the throne was taken by Guglielmo, count of

Capraia, a powerful family of the Valdarno linked to Pisa. Thus all four of the island's judicatures came to have sovereigns who were of mainland origin, as the destiny of Sardinia became enmeshed in the clashing ambitions of the empire and the papacy. In Pisa itself, what became known as the 'Sardinian question' was at the centre of the commune's power struggles, particularly between the Visconti and the Gherardesca.

The end of the judicatures and Pisan Sardinia

The judge of Cagliari, Chiano di Massa, in an attempt to recover a degree of independence from an increasing Pisan presence, allied himself with Genoa, to whom he ceded control of both Santa Igia and Castel di Castro, while the Pisans succeeded in maintaining control of the port area. The Pisan reaction was rapid, and Chiano was killed in an attack on the capital. His successor, Guglielmo Cepola, strengthened links with Genoa, and another war was fought on the island between the two maritime powers, at the same time as the war that took place at Acre (1256–8). In Sardinia the battle was also won by Pisa. Santa Igia was razed, and with it the judicature came to an end. The western part of its territory was given to Count Donoratico della Gherardesca, the central part to Arborea, ruled by the counts of Capraia, and the eastern part to Gallura, ruled by Giovanni Visconti. Castel di Castro remained an administratively autonomous commune, politically dependent on Pisa—its inhabitants were almost exclusively Pisan or of Pisan origin, while around the walls developed quarters that were populated by Sardinians and immigrants from various places.

The Donoratico della Gherardesca, the Capraia, and the Visconti held their sections of the former judicature in feudal title, confirmed by the contribution of tributes to Pisa. These 'lords of Sardinia' (*domini Sardinee*), as they came to be known in Pisan statutes, called themselves the 'lords of the thirds of Cagliari'. At the same time the judicature of Torres (or Logudoro) had also completely disintegrated. The Doria, Spinola, and Malaspina had carved out for themselves vast, though not always contiguous, domains. The commune of Sassari, though still possessing broad autonomy, gravitated towards

Pisa, which sent a representative each year. Only the judicature of Arborea maintained its own statutory identity. It is therefore only for this period (from about 1250 to 1325) that one can speak of a 'Sardegna Pisana', and even then it never applied to the entire island. This goes against the better part of contemporary historiography, which has absorbed the propaganda of medieval Pisa: the notion of a centuries-long Sardinian dependence on Pisa.

In fact, the way the lords of Sardinia conceived of their power and their interests led to their break with the commune of Pisa, in which government had been assumed by the people. In 1270 the judge Giovanni Visconti and Count Ugolino della Gherardesca, rather than recognize the commune's authority over their Sardinian territories, exiled themselves from Pisa and formed a Guelf faction in Pisan politics, which had traditionally been Ghibelline and pro-empire. The commune used force to take Gallura and the eastern part of the judicature of Cagliari away from the Visconti. Later on, after the tragic end in 1288 of the brief Pisan lordship of Count Ugolino (made famous by Dante's *Commedia*), his sons Guelfo and Lotto, supported by Genoa, rebelled against Pisa. Again Pisa managed, with the help of the judge of Arborea, to quell the revolt. Thus part of Sardinia passed into direct government by the Tuscan commune.

Pisan and Genoese economic activity in Sardinia: modes and consequences

Documents from the second half of the eleventh century and the first years of the twelfth century indicate two separate aspects of the Pisan and Genoese economic penetration of Sardinia: the seeking of privileges for merchants; and the acquisition, thanks to donations, of property on the part of ecclesiastical organizations based in the two cities. In reality there are connections between the two phenomena, not least because the operations of the two cities' cathedrals were also, to a certain extent, expressions of the civil communities they represented. Nor should merchants be regarded as a precisely defined group: representatives of many social groups were involved in the maritime activities of Pisa and Genoa.

A document in Sard, datable between 1080 and 1085, whose authenticity has recently been confirmed, details the exemption from the trade tolls obtained by the Pisans in the judicature of Torres. A few years later, as a counter-initiative to the politico-military actions of the commune, the Opera del Duomo of Pisa obtained the first territorial concessions on the island, at the same time as those obtained by the Genoese cathedral.

Pisan and Genoese merchants did not limit themselves to visits to the ports and intermediary commercial activities between the island (on which the exchange economy had had limited development, as indicated by the monastic registers known as *condaghi*) and the Italian mainland. Merchants, using the landed possessions of the ecclesiastical bodies (known as *donnicalie*), penetrated the hinterlands, acquiring agricultural and pastoral products directly, offering loans, and introducing a money economy. This explains the fact that two cardinals, sent to the island by the pope in 1176 to try to negotiate peace between Pisa and Genoa, condemned the cities' activities on the island as usurious. The condemnation remained a dead letter: over the decades penetration by mainland interests broke down the social and economic traditions of the island, and stimulated rapid and profound changes in its society.

One of the major indications of these changes was the development of urban areas, which in twelfth-century Sardinia was well behind trends in Mediterranean Europe more generally. Pisan and Genoese influence gave rise to significant urban development along Sardinia's coasts in the thirteenth century.

Castel di Castro (Cagliari) was founded by the Pisans in 1216, as we have seen, and grew rapidly, thanks to its position in the western Mediterranean. The Pisan port and its commercial activities came to be of primary importance for traffic with Majorca and Africa. Within the walls the population was exclusively Pisan or of Pisan origin, but outside the walls there developed large areas, known as *appendici*, with artisanal, market-garden, and port areas. Also of Pisan origin was the mining city of Villa di Chiesa (Iglesias); founded in 1258 by Count Ugolino, he gave it a statute (the *Breve*) which promoted the development of mining and metallurgical activity, and guaranteed the liberty of the Sardinian natives, who were joined by immigrants, particularly from Corsica. Nevertheless, the foremen, who came from the *borghese* class (as detailed in the *Breve*), were all of Pisan origin.

More autonomous, in terms of both driving force and ethnic composition, was the development of Sassari. Still a simple *curtis* under monastic ownership in the twelfth century, by the early decades of the thirteenth century it was a rapidly growing city with a mercantile class largely of Sardinian origin. Soon this class would be divided into two factions, the first supporting Pisa, the second Genoa. Even more independent was the development of Oristano, even though there were significant immigrations, first from Pisa, and later from Genoa. On the north-eastern coast, on the site of the ancient city of Olbia, grew Terranova, which a Pisan document of the thirteenth century describes as *quasi civitas*. In the north-west, the Doria family reputedly founded Alghero, which would later be taken over by the Catalans, as would Cagliari. In the first case the Catalan population would replace that from Genoa; in the second case, the Catalans replaced those from Pisa.

Documentation that would allow an estimate of the population numbers in these urban centres (and a large number of not insignificant minor towns), and even of the whole island, is both scarce and difficult to interpret. This explains the divergent figures given by scholars of Sardinian demographic history; but it seems reasonable to suppose that at the beginning of the fourteenth century the population of Cagliari was about 10,000, and Villa di Chiesa approached that figure, while Sassari and Oristano had about 7,000. The total population of the entire island was perhaps around 300,000.

Contrary to some scholarly arguments, the rapid and sustained urban development mentioned above did not automatically result in the decadence of rural structures. Until the great crisis of the mid-fourteenth century (with the consequential introduction of feudal relationships of the type familiar from continental Europe), and the extension to the entire island of the war that had been going on in the north from the beginning of Catalan–Aragonese rule, there are no signs of abandonment of villages. It is worth keeping in mind the contribution of immigration from the mainland and Corsica to the cities, and the demographic dynamics of rural Sardinia, both of which were growing strongly, albeit within the general context of underpopulation and endemic plague throughout the island's history.

Urban development and the economic penetration of Sardinia's hinterland by Pisans and the Genoese, with the concomitant introduction of an economy based on money and exchange, exercised a profound transformation in the island's social and economic structures. At the beginning of the thirteenth century a good part of the rural population were serfs, tied not to the land, as in many parts, but to their work: they owed to their lords anything from a quarter to all of their work days. During the course of the century the population effectively acquired the possibility of movement, which undermined the capacity of their feudal lords to control and maintain the rural population in conditions of serfdom.

The Catalan–Aragonese conquest and the end of Pisan Sardinia

In 1295 the Treaty of Anagni crowned diplomatic arrangements initiated by Boniface VIII, seeking to put an end to the Mediterranean war that had ignited with the Sicilian Vespers revolt of 1282. James II of Aragon ceased his claims to Sicily, and entered formally into an alliance with the Church, of which he became an admiral. In return he obtained generous promises in relation to Sardinia. In 1297 these promises were given more precise shape with James's feudal investiture by Boniface VIII as king of the *regnum Sardinie et Corsice*, which the pope created on the basis of rights he believed were bequeathed by the Donation of Constantine, which has been discussed already in the chapter on papal Italy.

At this point James II's reign in Sardinia was no more than theoretical, but he began an intricate series of diplomatic initiatives aimed at making it more concrete, without the need to resort to arms. Pisa opened direct negotiations with the king of Aragon, but at the same time completed the fortifications of Castel di Castro by raising three imposing towers. Pisa also built the walls of Villa di Chiesa, and sent the old pulpit from the cathedral of Pisa to the cathedral of Cagliari, to underline the close relationship between the two cities; it is there to this day. In 1309 the negotiations even entertained the idea of James becoming feudal lord of Pisa itself, provided the city maintained control over Cagliari and its port. Pisa was soon preoccupied with the descent of the German emperor Henry VII into Italy, which reignited

Ghibelline hopes and passions, and James did not seriously consider this possibility, as he had no intention of entering into the complexities of Italian politics. His brother, on the other hand, who had remained king of Sicily despite the Anagni accords, oscillated between dynastic solidarity and the possibility of becoming a point of reference for Ghibelline Italy.

The situation was aggravated in 1323 when the judge of Arborea, Ugone, abandoned Pisa and made an agreement with the crown of Aragon accepting tenure of his judicature in fief from James II. This agreement was bound to lead to conflict: while for the judge it was supposed to regulate international relationships and constitute the basis for his future role in central Sardinia, from the point of view of the Aragonese king the arrangement turned the judge into one of several vassals among whom power on the island would be shared. It should be added that in Sardinia, especially among the clergy, but also in Sassari, a group with pro-Catalan sentiments was forming, among whose protagonists were the Doria and the Malaspina, powerful landowning families in the north of the island.

In Catalonia a great naval and military expedition was prepared, to be entrusted to the young Alfonso, heir to the throne. Ugone opened the hostilities by having hundreds of Pisans in his judicature killed. In June 1323, the Catalan fleet arrived in Sardinia, where Alfonso put Villa di Chiesa to siege. The city surrendered in February 1324, though with an agreement that permitted the mining city to maintain intact its population, its statutes, and a certain degree of administrative autonomy. Pisa mobilized for the war with an effort that reflected the importance control of Sardinia had for the city: among the many interests at stake, it is enough to cite a balance sheet of the commune from 1314 indicating that fiscal rights alone over Sardinia guaranteed a revenue of 100,000 florins, or roughly a third of the city's income. Nevertheless, Pisa was defeated on both land and sea. Cagliari capitulated in June 1324, and by 1325–6 all that remained of Pisan Sardinia were two small inland provinces.

In the north of the island, the city of Sassari and the Malaspina and the Doria families soon began to rebel against the new sovereign. The subdivision of the island into fiefs, with the exception of a few cities directly subject to the king of Aragon, rapidly led to generalized disaffection. This was exemplified by the judge of Arborea, who began a war that would become a protracted ethnic struggle between the *nació catalanesca* and the *nació sardesca*. Genoa entered into the conflict with the new Mediterranean power that had, so to speak, taken the place of its old rival, Pisa, which it had defeated in the decisive battle of Meloria (1284). But the history of Sardinia was already becoming separate from that of Italy, to become part of the history first of the crown of Aragon, and then that of Spain.

Conclusion

David Abulafia

The early fourteenth century is sometimes classified as 'the early Renaissance' in Italy. The aim of this book, however, has been to suggest that many of the features that are commonly associated with the civilization of the Italian Renaissance can already be identified in the twelfth and thirteenth centuries: the vibrant urban economies of the north of Italy, an area characterized by city-states which asserted their autonomy vocally and by force of arms; the rivalries between cities, often expressed in the use of the vague labels 'Guelf' and 'Ghibelline'; the emergence of territorial lords who established regional states in parts of northern Italy; the success of Venice and Genoa in establishing overseas dominions, as close to home as Sardinia and Dalmatia, and as far away as Crete and the Italian quarters in Acre; the existence in the south of a powerful kingdom which was intimately involved in the politics of northern Italy and the papacy, as well as harbouring ambitions right across the Mediterranean; the presence in Sicily and, a little later, in Sardinia of the increasingly vigorous Catalan merchants and armies, which laid the foundations of later Spanish imperial power in Italy. Outside the realms of politics, the twelfth and thirteenth centuries saw developments of long-term significance in the arts, where increasing attention to classical models by (for instance) the Pisanos set new artistic trends; the life of the charismatic thirteenth-century holy man, Francis of Assisi, provided the theme for the great frescoes of Giotto a hundred years later; and these were cultural movements that had an impact right across the peninsula and islands of Italy, at the court of Naples as well as in the basilicas of Umbria.

Associated with these developments was a considerable improvement in the standard of living, even if some conservative voices, such as that of Dante, reminisced nostalgically about older, simpler times. This is not to suggest that the improvements in the quality of life were evenly spread; townsmen fared better than country folk, on whom, indeed, they increasingly looked with scorn; princes and wealthy merchants did far better than the rest, as in any pre-industrial society, or as in many areas of the Third World today. Although the expansion of population peaked after 1300, and although the economy experienced increasing difficulties in the first half of the fourteenth century, the twelfth and thirteenth centuries witnessed the laying of the foundations for the Italian economy of the Renaissance period: the sophisticated structure of trade and banking, the spread of technology, particularly in the woollen, silk and metal industries, the increasing economic specialization in the countryside, were all visible by 1300. More difficult is the question of continuities in the Italian south. Here, rulers often saw their best hope of profit in the creation of strong ties with merchants and bankers from northern Italy and the Catalan lands. Although Naples and Palermo were among the largest Mediterranean cities, their contacts with the wider world were largely managed by Genoese, Catalans and Tuscans. But this is not to deny that a lively internal market for grain, cotton and other goods persisted, and that certain parts of the south, such as Capitanata on the mainland and western Sicily, had an exceptional reputation for the productivity of their soils. Even Sardinia, often regarded as a mere backwater, possessed useful agricultural resources that attracted Pisan and Genoese businessmen and settlers, and Cagliari, Sassari and Alghero became significant centres of population.

There were, then, common features of the civilization of northern and central Italy, and ties linking the south to the rest of Italy, all of which do make it possible to speak of 'Italy' as an entity that was more than a geographical expression. It is true that there was no linguistic unity, and that the south, in particular, possessed striking ethnic and religious variety, though the newest element in the southern mosaic, Islam, was extirpated with the suppression of the Saracens first in Sicily and then among the Sicilian exiles at Lucera, in 1300. Italy, particularly southern Italy and Sicily, was buffeted by all the cross-currents of the Mediterranean. Both northern and southern Italy enjoyed close economic, cultural, dynastic and religious links to Europe across the Alps as well. Nonetheless, within Italy, north and south, the memory of the Roman past remained stronger than elsewhere in Europe: the remains of the past were in front of everyone's eyes, and Rome, seat of the pope, was also, at least in theory, the seat of Empire. The coming together of these impulses laid the foundations for the era of the early Italian Renaissance.

Further reading

The aim of this reading list is to introduce the most important literature, particularly in English. Sometimes the literature in English is very sparse, as in the case of medieval Sardinia, and it has been necessary to cite titles mainly in Italian. Sometimes there is an excellent literature in English, but there are fundamental works in Italian or other languages that simply must be mentioned. One function of this book is to act as a bridge between the literature in Italian and that in English, but in such a crowded field as Italian medieval history what is offered here is necessarily only a small selection.

Introduction

Bearing in mind their persistent emphasis on the north of Italy, the standard introductions to Italy in this period in English are: J. K. Hyde, *Society and Politics in Medieval Italy: The Evolution of the Civil Life, 1000–1350* (London, 1973); D. P. Waley, *The Italian City-Republics* (three editions, of which the first is remarkable for its coloured maps and illustrations: London, 1969, 1978, 1988); G. Tabacco, *The Struggle for Power in Medieval Italy: Structures of Political Rule*, trans. Rosalind Brown Jensen (Cambridge, 1989); B. Pullan, *A History of Early Renaissance Italy from the Mid-Thirteenth to the Mid-Fifteenth Century* (London, 1973). Mention should also be made of two controversial books by J. Heers: *Family Clans in the Middle Ages* (Amsterdam, 1979) and *Parties and Political Life in the Medieval West* (Amsterdam, 1977). A special place of honour must be accorded to P. J. Jones, *The Italian City-State* (Oxford, 1997). Works with a southern focus are mentioned in the bibliography for Chapter 2, but general surveys of the history of the Italian south, can be found in D. Abulafia, *The Western Mediterranean Kingdoms, 1200–1500: The Struggle for Power* (London, 1997, Italian edn., Bari-Rome, 1999), and in S. Tramontana, *Il Mezzogiorno medievale* (Rome, 2000), which includes a fair amount on the Norman period as well.

Helpful surveys of Italian history, mainly political, can be found in the *New Cambridge Medieval History*, iv. *c.1024–c.1198*, 2 parts, ed. D. Luscombe and J. Riley-Smith (Cambridge, 2004) and in vol. v, *c.1198–1300*, ed. D. Abulafia (Cambridge, 1999). These volumes also contain bibliographies of varying range.

Chapter 1

P. J. Jones's *Italian City-State: From Commune to Signoria* (Oxford, 1997) is the most comprehensive modern treatment of the city communes in English.

D. P. Waley, *The Italian City-Republics* (3rd edn., London, 1988) and John Kenneth Hyde, *Society and Politics in Medieval Italy: The Evolution of the Civil Life, 1000–1350* (London, 1973) are accessible to the beginner, though both are now in part superseded by more recent research. In Italian, R. Bordone's *La società cittadina del regno d'Italia. Formazione e sviluppo delle caratteristiche urbane nei secoli XI e XII* (Turin, 1987) is unrivalled in terms of its insights on all aspects of communal history covered in this chapter. The *New Cambridge Medieval History* contains valuable new work on the subject, including L. Green, 'Florence', and T. Dean, 'The Rise of Signori', in vol. v *(c.1198–1300)*, ed. D. Abulafia (Cambridge, 1999). C. Wickham, *Early Medieval Italy: Central Power and Local Society 400–1000* (London, 1981), chapter 6, and P. Cammarosano, *Storia dell'Italia medievale. Dal VI al XI secolo* (Rome, 2001) are useful on the background to the rise of the communes. J. Larner's evocatively written *Italy in the Age of Dante and Petrarch, 1216–1380* (London, 1980) covers the thirteenth century. For communal origins see C. Wickham, 'The sense of the past in twelfth-century city chronicles', in P. Magdalino (ed.), *The Perception of the Past in Twelfth Century Europe* (London, 1992), pp. 173–89, reprinted in C. Wickham, *Land and Power: Studies in Italian and European Social History, 400–1200* (London, 1994), pp. 295–312. Giovanni Tabacco, *The Struggle for Power in Medieval Italy: Structures of Political Rule*, trans. R. Brown Jensen (Cambridge, 1989), pp. 182–344, provides a close analysis of the institutional and socio-political structures of the communes which is further refined in his 'La genesi culturale del movimento comunale italiano' and 'Le istituzioni di orientamento comunale nel XI secolo', both in *Sperimentazione del potere nell'alto medioevo* (Turin, 1993), pp. 320–38, 229–68. H. Keller, *Signori e vassalli nell'Italia delle città* (Turin, 1995) (original German edition, *Adelsherrschaft und städtische Gesellschaft in Oberitalien, 9. bis 12. Jahrhundert* (Tübingen, 1979)) is a massive and controversial study of the nobility and ruling classes in the early communal era. On urban elites see R. Bordone, 'Le "elites" cittadine nell'Italia comunale (XI–XII secolo)', in *La Prosopographie. Problèmes et méthodes*, published as *Mélanges de l'École française de Rome—Moyen âge*, 100 (1988), pp. 47–53; P. Cammarosano, 'Elites sociales et institutions politiques des villes libres en Italie de la fin du XIIe au début au XIVe siècle', in *Les Elites urbaines au Moyen âge* (Rome, 1997), pp. 193–200. T. Dean and C. Wickham (eds.), *City and Countryside in Late Medieval Italy: Essays Presented to Philip Jones* (London, 1990), is a volume of essays covering a variety of aspects of the relations between city and *contado*. See also on this topic G. Chittolini, 'A geography of "contadi" in Communal Italy', in S. K. Cohn and S. A. Epstein (eds.), *Portraits of Medieval and Renaissance Living: Essays in Memory of David Herlihy* (Ann Arbor, 1996); R. Comba and A. Settia (eds.), *I borghi nuovi* (Cuneo, 1993). The best treatment of war is A. Settia, *Comuni in guerra: armi ed eserciti nell'Italia delle città* (Bologna,

1993). On civic identity see E. Coleman, 'Sense of community and civic identity in the Italian communes', in Joyce Hill and Mary Swan (eds.), *The Community, the Family and the Saint: Patterns of Power in Early Medieval Europe* (Turnhout, 1998), pp. 45–60. D. Webb, *Patrons and Defenders: The Saints in the Italian City States* (London, 1996), is a study of civic patron saints and their cults. J. C. Maire-Vigueur (ed.), *I podestà dell' Italia comunale*, pt. i (Rome, 2000) is a massively researched directory. The theme of cities and communes is examined regionally in the series *Storia d'Italia* edited by Giuseppe Galasso and published by UTET in Turin, the volumes of particular relevance being vol. iv, *Comuni e signorie* (1981); vol. v, *Comuni e signorie nell'Italia settentrionale. Il Piemonte e la Liguria* (1986); vol. vii/1, *Comuni e signorie nell'Italia nord orientale e centrale. Veneto, Emilia Romagna, Toscana* (1987); vol. vii/2, *Comuni e signorie nell'Italia nord orientale e centrale. Lazio, Umbria, Marche, Lucca* (1987); *Comuni e signorie nell'Italia settentrionale. La Lombardia* (1998). Fundamental on documentation for this, as for other themes in Italian medieval history, is P. Cammarosano, *Italia medievale: struttura e geografia delle fonti scritte* (Rome, 1991). T. Dean, *The Towns of Later Medieval Italy* (Manchester, 2000), provides English translations of selected documents relevant to the history of the city commune. R. Bordone, *La società urbana nell'Italia comunale (secoli XI–XIV)* (Turin, 1984) is a useful collection of Italian translations of documents. Recent book-length studies in English of particular cities include: G. Bruckner, *Florence, the Golden Age 1138–1737* (London, 1984); S. A. Epstein, *Genoa and the Genoese, 958–1528* (Chapel Hill, NC, 1996); C. Lansing, *The Florentine Magnates: Lineage and Faction in a Medieval Commune* (Princeton, 1991); Daniel Waley, *Siena and the Sienese in the Thirteenth Century* (London, 1991). For further bibliographical references see E. Coleman, 'The Italian communes: recent work and current trends', *Journal of Medieval History*, 25 (1999).

Chapter 2

There is a steadily growing literature here. A readable narrative is provided by J. J. Norwich, *The Normans in the South* (London, 1967), and *The Kingdom in the Sun* (London, 1970); repr. as *The Normans in Sicily* (London, 1992). A fine analytical study encompassing the period of the conquest and of the kingdom is J.-M. Martin, *Italies normandes, XIe–XIIe siécles* (Paris, 1994). For the eleventh century, G. A. Loud, *The Age of Robert Guiscard: Southern Italy and the Norman Conquest* (Harlow, 2000), is excellent; see too G. A. Loud and A. Metcalfe, *The Society of Norman Italy* (Leiden, 2002), for recent work on all aspects of Norman Italy. J. Drell, *Kinship and Conquest* (Ithaca, NY, 2002), looks at Salerno at the time of the Norman conquest; for Gaeta see the fine work of P. Skinner, *Family Power in Southern Italy* (Cambridge, 1995).

D. Matthew, *The Norman Kingdom of Sicily* (Cambridge, 1992), has some rather quirky views; better is H. Houben, *Roger II: A Ruler between East and West* (Cambridge, 2002). On administration, see H. Takayama, *The Administration of the Norman Kingdom of Sicily* (Leiden, 1993); also J. Johns, *Arabic Administration in Norman Sicily* (Cambridge, 2002), and L.-R. Ménager, *Ammiratus-Ἀμηρᾶς: l'Émirat et les origines de l'Amirauté* (Paris, 1960), without forgetting the classic and very substantial work of E. Jamison, 'The Norman administration of Apulia and Capua', *Papers of the British School at Rome*, 6 (1913), repr. in her *Studies on the Medieval History of Sicily and South Italy* (Aalen, 1992). On politics and culture, see E. M. Jamison, *Admiral Eugenius of Sicily* (London and Oxford, 1957), though with reservations. On politics and art, see E. Borsook, *Messages in Mosaic: The Royal Programmes of Norman Sicily, 1130–1187* (Oxford, 1990), and W. Tronzo, *The Cultures of his Kingdom* (Princeton, 1997), which looks at the Palatine Chapel in Palermo. On the wars in Africa, see D. Abulafia, 'The Norman kingdom of Africa', *Anglo-Norman Studies*, 7 (1985), pp. 26–49, repr. with other studies of Norman and Hohenstaufen Sicily in D. Abulafia, *Italy, Sicily and the Mediterranean, 1100–1400* (London, 1987). On the economy, see D. Abulafia, *The Two Italies: Economic Relations between the Norman Kingdom of Sicily and the Northern Communes* (Cambridge, 1977).

On Frederick II, see the mystical work of E. Kantorowicz, *Frederick the Second, 1194–1250*, trans. E. O. Lorimer (London, 1931), on which consult David Abulafia, 'Kantorowicz and Frederick II', *History*, 62 (1977), pp. 193–210, repr. in *Italy, Sicily and the Mediterranean* (cited above), and the excellent study of M. Ruehl, 'In this time without emperors: the politics of Ernst Kantorowicz's *Kaiser Friedrich der Zweite* Reconsidered', *Journal of the Warburg and Courtauld Institutes*, 63 (2000), pp. 187–242. See D. Abulafia, *Frederick II: A medieval Emperor* (London, 1988, 3rd edn., 2002), for a revisionist viewpoint. W. Stürner, *Friedrich II.*, 2 vols. (Darmstadt, 1992–2000), is very learned. T. C. Van Cleve, *The Emperor Frederick II of Hohenstaufen* (Oxford, 1972), is disappointing. On intellectual life and also the wider background, see W. Tronzo (ed.), *Intellectual Life at the Court of Frederick II Hohenstaufen* (Studies in the History of Art, 44, Center for Advanced Study in the Visual Arts, Symposium papers xxiv, National Gallery of Art, Washington DC, 1994). On the Church, H. J. Pybus, 'The Emperor Frederick II and the Sicilian Church', *Cambridge Historical Journal*, 3 (1929/30), pp. 134–63, is still worthwhile; see also J. M. Powell, 'Frederick II and the Church in the Kingdom of Sicily, 1220–40', *Church History*, 30 (1961), pp. 28–34, and 'Frederick II and the Church: a revisionist view', *Catholic Historical Review*, 44 (1962/3), pp. 487–97; P. Herde, 'Literary activities of the imperial and papal chanceries during the struggle between Frederick II and the papacy', in Tronzo (ed.), *Intellectual Life at the Court of Frederick II* (see above), pp. 227–39.

For the era of Charles of Anjou, a classic narrative is that of S. Runciman, *The Sicilian Vespers: A History of the Mediterranean World in the Thirteenth Century* (Cambridge, 1958); there is a sober account in German by P. Herde, *Karl I. von Anjou* (Stuttgart, 1979), which can also be found in Italian in the *Dizionario Biografico Italiano*, s.v. 'Carlo·I d'Angiò'. A good thematic study is that of J. Dunbabin, *Charles I of Anjou: Power, Kingship and State Making in Thirteenth-Century Europe* (London, 1998). The Angevin–Aragonese feud is the theme of D. Abulafia, *The Western Mediterranean Kingdoms, 1200–1500: The Struggle for Dominion* (London, 1997). For an approach emphasizing continuity, see L. Cadier, *Essai sur l'administration du royaume angevin de Sicile* (Paris, 1891; new Italian edn. prepared by F. Giunta, *L'amministrazione della Sicilia angioina*, Palermo, 1974). On the wider political setting, N. Housley, *The Italian Crusades: The Papal-Angevin Alliance and the Crusades Against Christian Lay Powers, 1254–1343* (Oxford, 1982), is valuable. On Lucera see the items listed under Chapter 11, which now include J. Taylor, *Muslims in Medieval Italy: The Colony at Lucera* (Lanham, Md., 2003). A superb study of a later Angevin king is S. Kelly, *The New Solomon* (Leiden, 2003), which looks at ideas of kingship under Robert the Wise (1309–43). A great explosion of Angevin studies in France has resulted in several volumes of conference proceedings that address the period from the thirteenth to the fifteenth century in Anjou, Provence, Italy, and beyond, beginning with *L'État angevin* (Rome, 1998), and continuing with *La Noblesse das les états angevins* (Rome, 2000); also *Les Princes angevins du XIIIe au XVe siècle* (Rennes, 2003). On Charles I and the Greek world, see D. J. Geanakoplos, *Michael VIII Palaeologus and the West, 1258–1282* (Cambridge, Mass., 1959), pp. 92–115. On Sicily under Charles, an important book is that of L. Catalioto, *Terre, baroni e città in Sicilia nell'età di Carlo I d'Angiò* (Messina, 1995). Several intriguing articles of the French scholar H. Bresc are reprinted in *Politique et société en Sicile, XIIe–XVe siècles* (Aldershot, 1990), and there is a wealth of precious material in his vast study *Un monde méditerranéen. Économie et société en Sicile, 1300–1450*, 2 vols. (Rome and Palermo, 1986). On the economy of mainland southern Italy, an influential older work is that of G. Yver, *Le Commerce et les marchands dans l'Italie méridionale* (Paris, 1903); see also D. Abulafia, 'Southern Italy and the Florentine economy, 1265–1370', *Economic History Review*, ser. 2, vol. 33 (1981), pp. 377–88, repr. in *Italy, Sicily and the Mediterranean*. On Aragonese Sicily, see C. Backman, *The Decline and Fall of Medieval Sicily: Politics, Religion and Economy in the Reign of Frederick III, 1296–1337* (Cambridge, 1995). S. R. Epstein, *An Island for Itself: Economic Development and Social Change in Late Medieval Sicily* (Cambridge, 1992) challenges the work of Bresc but is mainly concerned with later centuries.

P. Grierson and L. Travaini, *Medieval European Coinage, with a Catalogue of the Coins in the Fitzwilliam Museum, Cambridge*, xiv. *Italy*, part 1, *South*

Italy, Sicily and Sardinia (Cambridge, 1998), contains excellent surveys of political and economic developments throughout the Norman, Hohenstaufen, and Angevin periods.

Chapter 3

The background to, and Carolingian context of, papal Italy is best established by T. F. X. Noble, *The Republic of St Peter: The Birth of the Papal State, 680–825* (Philadelphia, 1984). Two complementary and vital studies are those by P. Partner, *The Lands of St Peter: The Papal State in the Middle Ages and the Early Renaissance* (London, 1972), and D. Waley, *The Papal State in the Thirteenth Century* (London, 1961). Turning to literature mainly in other languages: older but still valuable is G. Falco, 'I comuni della Campagna e della Marittima nel Medio Evo. I. Le origine e il primo comune (sec. XI–XII)', *Archivio della R. Società Romana di Storia Patria*, 42 (1919), pp. 537–605; G. Falco, 'I comuni della Campagna e della Marittima nel Medio Evo. II. La maturità del comune (sec. XIII)', ibid., 47 (1924), pp. 117–87. The indispensable work for the eleventh and twelfth centuries are the magisterial volumes of P. Toubert, *Les Structures du Latium médiéval*, 2 vols. (Rome, 1973). Itineration is dealt with in A. Paravicini-Bagliani's, 'La mobilità della Curia Romana nel secolo XIII. Riflessi locali', *Società e istituzioni dell'Italia comunale: l'esempio di Perugia (secoli XII-XIV), Atti del congresso storico internazionale, Perugia, 6–9 novembre 1985* (Perugia, 1988), pp. 155–278. A much shorter English version is A. Paravicini-Bagliani, *The Pope's Body*, trans. David S. Peterson (Chicago, 2000). Also valuable, particularly for the early thirteenth century, are: M. T. Caciorgna, *Marittima medievale: territori, società, poteri* (Rome, 1996); M. Maccarrone, *Studi su Innocenzo III*, Italia Sacra, 17 (Padua, 1972); Christian Lackner, 'Studien zur Verwaltung des Kirchenstaates unter Papst Innocenz III.', *Römische Historische Mitteilungen*, 29 (1987), pp. 127–214; B. Bolton, '"Except the Lord keep the city": towns in the papal states at the turn of the twelfth century', in D. Abulafia, M. Rubin, and M. Franklin (eds.), *Church and City: Studies in Honour of Christopher Brooke* (Cambridge, 1991). A. Cortonesi, 'La *silva* contesa. Uomini e boschi nel Lazio del Duecento', in B. Andreolli and M. Montanari, (eds.) *Il Bosco nel medioevo*, Biblioteca di Storia Agraria Medievale, 4 (Bologna, 1989), pp. 305–19, is an excellent study of a neglected subject. There is also Cortonesi's *Terre e signori nel Lazio medioevale. Un'economia rurale nei secoli XIII–XIV* (Naples, 1988). See also: B. Bolton, '*Nova familia beati Petri*: Adrian IV and the Patrimony', in B. Bolton and Anne J. Duggan (eds.), *Adrian IV, the English Pope (1154–1159)* (Aldershot, 2003), pp. 157–79; B. Bolton, 'Carthusians at San Bartolomeo di Trisulti: Innocent III's troublesome gift', in P. De Leo, (ed.), *L'Ordine Certosino*, 2 vols. (Rende, 2003), vol. i, pp. 235–60.

Strictly on Rome, useful works include R. Brentano, *Rome before Avignon: A Social History of Thirteenth-Century Rome* (London, 1974); R. L. Benson, 'Political *Renovatio*: Two Models', in R. L. Benson, G. Constable, and C. D. Lanham (eds.), *Renaissance and Renewal in the Twelfth Century* (Oxford, 1982); S. Twyman, *Papal Ceremonial at Rome in the Twelfth Century*, The Henry Bradshaw Society, Subsidia 4 (Woodbridge, 2002). For art and architecture, R. Krautheimer, *Rome: Profile of a City, 312–1300* (Princeton, 1980); A. M. Romanini (ed.), *Roma nel Dugento: l'arte nel città dei papi da Innocenzo III a Bonifacio VIII* (Turin, 1991); H. L. Kessler and J. Zacharias, *Rome 1300: On the Path of the Pilgrim* (New Haven, 2000); G. A. Loud, *Montecassino and Benevento in the Middle Ages: Essays in South Italian Church History* (Aldershot, 2000); D. Webb, 'The Pope and the cities: anticlericalism and heresy in Innocent III's Italy', *Studies in Church History*, Subsidia 9, *The Church and Sovereignty c.590–1918: Essays in Honour of Michael Wilks*, ed. D. Wood (Oxford, 1991), pp. 135–52; M. Stroll, *Symbols as Power: The Papacy following the Investiture Contest* (Leiden, 1991); L. Hamilton, 'Memory, symbol, and arson: was Rome "Sacked" in 1084?', *Speculum*, 78 (2003), pp. 378–99; J. Mitchell, 'St. Silvester and Constantine at the SS. Quattro Coronati', in *Federico II e l'Arte del Duecento Italiano, Atti della III Settimana di Studio di Storia dell'Arte Medievale dell'Università di Roma (15–20 maggio 1978)*, 2 vols. (Galatina, 1980), pp. 15–32.

Chapter 4

A good place to begin is D. M. Bueno de Mesquita, 'The place of despotism in Italian politics', in J. Hale, R. Highfield, and B. Smalley (eds.), *Europe in the Late Middle Ages* (London, 1965); also T. Dean, 'The rise of the *Signori*', *New Cambridge Medieval History*, vol. v, pp. 458–78, and bibliography, pp. 899–905. The later sections of P. J. Jones, *The Italian City-State* (Oxford, 1997) are fundamental; see also his *Economia e società nell'Italia medievale* (Turin, 1980). G. Chittolini, 'La crisi delle libertà comunali e le origini dello stato territoriale', *Rivista storica italiana*, 82 (1970), comes from the pen of a leading Italian scholar.

On individual dynasties in the period of this book (bearing in mind that the literature grows for the late fourteenth and fifteenth centuries, and citing works in English as far as possible), key studies include the following, which are arranged in rough geographical order from the north-east clockwise round to Milan: for Verona: G. M. Varanini (ed.), *Gli Scaligeri 1277–1387* (Verona, 1988); for Padua: J. K. Hyde, *Padua in the Age of Dante* (Manchester, 1966), and B. Kohl, *Padua under the Carrara, 1318–1405* (Baltimore, 1998); for Mantua: M. Vaini, *Dal comune alla signoria: Mantova dal 1200–1328* (Milan, 1986); for Ferrara, T. Dean, *Land and Power in Late Medieval Ferrara: The Rule of the Este* (Cambridge, 1987), and L. Chiappini, *Gli Estensi* (Varese, 1967); for the Romagna, J. Larner, *The Lords of Romagna: Romagnol Society and the Origins of the Signorie* (London, 1965), and P. J. Jones, *The Malatesta of Rimini and the Papal State* (Cambridge, 1974); for central Italy: D. Waley, *The Papal State in the Thirteenth Century* (London, 1961); for Piacenza: P. Racine, *Plaisance du Xe à la fin du XIIIe siècle*, 2 vols. (Lille, 1979–80); for Milan, D. E. Muir, *A History of Milan under the Visconti* (London, 1924), an old work that represents a generation of British historians of Italy, many of them women, of whom the most distinguished was perhaps C. M. Ady; important is the Treccani *Storia di Milano*, vol. iv, *Dalle lotte contro il Barbarossa al primo signore (1152–1310)* (Milan, 1954).

Chapter 5

A good place to begin is the discussion of the relationship between the sea and the movement of fleets by J. H. Pryor, *Geography, Technology and War: Studies on the Maritime History of the Mediterranean* (Cambridge, 1988). For background see the massive revisionist work of M. McCormack, *Origins of the European Economy* (Cambridge, 2001). On Amalfi there is little in English; two fundamental works in Italian are A. Citarella, *Il commercio di Amalfi nell'alto medioevo* (Salerno, 1977), and M. del Treppo and A. Leone, *Amalfi medioevale* (Naples, 1977); but also B. Kreutz, 'The ecology of maritime success: the puzzling case of Amalfi', *Mediterranean Historical Review*, 3 (1988), pp. 103–13. For an overview of Italian trade, see M. Tangheroni, *Commercio e navigazione nel medioevo* (Rome and Bari, 1996); an older work in English is R. S. Lopez, *The Commercial Revolution of the Middle Ages, 950–1350* (Englewood Cliffs, NJ, 1971). R. S. Lopez and I. W. Raymond, *Medieval Trade in the Mediterranean World* (New York, 1955) is a collection of key documents with commentaries. Useful collection of essays are: B. Garí (ed.), *El mundo mediterráneo de la edad media* (Barcelona, 1987), with essays by Pistarino, Lopez, Goitein, and others; M. Balard (ed.), *État et colonisation au moyen âge et à la Renaissance* (Lyons, 1989); M. Balard and A. Ducellier (eds.), *Le Partage du monde: échange et colonisation dans la Méditerranée médiévale* (Paris, 2000); G. Airaldi (ed.), *Gli Orizzonti aperti: profili del mercante medievale* (Turin, 1997), a collection of reprinted essays by Le Goff, Lopez, Sapori, Heers, Abulafia, and others. The society and economy of Pisa are examined in D. Herlihy, *Pisa in the Early Renaissance* (New Haven, 1958); a classic study is G. Volpe, *Studi sulle istituzioni comunali a Pisa* (new edn., Florence, 1970); and also C. Violante, *Economia, società, istituzioni a Pisa nel medioevo* (Bari, 1980). F. C. Lane, *Venice: A Maritime Republic* (Baltimore, 1973), remains the standard history of Venice, though somewhat adulatory in tone. On Genoa see especially S. A. Epstein, *Genoa and the Genoese, 958–1528* (Chapel Hill, NC, 1996); classic older works are E. Bach, *La Cité de Gênes au XIIe siècle* (Copenhagen, 1955), and E. H. Byrne, *Genoese Shipping in the Twelfth and*

Thirteenth Centuries (Cambridge, Mass., 1930); and (though later in emphasis) there is much of value in J. Heers, *Gênes au XVe siècle: civilisation méditerranéenne, grand capitalisme, et capitalisme populaire* (Paris, 1971; or the longer version of the same work, Paris, 1961). Relations between Genoa and Sicily dominate the study by D. Abulafia, *The Two Italies: Economic Relations between the Norman Kingdom of Sicily and the Northern Communes* (Cambridge, 1977; Italian edn., Naples, 1991); and Genoese relations with the remnants of Byzantium are studied with great expertise in M. Balard, *La Romanie génoise, XIIIe–début du XVe siècle*, 2 vols. (Rome and Genoa, 1978). For Venice, Crete, and the Byzantine lands see F. Thiriet, *La Romanie vénitienne au moyen âge* (Paris, 1975). On the Latin East, see G. Airaldi and B. Z. Kedar (eds.), *I comuni italiani nel regno di Gerusalemme* (Genoa, 1987), with articles in Italian, English, and other languages, by Tangheroni, Abulafia, Figliuolo, etc. For the role of trade with the Iberian lands, see O. R. Constable, *Trade and Traders in Muslim Spain: The Commercial Realignment of the Iberian Peninsula, 900–1500* (Cambridge, 1994), and D. Abulafia, *A Mediterranean Emporium: The Catalan Kingdom of Majorca* (Cambridge, 1994). On warehouses and other facilities for travelling merchants, as well as a great amount of information about Italian trade concessions throughout the Mediterranean, see O. R. Constable, *Housing the Stranger in the Mediterranean World* (Cambridge, 2004). On banking, see E. S. Hunt, *The Medieval Super-Companies: a Study of the Peruzzi Company of Florence* (Cambridge, 1994) and E. S. Hunt and J. M. Murray, *A History of Business in Medieval Europe 1200–1550* (Cambridge, 1999).

Chapter 6

Most of the sources quoted are to be found in edited translation in R. S. Lopez and I. W. Raymond (eds.), *Medieval Trade in the Mediterranean World* (New York, 1955). An overview of the trade of the period is in R. S. Lopez, *The Commercial Revolution of the Middle Ages, 950–1350* (2nd edn., Cambridge, 1976). A rich source of illustrative evidence for southern Italian material of the period is the catalogue, *I Normanni: popolo d'Europa*, ed. M. d'Onofrio (Venice, 1994). On dowry items see P. Skinner, 'Women, wills and wealth in medieval southern Italy', *Early Medieval Europe*, 2 (1993). Public health is discussed in P. Skinner, *Health and Medicine in Early Medieval Southern Italy* (Leiden, 1997). A summary of recent work on domestic architecture is R. Santangeli Valenzani, 'Residential building in early medieval Rome', in J. M. H. Smith (ed.), *Early Medieval Rome and the Christian West* (Leiden, 2000), pp. 101–12. A stimulating discussion of the trading relationship between north and south, including references to the commodities carried, is D. Abulafia, *The Two Italies: Economic Relations between the Norman Kingdom of Sicily and the Northern Communes* (Cambridge, 1977).

On more specialist themes: M. Mazzaoui, 'The cotton industry of northern Italy in the late middle ages', *Journal of Economic History*, 32 (1972), and her *The Italian Cotton Industry in the Later Middle Ages, 1100–1600* (Cambridge, 1981). A general overview of the Italian economy, though a little dated, is that of G. Luzzatto, *An Economic History of Italy from the Fall of the Roman Empire to the Beginning of the Sixteenth Century*, trans. P. J. Jones (London, 1971).

On ceramics, see F. D'Angelo, 'La ceramica normanna nella Sicilia', *Atti del Congresso internazionale di studi sulla Sicilia normanna, Palermo, 1972* (Palermo, 1973); D. Abulafia, 'The Pisan *bacini* and the medieval Mediterranean economy: a historian's viewpoint', *Papers in Italian Archaeology*, iv. *The Cambridge Conference*, pt. 4, *Classical and Medieval Archaeology*, ed. C. Malone and S. Stoddart, British Archaeological Reports, International Series, vol. 246 (Oxford, 1985), pp. 287–302, repr. in D. Abulafia, *Italy, Sicily and the Mediterranean, 1100–1400* (London, 1987). On other artefacts, see F. E. de Roover, 'Lucchese silks', *CIBA Review*, 80 (1950); and C. N. L. Brooke and R. H. Pinder-Wilson, 'The reliquary of St Petroc and the ivories of Norman Sicily', *Archaeologia (Society of Antiquaries of London)*, 104 (1973).

Chapter 7

There are two useful general surveys of rural Italy, both of which emphasize the role of urban capitalists: E. Sereni's classic *History of the Italian Agricultural Landscape* (Princeton, 1997; first Italian edn., 1961); and P. J. Jones's 'Medieval agrarian society in its prime: Italy', in M. M. Postan, (ed.), *The Cambridge Economic History of Europe*, i (2nd edn., Cambridge, 1966), pp. 340–431; see also P. J. Jones, 'From manor to Mezzadria: a Tuscan case-study in the medieval origins of modern agrarian society', in N. Rubinstein (ed.), *Florentine Studies: Politics and Society in Renaissance Florence* (London, 1968), pp. 193–241. Recent debates over the nature of rural life are central to G. Andenna's *Storia della Lombardia medioevale* (Turin, 1998) and G. Cherubini, *L'Italia rurale del basso medioevo* (Bari, 1985). A. Cortonesi and M. Montanari (eds.), *Medievistica italiana e storia agraria: risultati e prospettive di una stagione storiografica* (Bologna, 2001), is an excellent bibliography, unfortunately organized by region rather than by topic which obscures common issues and approaches.

On the issue of castles and the reorganization of the Italian countryside in the eleventh and twelfth centuries, the most important work is still P. Toubert, *Les Structures du Latium médiéval: le Latium méridional et la Sabine du IXe siècle à la fin du XIIe siècle*, 2 vols. (Rome, 1973). There are two important examinations of the issue in Italian: A. A. Settia, *Castelli e villaggi nell'Italia padana: popolamento, potere e sicurezza fra IX e XIII secolo* (Naples, 1984), and R. Comba and A. A. Settia (eds.), *I borghi nuovi: secoli XII–XIV* (Cuneo, 1993). There are also important essays in B. Andreolli, V. Fumagalli, and

M. Montanari (eds.), *Le campagne italiane prima e dopo il mille: una società in trasformazione* (Bologna, 1985). See also on the early construction of castles in Lombardy, E. Coleman, 'Incastellamento on the Po Plain: Cremona and its territory in the tenth century', *Reading Medieval Studies*, 17 (1991), pp. 77–102. The best discussions in English are C. Wickham, 'The terra of San Vincenzo al Volturno in the 8th to 12th centuries: the historical framework', in R. Hodges and J. Mitchell (eds.), *San Vincenzo al Volturno: The Archaeology, Art and Territory of an Early Medieval Monastery* (Oxford, 1985), pp. 227–58, and C. Wickham, *The Mountains and the City: The Tuscan Appennines in the Early Middle Ages* (Oxford, 1988), especially pp. 115–31.

On the influence of urban institutions on rural life see C. Wickham, *Community and Clientele in Twelfth-Century Tuscany: The Origins of the Rural Commune in the Plain of Lucca* (Oxford, 1998); F. Menant, *Campagnes lombardes du moyen âge: l'économie et la société rurales dans la région de Bergame, de Crémone et de Brescia du Xe au XIIIe siècle* (Rome, 1993); and J. P. Delumeau, *Arezzo: espace et sociétés, 715–1230: recherches sur Arezzo et son contado du VIIIe au début du XIIIe siècle* (Rome, 1996). For English-language studies on urban–rural relations in the later Middles Ages see D. Herlihy, 'Santa Maria Impruneta: a rural commune in the late Middle Ages', in N. Rubinstein (ed.), *Renaissance Florence* (London, 1968), pp. 242–76, and W. M. Bowsky, *The Finance of the Commune of Siena, 1287–1355* (Oxford, 1970), pp. 225–55.

On agriculture and the environment, there are numerous local studies, found in a number of important collections. B. Andreolli and M. Montanari (eds.), *Il bosco nel medioevo* (Bologna, 1988); M. Baruzzi and M. Montanari (eds.), *Porci e porcari nel medioevo: paesaggio, economia, alimentazione* (Bologna, 1981); M. Montanari, *Campagne medievali: strutture produttive, rapporti di lavoro, sistemi alimentari* (Turin, 1984); Rinaldo Comba and Francesco Panero (eds.), *Aziende agrarie nel medioevo: forme della conduzione fondiaria nell'Italia nord-occidentale, secoli 9–15* (Cuneo, 2000); and most recently, A. Malvolti and G. Pinto (eds.), *Incolti, fiumi, paludi: utilizzazione delle risorse naturali nella Toscana medievale e moderna* (Florence, 2003). On the special problems of agriculture in southern Italy, see H. Bresc, *Un monde méditerranéen: Économie et société en Sicile, 1300–1450* (Rome, 1986), and S. R. Epstein, *An Island for Itself: Economic Development and Social Change in Late Medieval Sicily* (Cambridge, 1992), especially pp. 1–24. Since both these works primarily cover the later Middle Ages, the reader also should consult the titles found in *Medievistica italiana e storia agraria*.

Chapter 8

Useful information on the family appears in general works on the history of the European family, in works on law, women, men, and children, as well as in most specialized studies on Italian cities and regions. The period 1100–1350 is not rich in sources, so studies of the Renaissance family can also be helpful on the earlier period. Good places to begin are G. Duby (ed.), *A History of Private Life: Revelations of the Medieval World* (Cambridge, Mass., 1988), and G. Duby and J. Le Goff, (eds.), *Famille et parenté dans l'Occident médiévale* (Rome, 1977); J. Heers, *Family Clans in the Middle Ages* (Amsterdam, 1977); D. Herlihy, *Medieval Households* (Cambridge, Mass., 1985) with references to his many essays on medieval Italian families, supplemented by D. Herlihy and C. Klapisch-Zuber, *Tuscans and their Families* (New Haven, 1985) and Klapisch-Zuber's essays in *Women, Family, and Ritual in Renaissance Italy* (Chicago, 1985). For legal issues see J. Brundage, *Law, Sex, and Christian Society in Medieval Europe* (Chicago, 1985). Specific studies on Italian themes are: H. Bresc, *Un monde méditerranéen: Économie et société en Sicile 1300–1450* (Rome, 1986); J. Day, *La Sardegna sotto la dominazione pisano-genovese* (Turin, 1987); S. A. Epstein, *Wills and Wealth in Medieval Genoa, 1150–1250* (Cambridge, Mass., 1984); D. Kertzer and R. Saller, *The Family in Italy from Antiquity to the Present* (New Haven, 1991); P. Skinner, *Women in Medieval Italian Society 500–1200* (Harlow, 2001); P. Toubert, *Les Structures du Latium médiéval*, 2 vols. (Rome, 1973).

Chapter 9

For an overview of the linguistic situation in the area that would later become Italy, see A. Varvaro, 'L'Italiano dell'anno 1000', in the conference proceedings of the *Società di Linguistica Italiana*, held in Florence in 2000, forthcoming. A fundamental text, particularly for Tuscany and the central areas, is vol. i (so far the only one published), of A. Castellani, *Grammatica storica della lingua italiana*, (Bologna, 2000). General information on Italian literature and culture of the period can be found in A. Asor Rosa (ed.), *Letteratura italiana* (Turin, 1982), and E. Malato (ed.), *Storia della letteratura italiana* (Rome, 1995). For the cultural background, important contributions are available in English in A. Petrucci, *Writers and Readers in Medieval Italy* (New Haven, 1995), pp. 169–235. On medieval Latin works, the most recent volume is C. Leonardi (ed.), *Letteratura latina medievale (secoli VI–XV)* (Tavarnuzze, 2002).

On earlier vernacular texts, see A. Castellani, *I più antichi testi italiani* (Bologna, 1973), and *La prosa italiana delle origini*, 2 vols. (Bologna, 1982). They are also examined in Livio Petrucci, 'Il problema delle origini e i più antichi testi italiani', in L. Serianni (ed.), *Storia della lingua italiana*, iii (Turin, 1994), pp. 5–73. There are English anthologies of these texts, but they are now rather out of date: C. Dionisotti and C. Grayson, *Early Italian Texts* (Oxford, 1965); R. Sampson, *Early Romance Texts* (Cambridge, 1980); neither of these mentions, of course, the most recently discovered texts. The *canzone* of the end of the twelfth century was published by A. Stussi in 'Versi d'amore in volgare tra la fine del secolo XII e l'inizio del XIII', *Cultura neolatina*, 59 (1999), pp. 1–69, and later in the appendix to C. Segre and C. Ossola (eds.), *Antologia della poesia italiana*, i (Turin, 1999), pp. 607–20. The text by Giacomino Pugliese was edited and published in G. Brunetti, *Il frammento inedito* Resplendiente stella de albur *di Giacomino Pugliese e la poesia italiana delle origini* (Tübingen, 2000). The codices of thirteenth-century poetry were reproduced photographically and published with a commentary by L. Leonardi, *I canzonieri della lirica italiana delle origini*, 4 vols. (Tavarnuzze, 2000). The most authoritative collection of poetic texts of the thirteenth century remains that of G. Contini, *Poeti del Duecento*, 2 vols. (Milan and Naples, 1960). More up-to-date critical analyses can be found in the literary histories mentioned above.

In relation to Dante, see work by two English scholars: P. Boyde, *Dante Philomythes and Philosopher: Man in the Cosmos* (Cambridge, 1981); P. Boyde, *Perception and Passion in Dante's Comedy* (Cambridge, 1993); P. Boyde, *Human Vices and Human Worth in Dante's Comedy* (Cambridge, 2000); Z. Baranski, *'Sole nuovo, luce nuova': saggi sul rinnovamento culturale in Dante* (Turin, 1996); Z. Baranski, *Dante e i segni* (Naples, 2000).

On Sicilian Arabic and its Maltese legacy, see D. A. Agius, *Siculo-Arabic*, (London, 1996). For bibliographical news see the regular annual volumes of *Bibliografia generale della lingua e della letteratura italiana*, ed. E. Malato (Rome, 1993–).

Chapter 10

The literature on Greeks, Muslims, and Jews is, not surprisingly, multilingual, and modern books and articles can be found in Hebrew, Maltese, Arabic, Greek, and Japanese as well as English, Italian, French, and German. On the Greeks, much more needs to be done, but there are fundamental studies by A. Guillou: *Studies on Byzantine Italy* (London, 1970); *Culture et société en Italie Byzantine (VIe–XIe siècle)* (London, 1978); these volumes consist of essays mainly in French, otherwise in Italian. The important study by V. von Falkenhausen, *Untersuchungen über di byzantinische Herrschaft in Süditalien vom 9. bis ins 11. Jahrhundert* (Wiesbaden, 1969), is also accessible in an Italian edition. F. Giunta, *Bizantini e bizantinismo nella Sicilia normanna* (2nd edn., Palermo, 1974) was influential in its day, but it is now somewhat dated. Literature on ecclesiastical relations between East and West includes some old classics like S. Runciman, *The Eastern Schism* (Oxford, 1955), and D. Geanakoplos, *Byzantine East and Latin West* (Oxford, 1966). The strange episode of Byzantine dominion over Ancona is explored in D. Abulafia, 'Ancona, Byzantium and the Adriatic, 1155–1173', *Papers of the British School at Rome*, 52 (1984), pp. 195–216, repr. in D. Abulafia, *Italy, Sicily and the*

Mediterranean, 1100–1400 (London, 1987), and a key text is accessible in Boncompagno da Signa, *The History of the Siege of Ancona*, ed. and transl. A. F. Stone, Archivio del Litorale Adriatico, vi (Venice, 2002).

Literature on the Muslims has flourished recently: see first of all the comments of ibn Jubayr, in *The Travels of ibn Jubayr*, trans. R. J. C. Broadhurst (London, 1952); no less fascinating is Idrisi, *La Première Géographie de l'Occident*, ed. H. Bresc and A. Nef (Paris, 1999). N. Daniel, *The Arabs and Mediaeval Europe* (London and Beirut, 1975), questioned some fond myths about Norman Sicily as an island of tolerance. Further secondary literature includes D. Abulafia, 'The end of Muslim Sicily', in James M. Powell (ed.), *Muslims under Latin rule: A Comparative Perspective* (Princeton, 1990), pp. 103–33, repr. in D. Abulafia, *Commerce and Conquest in the Mediterranean, 1100–1500* (Aldershot, 1993); and a German dissertation, D. Schack, *Die Araber im Reich Rogers II.* (Berlin, 1969); also H. Bercher, A. Courteaux, and J. Mouton, 'Une abbaye latine dans la société musulmane: Monreale au XIIe siècle', *Annales: Économies, Sociétés, Civilisations*, 34 (1979), pp. 525–47. Since then, particularly important work has been that of A. Metcalfe, *Muslims and Christians in Norman Sicily: Arabic Speakers and the end of Islam* (London, 2002); fundamental are the books of H. Takayama, *The Administration of the Norman Kingdom of Sicily* (Leiden, 1993), and of J. Johns, *Arabic Administration in Norman Sicily* (Cambridge, 2002). W. Tronzo, *The Cultures of his Kingdom* (Princeton, 1997), looks at Roger II and the Palatine Chapel in Palermo from new angles that are relevant to this chapter. D. A. Agius, *Siculo-Arabic* (London, 1996), shows sensitivity to historical aspects of the study of language.

On the Muslims and the Jews, see two articles by D. Abulafia which treat them together, something that modern subject boundaries, not to mention modern political boundaries, have often prevented: 'Ethnic variety and its implications: Frederick II's relations with Jews and Muslims', *Intellectual Life at the Court of Frederick II Hohenstaufen*, Studies in the History of Art, 44, Center for Advanced Study in the Visual Arts, Symposium papers xxiv, National Gallery of Art, ed. W. Tronzo (Washington, DC 1994), pp. 213–24; 'Monarchs and minorities in the late medieval western Mediterranean: Lucera and its analogues', in S. L. Waugh and P. D. Diehl (eds.), *Christendom and its Discontents: Exclusion, Persecution and Rebellion, 1000–1500* (Cambridge, 1996), pp. 234–63.

In addition to the essay just cited, Lucera is the subject of an excellent article by J. M. Martin, 'La Colonie sarrasine de Lucera et son environnement: quelques réflexions', *Mediterraneo medievale: scritti in onore di Francesco Giunta*, 3 vols. (Soveria Mannelli, 1989), vol. ii, pp. 795–811. See also J. Taylor, *Muslims in Medieval Italy: The Colony at Lucera* (Lanham, Md., 2003). The condominium at Panetelleria has been examined by H. Bresc,

'Pantelleria entre l'Islam et la Chrétienté', *Cahiers de Tunisie*, 19 (1971), pp. 105–27, repr. in H. Bresc, *Politique et société en Sicile, XIIe–XVe siècles* (Aldershot, 1990), along with other very valuable studies by this author. Malta cannot be ignored, either: see A. T. Luttrell (ed.), *Medieval Malta: Studies on Malta before the Knights* (London, 1975), though some of his views are being challenged by literature (by C. Dalli and others) that is written as often in Maltese as in English.

On the Jews, as for the Muslims, there is an extensive new literature; the place to begin is a contemporary travel narrative, this time that of Benjamin of Tudela: *The Itinerary of Benjamin of Tudela*, ed. M. N. Adler (London, 1907; new edn. with additional material by M. Signer, New York, 1983). S. Simonsohn, *The Jews in Sicily*, i. *383–1300* (Leiden, 1997), provided essential documentary source-material. A stimulating work published in French and Italian editions is H. Bresc, *Arabi per lingua, Ebrei per religione: l'evoluzione dell'ebraismo siciliano in ambiente latino dal XII al XV secolo* (Messina, 2001; French edn., Paris, 2001). For a survey in Italian, see three consecutive essays by D. Abulafia, 'Il Mezzogiorno peninsulare dai bizantini all'espulsione (1541)', 'Le comunità di Sicilia dagli arabi all'espulsione (1493)', and 'Gli ebrei di Sardegna', in *Storia d'Italia, Annali*, 11, part 1, *Gli Ebrei in Italia*, ed. C. Vivanti (Turin, 1996), pp. 5–94. The older work of C. Roth, *The History of the Jews of Italy* (Philadelphia, 5706/1946) has fairly extensive material on the south of Italy in the Middle Ages, and another classic, by R. Straus, has recently appeared in Italian translation from the German original: *Gli ebrei di Sicilia dai Normanni a Federico II*, tran. S. Siragusa (Palermo, 1992). More up-to-date research can be found in *Italia Judaica 5: Gli Ebrei in Sicilia sino all'espulsione del 1492. Atti del V Convegno internazionale, Palermo, 15–19 giugno 1992*, Pubblicazioni degli Archivi di Stato, Saggi, 32 (Rome, 1995); also in the early chapters of B. D. Cooperman and B. Garvin (eds.), *The Jews of Italy: Memory and Identity* (College Park, Md., 2001), and now in a handsome volume produced by the Sicilian regional government, *Ebrei e Sicilia* (Palermo, 2003).

Chapter 11

There is very little to read on Sardinia in English apart from M. Tangheroni, 'Sardinia and Corsica from the mid-twelfth to the mid-fourteenth century', in D. Abulafia (ed.), *New Cambridge Medieval History*, v. *c.1198–1300* (Cambridge, 1999), pp. 447–57. For an accessible bibliography of works in Italian, see pp. 898–9 of the same volume. A few comments may be found in D. Abulafia, 'Southern Italy, Sicily and Sardinia in the medieval Mediterranean economy', in D. Abulafia, *Commerce and Conquest in the Mediterranean, 1100–1500* (Aldershot, 1993). A straight narrative of Sardinian political history is provided by F. Artizzu, *La Sardegna pisana e genovese* (Sassari, 1985), followed in the same series by F. C. Casula, *La Sardegna aragonese*, 2 vols. (Sassari, 1990), but there is still much merit in E. Besta, *La Sardegna medievale*, 2 vols. (Palermo, 1908–9). John Day's contribution to the UTET *Storia d'Italia*, edited by G. Galasso, 'La Sardegna e i suoi dominatori dal secolo XI al secolo XIV', in *La Sardegna medioevale e moderna* (Turin, 1984), was republished separately as *La Sardegna sotto la dominazione pisano-genovese* (Turin, 1986); and several of his essays on Sardinia appeared in English in his book *The Medieval Market Economy* (Oxford, 1986). For the history of Sardinia in the late Middle Ages an invaluable collection of studies is the acts of the *XIV Congresso di Storia della Corona d'Aragona, Sassari/Alghero/Nuoro, 19–24 maggio 1990*, devoted mainly to *Il 'Regnum Sardiniae et Corsicae' nell'espansione mediterranea della Corona d'Aragona (sec. XIV–XVIII)*, 6 vols. (Sassari, 1995).

Glossary

Albergo: Clan or confederation of families in late medieval Genoa.

Arti: Often translated 'guilds'; organizations bringing together investors in trade and industry, workshop proprietors, and the wealthier artisans in the Italian cities. The *Arti maggiori* encompassed relatively prestigious areas such as banking, legal practice, and mercery (e.g. the *Arte della Calimala* in Florence); while the *Arti minori* would include bakers, butchers, and so on.

Augustales: Gold coins of southern Italy and Sicily, first minted by Frederick II in 1231; later known as *carlini*.

Bacini: Highly glazed and decorated ceramic dishes inserted for decoration in the fabric (e.g. towers and façade) of churches in Pisa, Rome, and elsewhere, often produced in Spain, north Africa, Sicily, and the Levant.

Borghi nuovi: New towns founded in the twelfth and thirteenth centuries to help the cities cope with growing population and the need to maximize returns from the countryside.

Camerarius: Chamberlain, an important official in the papal Curia (q.v.).

Capitanei: High-ranking social group in eleventh-century Milan.

Carroccio: Cart drawn by oxen carrying the banners and often the holy relics of a city, taken into battle on the model of the cart carrying the Ark of the Covenant described in the Bible.

Castellum or *castrum*: Fortified settlement, as much a village as a castle; see *incastellamento*.

Colleganza: Type of trade contract widely used in Venice, similar to the *commenda* (q.v.).

Commenda or *accomendacio*: Widespread type of trade contract in which a sleeping partner invests capital with a travelling partner, who receives a share of any profits in return for his labour.

Commune: System of city-government in which power is shared among the city elite or among the representatives of the *Arti* (q.v.); may loosely be translated as 'republic', and is often used to mean the north Italian cities themselves (as in 'the Lombard communes').

Condaghe: Legal document from Sardinia listing in detail the possessions, in land and livestock, of Sardinian monasteries, written in the Sard language.

Consorteria: Descent group of nobles who hold their property in common.

Curia: Literally, 'court'; the papal Curia was the seat of government (and intrigue) of the Catholic Church, offering career opportunities to canon lawyers of Bologna and elsewhere.

Dazio: Direct tax based on estimates of wealth.

Dictatus Papae: Controversial list of the rights of the papacy set out by Pope Gregory VII in 1075 and copied into the register of his acts preserved in the Vatican Archives, though never officially published; includes the proviso 'the pope can depose emperors'.

Diwan or duana: Government office in Norman Sicily, based on Arabic models; the *duana de secretis, mega sekreton*, or *dîwân at-taḥqîq al-ma'mûr* dealt with the king's revenue and his Sicilian estates, while the *duana baronum* was mainly concerned with the mainland territories.

Familiares Regis: Group of intimate advisers to the king in Norman Sicily, exercising considerable power under William I and II.

Fodrum: Imperial hospitality tax paid by imperial vassals in cash, one of the focal points of the conflict between Frederick Barbarossa and the Lombard cities in the 1160s.

Fustian: Wool and cotton mixed weave, widely produced in northern Italy, often using Sicilian cottton.

Ghibelline: Derived from 'Waiblingen', a castle of the imperial family of Hohenstaufen, and signifying in general those who favoured a pro-imperial alliance in northern and central Italy (but cf. the 'Ghibellines of the party of the Church' in Todi, *c.*1300).

Guelf: Derived from 'Welf', the family name of the rivals of the Hohenstaufen, but generally signifying those factions in northern and central Italy who were favourable to the papacy and its major ally, the Angevin king of Naples; often divided between 'Black' and 'White' factions, especially in Tuscany, the former more enthusiastic about the pro-papal alliance, the latter including 'reformed' Ghibellines.

Incastellamento: The move of the population in the eleventh and twelfth centuries away from the plains into fortified *castella* or *castra* (q.v.), decisively changing settlement patterns in medieval Italy.

Laudes or lodi: Literally 'praises'; used in particular for religious songs in Latin and the vernacular extolling the Virgin Mary and the saints.

Mezzogiorno: The Italian south, often including Sicily and Sardinia.

Palazzo Pubblico: Term sometimes used for the seat of communal government (e.g. in Siena); also often termed *Palazzo del Comune*; often a substantial building with a tower and frescoes.

Patarini: Generic term for dissidents in the Italian Church, first of all in eleventh-century Milan and Lombardy, though later applied widely to such heretics as Cathars and Waldensians.

Podestà: Head of city government appointed generally for one year to bring internal peace to the commune and provide military leadership, legal advice, etc., nearly always drawn from outside, with noble and/or legal background.

Popolo: Literally, 'the People'; often employed for an alliance of the *Arti* (q.v.), and led by a Captain of the *Popolo*; in many communes the *Popolo* gained power, but the term might also mean the entire citizen body in contrast to a small oligarchy; it should not be understood to include the proletariat, though the term *Popolo minuto* was sometimes used to encompass the wider workforce.

Proskynesis: Prostration in the presence of a ruler, practised in Norman Sicily and based on Byzantine and Persian models.

Regalia: The rights claimed by the Holy Roman Emperor in the north of Italy, mainly taxes such as the *fodrum* (q.v.).

Regno: Literally, 'the Kingdom'; used for the kingdom of Sicily and southern Italy, as the only seat of royal government in Italy (but cf. *regnum italicum*); after 1282 generally used solely for the Angevin kingdom of Naples, rather than the Aragonese kingdom of Sicily.

Regnum italicum: The 'Italian kingdom', part of the Holy Roman Empire along with Germany and Burgundy, but without a seat of government; mainly a collection of rights claimed by the German emperors in the Lombard cities, without continuous practical expression, though the cities (apart from Venice) were nominally subject to imperial suzerainty.

Servi camere: 'Servants of the [royal] chamber', a term applied from the time of Frederick II to Jews in Germany and Sicily/southern Italy and to Muslims in Sicily/southern Italy to indicate their direct dependence on the crown.

Signoria: Literally 'lordship', but often indicating a system of government in which a hereditary lord gains control of a commune or communes and the surrounding countryside; the norm in most of northern and central Italy after c.1300.

Signore: Literally, 'lord', often mistranslated 'despot' or 'tyrant'; a generally hereditary lord who establishes mastery over a city, sometimes leaving the commune intact as a form of local government, and sometimes exercising overpowering influence rather than taking high office.

Sistema curtense: System of estates and manors.

Societas: 'Society', 'partnership', 'company', a term used for everything from the Lombard League of cities to a Genoese business partnership in which two parties invest varying proportions of money, sharing the profits equally.

Valvassores: Middle-ranking members of the ruling classes in eleventh-century Milan.

Chronology

1013–17 Norman adventurers begin to appear in southern Italy as mercenaries supporting Longobard rebellion against Byzantine rule

1015–16 Mujahid's Muslim armies expelled from Sardinia by Pisa and Genoa

1030 Normans receive first grant of a county at Aversa in southern Italy

1046 Emperor Henry III resolves dispute over who should be pope at Synod of Sutri, thereby stimulating resentment at imperial intervention in Church affairs

1054 Overt quarrel between the papal legate Cardinal Humbert of Silva Candida and the Patriarch of Constantinople leads to public breach between Greek and Latin Churches

1060 Normans invited to intervene in Muslim Sicily by ibn ath-Thumnah, emir of Catania, who hopes to use them against his rivals on the island

1071 Fall of Bari to Robert Guiscard ends Byzantine rule in southern Italy

1072 Fall of Palermo gives Normans (and Roger I in particular) effective control of most of Norman Sicily

1073 Reformer Hildebrand accedes to the papacy as Gregory VII, championing the independence of the papacy from imperial interference

1082 Byzantine emperor confers exceptional trading privileges on Venetian merchants and grants Venice a quarter in Constantinople and Durazzo

1085 Robert Guiscard dies in Cephalonia during a raid on Byzantine territory

1087 Pisans and Genoese sack trading centre of Mahdia in north Africa, after receiving papal blessing for their act of holy war

1090 Capture of Noto, last Muslim stronghold in Sicily, consolidating Roger I's hold on the island

1098 Genoese form commune ('Company') for three years and participate in First Crusade; the Company is thereafter regularly renewed, and the reward for helping the crusaders is a sequence of trading privileges in the Holy Land

1124	Venice rewarded for helping the Franks of Jerusalem to conquer Tyre in 1123 with handsome trade privileges and rights in part of the town and its countryside
1130	Roger II receives royal title from Pope Anacletus II, of the Pierleoni family, whose claim to the papal title is contested by Innocent II
1139	Anacletus II's rival, Pope Innocent II, confirms Roger II's royal title after falling into Roger's hands
1144–5	Roman commune in revolt against the papacy, seeking to re-establish the Senate under its authority
1146	Roger II's fleet captures Tripoli (in modern Libya)
1147–8	Genoese naval campaigns in Spain result in the capture of Almería and Tortosa from the Muslims
1148	Roger II's fleet captures Mahdia (in modern Tunisia) and raids Byzantine territory as well
1152	Frederick I Barbarossa becomes German king and begins to develop ambitious Italian policy
1154	Roger II dies, to be succeeded by his youngest son William, who adopts a hands-off approach to government
1154–64	Earliest fragments of Genoese notarial cartularies to survive, documenting trade, land sales, wills, and other aspects of Genoese life over many centuries
1155	Frederick crowned Roman emperor in Rome, amid squabbles about the deference due from the emperor to the pope
1156	Treaty of Benevento secures recognition of King William I of Sicily by Pope Hadrian IV after the pope at first declines to accept his title and is then captured by the king
1156	Genoa secures extensive trading privileges in the kingdom of Sicily in return for trade concessions, helping it to develop its trade in grain and cotton
1158	Diet of Roncaglia demands taxes from Lombard cities, in accordance with the rights of Frederick Barbarossa as heir to the ancient Roman emperors
1160	Fall of Mahdia to the Almohad Berbers, after twelve years in Norman Sicilian hands, leading to severe criticism of the government of Sicily for not reacting; murder later that year of Maio of Bari, William's chief minister, and severe unrest in Sicily
1162	Destruction of Milan by Barbarossa as punishment for treason in rebelling against its overlord the emperor

1163	League of Verona unites cities of eastern Po valley in opposition to Barbarossa, forming kernel of later 'Society of Lombards', or Lombard League
1166	William I of Sicily dies, to be followed by period of regency in Sicily
1167	Lombard League rebuilds Milan in defiance of Barbarossa
1168	Lombard League usurps imperial right to establish cities by building Alessandria in Piedmont, named after Pope Alexander III
1173	Frederick Barbarossa unsuccessfully besieges Ancona, ally of the Byzantine emperor, and a funnel through which Greek gold was reaching the Lombards
1176	Defeat of Barbarossa at the battle of Legnano, bringing the German emperor to the negotiating table
1177	Peace of Venice between Barbarossa, the Lombards, and the king of Sicily, with Barbarossa accepting for the first time the legitimacy of the Sicilian kingdom
1182	Massacre of Italian merchants in Constantinople testifies to difficult relations between Italians and Byzantines at imperial and popular levels
1183	Treaty of Constance defines relationship between the Holy Roman Emperor and Lombard cities; marriage arranged linking Sicilian and German royal families (Constance and Henry: see below, 1189)
1185	William II sends massive fleets against Thessalonica and Durazzo in the Byzantine Empire, claiming he will restore the deposed emperor Alexios, but fails in his objectives
1189	Barbarossa dies on crusade, hoping to recover Jerusalem, lost two years previously to Saladin; William II of Sicily dies, leaving succession contested between his cousin Tancred and Henry VI, German ruler and husband of Roger II's daughter Constance
1189	Further privileges to the Italian republics for trade in the Holy Land, as a result of aid to the Third Crusade; position of Italian merchants continues to be consolidated
1194	Barbarossa's son Henry VI of Hohenstaufen is crowned at Palermo on Christmas Day; the next day his son, the future Frederick II, is born at Jesi
1197	Henry VI dies in Sicily following local unrest and ruthless suppression of the rebels

1198	Election of the dynamic Roman nobleman Lotario de'Segni as Pope Innocent III
1198	Henry's wife Constance dies in Sicily, leaving Frederick as a ward of the pope and German warlords or Genoese pirates in effective charge of large areas of the kingdom
1204	Venice plays a major role in the capture of Constantinople by the Fourth Crusade; division of Byzantine Empire brings Venice extensive territories, eventually including Crete
1214	Battle of Bouvines is a victory for Frederick II and Philip II, king of France, over Otto IV the Welf, their rival for rule over Germany and Italy; Otto's power wanes but his name lives on as the term 'Guelf'
1215	Fourth Lateran Council under the presidency of Pope Innocent III, including important legislation concerning Jews and heretics
1215	Reputed date of Buondelmonte murder in Florence, which, according to the chroniclers, is the start of the rivalry of Guelfs and Ghibellines in the city
1217	Pisans found Castel di Castro, or Cagliari, as the centre of operations in southern Sardinia
1220	Frederick II crowned emperor by Pope Honorius III
1228–36	Ezzelino da Romano takes control of Verona, Padua, and Vicenza, establishing a ruthless regime seen as tyrannical
1229	Frederick II repulses papal armies in southern Italy on his return from crusade
1230	Peace of San Germano between Frederick II and Pope Gregory IX leading to wary peace between both sides till c.1237 battle of Cortenuova
1231	Constitutions of Melfi (later known as *Liber Augustalis*), a general law code for Sicily and southern Italy, issued by Frederick II and reutilizing earlier Norman legislation; Frederick seeks to restore order in the kingdom
1231	Frederick II begins minting *augustalis* coins in the kingdom of Sicily, portraying himself as a Roman emperor in classical style
1239	Alarmed at the growth of Frederick's influence in northern and central Italy, Gregory IX excommunicates Frederick II and declares a crusade against him
1245	Innocent IV declares Frederick II deposed at Council of Lyons, to the consternation of most European rulers
1248	Frederick II defeated by Lombard rebels at Parma

1250	Frederick II dies in southern Italy with Lombard wars still raging
1250	Exiled Guelfs recalled to Florence
1252	Florence and Genoa begin minting of gold coinage
1254	Farinata degli Uberti and Florentine Ghibellines move to Siena
1256–8	War of St Sabas in Acre pitches Genoese against Venetians in the Holy Land and results in Genoese evacuation of Acre; Genoese move to Tyre
1258	Foundation of Iglesias (Villa di Chiesa), centre of silver mining in Sardinia
1258	Manfred of Hohenstaufen, illegitimate son of Frederick II, is elected king of Sicily and becomes active in Tuscan politics on Ghibelline side
1259	Della Torre family become lords of Milan (until 1277 and again in early fourteenth century)
1259	Death of Ezzelino da Romano, lord of Verona and neighbouring cities
1260	Florentine Guelfs are defeated by Sienese at Montaperti and leave Florence; Farinata prevents the destruction of Florence (an event commemorated by Dante)
1261	Genoese assist Michael VIII Palaiologos in the recovery of Constantinople by Greek forces, leading to commercial privileges and the opening of the Black Sea to Genoese trade
1266	King Manfred is killed in battle with Charles I of Anjou at Benevento, and Charles seizes control of southern Italy and Sicily as a papal vassal and champion of the Guelf cause in Italy
1268	Charles I of Anjou defeats the army of the boy-king Conradin of Hohenstaufen, last male heir of Frederick II, who is executed, arousing widespread horror
1270	Charles I of Anjou joins the crusade of his brother Louis IX, king of France, against Tunis, initiating ambitious policies in the waters around his kingdom
1274	Council of Lyons attempts to solve rift between Latin and Greek Churches, but leaves dissatisfied those who do not trust the Greek Church and emperor (e.g. Charles I of Anjou)
1277	First evidence of direct sailing by Genoese ships from the Mediterranean to Flanders

1279	Cardinal Latino is sent by Pope Nicholas II to make peace between warring factions in Florence
1281	First reference to Genoese (and Catalan) shipping in the Port of London
1281	Charles of Anjou's army suffers major defeat at Berat (Albania) by Michael VIII Palaiologos
1282	Revolt of the Vespers in Palermo (March) and the invasion of Sicily by King Peter III ('the Great') of Aragon (August), leading to the loss of Sicily by Charles I of Anjou
1284	Defeat of Pisan fleet by Genoese at battle of Meloria, leading to temporary loss of Elba
1285	Death of Peter the Great of Aragon and Charles I of Anjou, whose heir Charles remains until 1289 a captive in Aragonese hands; Sicily is bequeathed by Peter to his second son, James
1289	Florence defeats Arezzo at Campaldino and begins to gain hegemony in Tuscany
1290 (approx.)	Severe persecution of south Italian Jews by Charles II, king of Naples, on his return to Naples from captivity (see above, 1285)
1293	Ordinances of Justice in Florence, issued in April at the behest of Giano della Bella, discriminating against so-called Magnate families, but leading to a reaction and the fall of della Bella
1296	Frederick, third son of Peter the Great, elected king of Sicily against the wishes of his brother James, now King James II of Aragon, who hoped to exchange it for Sardinia, Cyprus, or Albania; Sicily technically at war with Aragon as well as Naples
1297	Serrata or closing of the ranks of the aristocracy in Venice, after which it becomes much more difficult for new families to claim a place in government
1297	Pope Boniface VIII creates a 'Kingdom of Sardinia and Corsica' which he confers on James II of Aragon in return for promises to evacuate Sicily
1298	Defeat of Venice at the hands of Genoa at battle of Curzola (Korcula); Marco Polo is carried off to Genoese prison
1300	Charles II of Naples sells the Muslim inhabitants of Lucera as slaves, in a fit of religious ardour and in the hope of raising money for his wars

1300   Rivalries between Black and White Guelfs explode on the
        streets of Florence with inter-noble violence

1302   Treaty of Caltabellotta, brokered by Pope Boniface VIII,
        officially ends twenty-year war between Aragonese and
        Angevins for control of Sicily

1303   Death of Pope Boniface VIII following his arrest by the
        Colonna, allies of King Philip IV of France

1309   Robert the Wise succeeds to the kingdom of Naples
        following its renunciation by his two elder brothers, and
        forges close links with the papacy (at Avignon) and the
        Guelfs of Florence

1311   Emperor Henry VII of Luxembourg enters Italy with dreams
        of making peace between the contending parties, but gains
        support mainly among the Ghibellines (they being weaker
        and looking for a protector)

1313   Death of Henry VII, who wins praise for his good manners
        even from Guelf writers

Map section

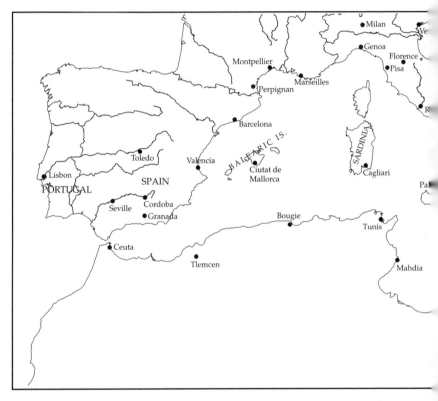

Map 1 The medieval Mediterranean

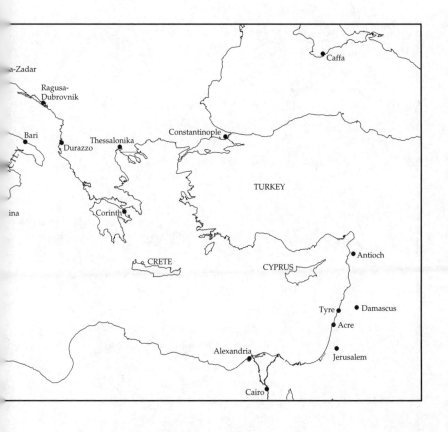

Map 2 Italy in the Central Middle Ages

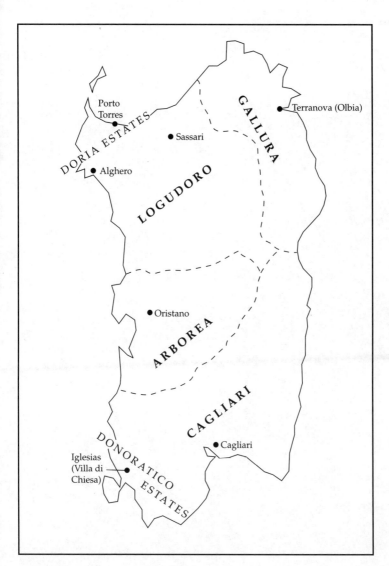

Map 3 Sardinia in the Central Middle Ages

Index